COUNT THEM ONE BY ONE

COUNT THEM ONE BY ONE

Black Mississippians Fighting for the Right to Vote

Gordon A. Martin, Jr.

UNIVERSITY PRESS OF MISSISSIPPI • JACKSON

Margaret Walker Alexander Series in African American Studies

www.upress.state.ms.us

The University Press of Mississippi is a member of the Association
of American University Presses.

First printing 2010

∞

Library of Congress Cataloging-in-Publication Data

Martin, Gordon A.
Count them one by one : Black Mississippians fighting for the right to vote /
Gordon A. Martin.
p. cm. — (Margaret Walker Alexander series in African American studies)
Includes bibliographical references and index.
ISBN 978-1-60473-789-9 (cloth : alk. paper) — ISBN 978-1-60473-790-5 (ebook)
1. African Americans—Suffrage—Mississippi—History. 2. Suffrage—
Mississippi—History. I. Title.
JK1929.M7M37 2010
324.6'2089960730762—dc22   2010013096

British Library Cataloging-in-Publication Data available

For my daughter, Constance, who as a baby moved to Washington with Stephanie and me and who never lost interest in this book

PREFACE

On January 20, 2009, Barack Obama was inaugurated as President of the United States, the first African American to win that office. How did it happen? It can't be traced to his stirring announcement of candidacy in Springfield, Illinois, two years earlier, or even to his memorable keynote address in Boston at the 2004 Democratic National Convention. Certainly his campaign organization was superb. But what gave any African American the opportunity to put together such a broad-based popular coalition?

The antecedents of his victory go back to the Civil War and its aftermath. The Thirteenth, Fourteenth, and Fifteenth Amendments to the Constitution, which were ratified in the flush of Reconstruction between 1865 and 1870, were the first amendments to give our federal government new powers.[1] The Thirteenth abolished slavery and involuntary servitude. Due process and equal protection were guaranteed to all by the Fourteenth. The language of the Fifteenth could not have been clearer:

1. The right of citizens of the United States to vote shall not be denied or abridged by the United States or by any State on account of race, color, or previous condition of servitude.
2. The Congress shall have power to enforce this article by appropriate legislation.

The United States Supreme Court was in accord in 1886, characterizing the right to vote as a fundamental right because it was "preservative of all rights."[2] It just was not enforced for African Americans in the South once Reconstruction ended. It was not until 1957 that enforcement legislation was passed,[3] and neither that statute nor follow-up legislation in 1960, though path- breaking, was sufficient.

What completed the job was the Voting Rights Act of 1965, the greatest civil rights legislation since Reconstruction.[4] This is the story of the people involved in *United States v. Theron Lynd*, a civil rights trial in Mississippi that helped bring about the passage of the Voting Rights Act by demonstrating the limitations of the 1957 and 1960 statutes. Marian Wright Edelman, who, as a young lawyer, courageously represented Mississippi blacks, has described people such as our African American witnesses in the *Lynd* case as "ordinary people of grace with extraordinary courage."[5] I write as one of the lawyers who prepared their case.

Twenty-seven years after that first *Lynd* trial, I returned to Mississippi to talk again to the brave witnesses with whom I had worked preparing for their testimony in 1962. They are not household names, not even Vernon Dahmer, who was murdered because of his pursuit of the cause of voting rights. But they had stayed vividly in my memory during the intervening years. In this book you will learn what made them tick, their hopes, and their aspirations. There would have been no *Lynd* case without their courage, without their tenacity in going back over and over again to attempt to register to vote. Without them and without their counterparts in some other Deep South counties and parishes, the Justice Department could not have acted. There would have been no Voting Rights Act, and there would have been no Obama presidency. But the *Lynd* case was first. It was the first case brought to trial in Mississippi by the Justice Department, taking on a seemingly omnipotent registrar's denial of the right to vote to African Americans.

Since that time I have interviewed many people in Forrest County, Mississippi, and elsewhere and reexamined the evidence, so that I can present this case from multiple points of view, the personal as well as the legal.

It was February 1962. I had passed the bar a year and a half before. I had been with the Civil Rights Division of the U.S. Department of Justice for less than four months when I went down to Mississippi for the first time to help prepare *United States v. Theron Lynd*. My role was to find new witnesses and talk with those we had already identified whose testimony would demonstrate the systemic discrimination against the county's black citizens.

Four years before, David Roberson, born the same month I was in 1934, had returned home to Mississippi, after serving with the U.S. Army in Korea. A college graduate, intelligent and well read, Roberson had gotten a job teaching science at Rowan High School in Hattiesburg, in the southeast part of the state. But when he tried to register to vote, he could not, because of his dark skin. David Roberson would be one of our witnesses.

In Mississippi, in 1962, African Americans were denied benefits of citizenship in a way unimaginable today. They could not eat in the same restaurants as whites, sit down next to them in a movie theater, or enroll at any state university. For them there were only underfunded black colleges with no graduate programs. Grown men were called "Boy." The Klan imperial wizard Sam Bowers was riding high, free to plan the murder of law-abiding African American citizens and their supporters, if he so chose.

African Americans had little power to change this. With few exceptions, they were not permitted to vote. As Vernon Dahmer liked to say: "If you can't vote, you don't count."

The denial of voting rights gave the lie to the myth that the "southern way of life" enshrined some decent "separate but equal" status for whites and African Americans. And white leaders were determined to deny them the vote. For once they could vote, how could a governor of Mississippi publicly and personally turn away a qualified African American student from the leading state university—as Governor Ross Barnett did in 1962?

The Kennedy administration, for which civil rights aspirations had scarcely been a priority, concluded that the best way to improve the lot of African Americans in the South was to help them secure the right to vote.[6] That became the administration's great civil rights goal. The Justice Department's three-year-old Civil Rights Division sent a dozen or so lawyers into the South to try to bring this about. I was one of those lawyers.

It was not a simple matter. Each of Mississippi's eighty-two counties had a separate registrar of voters who had to be tackled individually. But *United States v. Lynd* put Forrest County, and ultimately the whole South—and the United States of America—on the road to permanent change.

My story has some white "heavies" in its cast: Theron Lynd, the registrar; M. M. Roberts, his lawyer; and Harold Cox, the federal judge who presided over the trial. Much of their behavior was repugnant to anyone with a sense of fairness.

But the story has sympathetic white characters, too, like Huck Dunagin, the union's chief steward at Hercules Powder Company, and Judges Tuttle, Wisdom, Brown, and Rives—the great judges of the U.S. Court of Appeals for the Fifth Circuit. Those judges kept the U.S. district judges of their circuit on track as best they could.

The real heroes of the story, of course, are David Roberson and the other African American citizens who risked their jobs, their health, even their lives, to attempt to register to vote, and then to testify in federal court about their rejection as voters for no reason other than the color of their skin. And risk their lives they did. Vernon Dahmer, leader of Forrest County's small NAACP chapter, was, as noted, murdered by the White Knights of the Ku Klux Klan in 1966.

When, in 1965, the Voting Rights Act was challenged in the Supreme Court by six southern states, Chief Justice Earl Warren, writing for the Court, pointed to Roberson and our other teacher-witnesses as proof that radical federal legislation was needed: "In Forrest County, Mississippi, the registrar rejected six Negroes with baccalaureate degrees, three of whom were also Masters of Arts."[7] That was the difference. All sixteen of our African American witnesses were courageous, competent human beings, but Theron Lynd's rejection of teachers with such credentials was ludicrous on its face. It flagged the whole registration process as a farce. When Judge Cox did not immediately order their registration, it was incumbent upon us to appeal without delay to the reconstituted Court of Appeals for the Fifth Circuit, and that is what we did—successfully.

The Student Non-Violent Coordinating Committee (SNCC) bravely performed necessary work encouraging potential Negro voters in many southern counties, and SNCC workers came to Forrest County as well—after our sixteen African American witnesses had risked their lives by attempting to register to vote and then traveling to Jackson twice to testify.

Many today were born after this time. Others lived through it, following news accounts. Some have seen movies. One young white man I met in Hattiesburg had learned about it on the History Channel. He told me, "I couldn't believe it happened right here in Mississippi!" This story brings them all inside and introduces them to the people who made change happen.

Vernon Dahmer did not die in vain. The "stringent new remedies" of the Voting Rights Act, "designed by Congress to banish the blight of racial discrimination in voting, which . . . infected the electoral process in parts of our country for nearly a century,"[8] did complete the job. Among those remedies was the suspension of literacy tests for five years.

Today, Hattiesburg, Forrest County's seat, has an African American mayor, as it has had many black councilors and representatives in the state legislature. In 2008, African American voters carried Barack Obama to resounding Democratic primary victories in Mississippi and other southern states and then were significant factors in his election in November. And the belated but successful state prosecution of Imperial Wizard Sam Bowers in 1998 for the murder of Vernon Dahmer had made clear to one and all that Mississippi no longer tolerated the killing of its African American citizens.

COUNT THEM ONE BY ONE

IN THE OFFICE OF REGISTRAR
LUTHER COX

"How Many Bubbles in a Bar of Soap?"

Black citizens of Forrest County, Mississippi, never knew what would happen when they went in to try to register to vote during the time Luther Cox was in charge. But they could be almost certain they would leave unregistered.

The women who worked for Luther Cox formed a protective buffer for the registrar, just as they did later for Lynd. "He's not in, he's not available" became a familiar refrain—though Cox might be standing at the back of the office.

For black applicants, Luther M. Cox, Jr., was the state of Mississippi. A one-time department store bookkeeper and deputy sheriff, a combat infantryman in World War I, Cox had been Forrest County's circuit clerk and registrar of voters since 1935. And Luther Cox was no longer content with what the crafters of the Mississippi Constitution had written in 1890.

Vernon Dahmer had been registered in the 1940s, but when a reregistration was ordered in 1949, a deputy clerk was in the process of making out his new registration card when Luther Cox called Dahmer out into the hall and told him he could not reregister.

Dahmer kept going back to try. State law authorized a registrar only to determine whether applicants could read a section of the Mississippi Constitution, or, if unable to read, interpret a section read to them. Luther Cox also questioned applicants about the "due process of law." Dahmer did not know what the phrase meant. He failed the registrar's test and left with an "air of rejection."[1] Cox had another question he liked to ask would-be black registrants: "How many bubbles in a bar of soap?"

Some fifty times Richard Boyd tried.[2] Boyd worked at the Hercules Powder Company, Hattiesburg's major employer. Monday was his day off. Just about every Monday for two years, Boyd went to Luther Cox's office in the courthouse to try to register.

Finally, in February 1954, Boyd had the chance to talk to Cox. "I'll tell you why it's important to me," he told the registrar. "I go to statewide meetings of the Worshipful Masters of Masonic Lodges. I'm asked each time if I'm registered to vote, and I'm embarrassed to have to keep saying I'm not."

Cox muttered that "those niggers in Jackson" should mind their own business, but he told Boyd to come back the next week. Finally, Cox let him sign the book.

In 1950, fifteen resolute leaders of Forrest County's black community, Dahmer included, brought suit against Cox for his administration of the voting laws. They were not waiting for outside help, governmental or private. U.S. district judge Sidney Mize dismissed the action, and the U.S. Court of Appeals for the Fifth Circuit declined to act until state administrative appeals were exhausted. A federal grand jury presentation based largely on the testimony of teacher Addie Burger was made by the local United States Attorney at the direction of the Civil Rights Section of the Justice Department's Criminal Division. But the grand jury refused to indict Luther Cox. The futility of attempting to deal with voting discrimination with inadequate federal criminal statutes and hostile white jurors was apparent.

About 10 A.M. Friday, April 11, 1952, nine black applicants were back again at Luther Cox's office. This group included the Reverend Wayne Kelly Pittman and Savannah Davis, who previously had been asked both how many bubbles were in a bar of soap and what the due process of law was.

The same two white women behind the counter who'd been registering white people said they couldn't register Reverend Pittman, Savannah Davis, and the others; they would have to come back when Mr. Cox was there. One black woman, Florine Love, waited another twenty minutes, and Cox finally appeared. But all he told her was that he wouldn't register her, and she should go to see T. Price Dale, the lawyer for the fifteen black plaintiffs. But these nine black men and women prepared affidavits about their experiences, which were sent to the National Association for the Advancement of Colored People (NAACP). At a time when SNCC, the Congress of Racial Equality (CORE), and the Southern Christian Leadership Conference (SCLC) were still unheard of, the NAACP was operating nationally, including small clandestine chapters in Mississippi.

Before the end of the month, the nine affidavits were on the New York desk of NAACP special counsel Thurgood Marshall. Marshall, who had

CONTENTS

succeeded in persuading the courts to strike down segregation in major higher education cases,[3] was already two years into his assault on segregated public education that would culminate in the *Brown* decision by the Supreme Court on May 17, 1954.[4]

He was not too busy, however, to send the affidavits to President Truman's last chief of the Justice Department's Criminal Division, requesting "an immediate investigation of these complaints and the necessary definitive action to insure the protection of the right of qualified Negro electors to register and vote in the State of Mississippi."[5]

There was paper response within two weeks, but meaningful action was painfully slow. However, Herbert Brownell, President Eisenhower's first attorney general, submitted one of the affidavits—the author's identity not revealed for her protection—to Congress in advocating for what became the Civil Rights Act of 1957. Finally, federal help was coming.

CHAPTER 1

RACE-HAUNTED MISSISSIPPI

As I grew up in Boston, becoming more and more conscious of public affairs, of the differences—and similarities—between North and South, one thing was clear to me: Mississippi was first in poverty and last in its treatment of its black citizens. Lynchings there were covered in the Boston papers.

Treatment of blacks in the country generally was far from perfect, as de facto housing segregation in my own city indicated. Yet, it was different in kind from the blanket denial of the right to vote to southern blacks, particularly in Mississippi.

In fields unrelated to civil rights, southern states produced positive national leaders. Georgia, my father's home state, had Senator Walter George, chair of the Senate Foreign Relations Committee. Georgia also had as a senator venerable, respected Richard Russell, for whom one of today's senate office buildings is named. Alabama's Lister Hill was a leader in health care legislation, and the state's other longtime senator, John Sparkman, had been Adlai Stevenson's running mate in 1952. And Arkansas had the internationalist Senator J. William Fulbright. These bright men did not rock the racial boat, but they did far more for their states and country than just cry race.

Mississippi senator John Stennis was a leader of the Armed Services Committee, but in 1948 the state's governor was Fielding L. Wright, the vice presidential candidate on Strom Thurmond's Dixiecrat ticket, which ran nationally in opposition to the strong civil rights plank inspired by Hubert H. Humphrey at the Democratic National Convention. Segregation and violence toward blacks thought not to "know their place" continued unabated. Most of all, the state was personified by cigar-chomping James O. Eastland, chairman of the Senate's Judiciary Committee,[1] appointed to succeed Senator Pat Harrison, who had died in 1941.

By early 1962 when I made my first foray into Mississippi as one of Robert Kennedy's civil rights lawyers, the societal structure for which Eastland was conducting a last holding action had become an anachronism in most of the country. In Chicago, Kansas City and Seattle blacks and whites sat side by side at lunch counters and next to each other in theaters. The question was what, if anything, the rest of the country was prepared to do about Mississippi.

The historian Neil McMillen has called the state in which he taught at the University of Southern Mississippi "this most race-haunted of all American states."[2] Before the Civil War, free blacks in the state were few in number and heavily restricted. The ballot had been limited to free white males. There had been 773 free blacks in Mississippi in 1860, and the state allowed no more to enter. Those already there were not permitted to travel within the state without a certificate authorizing such travel.[3]

But a revolution in racial mores was underway. In 1867, freedmen became registered to vote under military authority, and the color bar was dropped from the Reconstruction Constitution of 1868. With black support, a new legislature was elected that endorsed the Fourteenth and Fifteenth Amendments and brought Mississippi back into the Union in 1870. In the early 1870s, its Ohio-born Republican governor, Ridgley C. Powers, in the flush of Reconstruction, declared it the first state to guarantee "full civil and political rights to all her citizens, without distinction."[4]

Yet it was all illusory. While two blacks served in the United States Senate for a time,[5] and there were some other prominent black officeholders, whites continued to dominate the local power structures, and whites never accepted black suffrage.

After the 1876 election returns for president were repeatedly challenged, a supposedly bipartisan commission awarded the presidency to Republican Rutherford B. Hayes over Democrat Samuel J. Tilden in exchange for commitments by Hayes that included his withdrawing federal troops from the South. Southern blacks were on their own, and intimidation and election fraud perpetuated white domination until Mississippi's landmark Constitutional Convention made it "legal" in 1890. The state's voting-age population then was 271,080: 150,469 blacks and 120,611 whites.[6]

Convention president S. S. Calhoon led the way with his call "to exclude the negro."[7] Forthright approaches such as the exclusion from public office of anyone with "as much as one-eighth negro blood" did not carry the day,[8] but the convention majority cleverly found language that would codify existing mores without being so blatant as to cause northern interference. Article 12 of the constitution didn't mention race.

However, to vote in Mississippi after January 1, 1892, an adult male was required by Article 12 to be "duly registered," to have paid all taxes, including a two-dollar annual poll tax, not to have committed any number of crimes, and—most important—to be able to read any section of the Mississippi Constitution or to "be able to understand the same when read to him, or give a reasonable interpretation thereof."[9] Without further instructions, the registrars of voters of Mississippi's counties got the message. At the turn of the century, a local editor wrote: "The negroes are as far from participating in governmental affairs in this state as though they were [in] a colony in Africa."[10]

NAACP leader Roy Wilkins termed 1889–1945 the country's "lynching era." Mississippi had 476, more than any other state, and almost 13 percent of the national total of 3,786.[11] The country's leading black newspaper, the *Chicago Defender*, called Mississippi the "most brutal community in history."[12]

In 1922 Bert and Tom Hederman purchased the state's leading newspaper, the *Clarion-Ledger*. They and their sons would control the paper for the next sixty years, using it and their other papers to work with state government to maintain segregation. Bill Minor, the legendary Mississippi bureau chief of the *New Orleans Times-Picayune*, termed the sons "Bible-quotin', Bible-totin' racists."[13] A classic Hederman story I recall seeing was captioned "McComb Negro Hits Train."

The 1960 census reported that nonwhites made up 36.1 percent of the voting-age population of the state, but only 6.2 percent of them were registered to vote. Not a single African American was registered in thirteen of the eighty-two Mississippi counties.[14] Forrest County had twelve.[15]

In 1960, six years after the decision in *Brown v. Board of Education*[16] and two years after President Eisenhower sent in federal troops to support court-ordered integration of Little Rock's Central High School,[17] Ross R. Barnett, in his inaugural address as Mississippi's governor, declared to both racist whites and aggrieved blacks: "Our schools at all levels must be kept segregated at all costs."[18]

When my legal career brought me to Mississippi two years later, I worked in most of the southern half of the state. But I spent particular time and effort in Forrest County, in the southeast but north of the strip of counties along the Gulf Coast. The county seat was Hattiesburg.

While there were a few white settlers in the vicinity in the 1820s, a sign in front of the old federal courthouse on Pine Street credits Hattiesburg's founding to an entrepreneur named William Harris Hardy. Captain Hardy, a Confederate veteran and later a state senator and judge, was vice president of a proposed railroad from Meridian to New Orleans. In 1880, while plotting the railroad, he founded Hattiesburg and named it for his wife,

Hattie Lott. Forrest County, named for Nathan Bedford Forrest, the famed Confederate cavalry leader who founded the Ku Klux Klan, was formed twenty-eight years later.

A thriving post–Civil War community, blessed with a good railroad, great pine forests, and huge lumber mills, Hattiesburg should have been a town of progressive race relations. It had no base in slavery and lacked any scars from Reconstruction.

Even after the boom was over, much of the timber gone and its natural resources eroded, Forrest County was two-thirds white and had no reasonable fear of black political domination. Yet it was one of only three Mississippi counties with any significant urban population that barred virtually all blacks from voting.[19]

◆◆◆

On November 10, 1949, Forrest County's Board of Supervisors determined that the county's voter registration books were "so confused that a new registration of the voters of the County [was] necessary to determine clearly the names of the qualified electors of the County and the election districts and precincts of each of the said voters."[20] June 1, 1950, was the effective date of the new registration.[21]

The process presented a problem for the county's minority black population. It wasn't that the law was any worse. The voting requirements of the Mississippi Constitution had remained unchanged for sixty years. You still had to be able to read any section of the constitution *or* understand or interpret it when read to you. But Luther Cox, now in his fifteenth year as Forrest County registrar of voters, appeared no longer satisfied with the efforts of the crafters of the constitution.

On April 11, 1950, fifteen "native born colored citizens," led by the Reverend I. C. Peay of Mount Zion Baptist Church and future *Lynd* witness B. F. Bourn, filed suit against Cox in federal court. The case became known as *Peay v. Cox*. They were not waiting for assistance from the U.S. Department of Justice or anyone else, and they accused the registrar of making them interpret the constitution whether they could read or not. Most frequently Cox chose section 14: "No person shall be deprived of life, liberty or property except by due process of law."[22]

Bourn and Vernon Dahmer were the leaders of the handful of blacks who constituted Forrest County's NAACP chapter when it was founded September 9, 1946. The chapter's history declares: "There were burnings, intimidations, harassments, murders, even by those sworn to uphold the law. But through it all the Forrest County Branch never wavered or surrendered."

The Klan was aware of B. F. Bourn. One night, a wooden cross five feet high was burned on Old Airport Road, right in front of his house. Other incidents in his youth prompted B. F. to carry a pistol with him much of the time.

Another plaintiff was R. C. Jones, born in Hattiesburg on Christmas Day 1915, the second of ten children. His father was a railway baggage handler, his mother a strong member of the Morningstar Baptist Church. R. C. graduated from Eureka High School in 1934. If he hadn't missed so many classes helping out his family during the Depression, he could have been valedictorian. He did some teaching and enrolled in the noted black college, Morehouse in Atlanta.

Jones was drafted in 1943, serving in a medics support group assigned to the Quartermaster Corps in Europe. Honorably discharged in 1946, he studied civil engineering for a year under the GI bill at the University of New Mexico.

That same year he paid his first visit to the office of Circuit Clerk Luther Cox to try to register to vote. Cox "proceeded to ask questions,"[23] questions he was not entitled to ask of someone who could obviously read as Jones could. The first time, Cox asked about land titles and then told Jones that he had failed. The second time, Cox asked Jones what the due process of law was. Jones's answer was "any person charged with a crime could be tried in the proper court with the proper jury, whether it be civil or criminal."[24] It was certainly an example of due process. But R. C. Jones was rejected again. At least, he had gotten to see Cox. That was not always the case over the next three years.

In 1948 he was hired by Principal N. R. Burger to teach physics and math at Eureka High School. Now Jones got involved with other black leaders of Forrest County who wanted to vote. Their business and professional men's organization was the vehicle. Dr. Charles W. Smith, the druggist, and Milton Barnes, who ran the cleaning establishment over on Manning Avenue, joined with Jones, Bourn, Reverend Peay, the Reverend J. H. Mays, and others to raise the money to retain a lawyer. Alfonso Clark, a teacher and businessman, was their contact with the lawyer who had "nerve enough to take the case."[25]

No law school in Mississippi accepted blacks. Medgar Evers, then twenty-nine, a veteran of World War II service in a racially segregated army field battalion in England and France, applied to Ole Miss Law School in 1954.

Today a small exhibit at the law school commemorates his application, but in 1954, he was, of course, rejected.[26] There were only a handful of black lawyers in the state and none in Forrest County. What white lawyer would represent them?

T. Price Dale, an attorney in his late sixties, a former mayor of Columbia, Mississippi, and a chancery judge for sixteen years, was a member of the white establishment—but a renegade member. That was not the case with Dale's brother, Circuit Judge Sebe Dale, a Citizens' Council member and an associate of the late Theodore G. Bilbo. The Dale brothers were both lawyers and judges, but they were very different people.

Sebe Dale, who previously had been district attorney for eight years, was to be the trial judge in the notorious Mack Charles Parker case, the black former soldier accused of raping a young pregnant white woman. Dale had denied motions to dismiss the indictment because of the exclusion of blacks from the grand jury and to change the venue because of the deep local animosity toward Parker. In April 1959, Parker was taken out of the Poplarville jail by a mob, shot and thrown into the Pearl River, his body in chains. Bill Minor told me, "Dale's remarks were absolutely extreme. He minimized the whole thing, made it look like it was just all grandstanding. No one was ever charged."[27]

Four years later Judge Sebe Dale spoke in Connecticut for the Mississippi Sovereignty Commission, the agency charged with promoting the state's segregationist views. Asked whether Parker's killers would ever be brought to justice, Dale replied that three had died. Challenged over knowing who the killers were and doing nothing about it, Dale retorted that his job was fairness in the courtroom, not prosecution.[28]

T. Price Dale pulled no punches as he vigorously represented his black clients. Many of his plaintiffs, he declared, were college trained, and all of them could read any section of the Mississippi Constitution. Disparate treatment was alleged: "white citizens applying to defendant Registrar are not examined by him as to the meaning of any section of said Constitution," while colored citizens "without exception" were so examined.[29] The registration examinations were totally subjective and racially biased.

Courageous enough to represent the disfranchised blacks, T. Price Dale was well aware too of the complex appellate process established in Mississippi law. Written appeals had to be filed within five days with the board of election commissioners, which met in October.[30] An appellant was entitled to a hearing and could call witnesses.[31] Then one could post a $100 bond and go on, as to questions of law, to the circuit court, and ultimately to the Mississippi Supreme Court if one had the tenacity and the money for another $500 bond. But if the rejection was upheld, the bonds were applied to the county's costs.[32]

For blacks asserting their right to vote, it was a detailed, expensive charade that led nowhere. In emotional prose for a legal brief, Dale emphasized to the federal court that state law did not permit a rejected class to appeal and that imposing such a procedural burden on individual members of "a poor and unfortunate people . . . would be staggering and unconscionable and utterly unthinkable . . . that the very machinery provided by the Legislature for their relief from oppression would be the very instrumentality to crush them into the earth."[33]

Now that many blacks were receiving enough education to enable them to read the sections of the constitution itself, the registrar of a major county had erected his own illegal barrier, asking questions he was not entitled to ask, and ignoring correct answers at that. T. Price Dale had chosen to challenge the way Luther Cox applied the law rather than brand the law as unconstitutional.

Twenty-three Hattiesburg lawyers, including M. M. Roberts and Francis T. Zachary, signed Cox's answer to the complaint. On October 13, 1950, U.S. district court judge Sidney C. Mize, a Roosevelt appointee, dismissed the action, sustaining five of the six asserted defenses, including failure to have exhausted the state's administrative remedies.

Less than a decade later no district court judge in the Fifth Circuit would have been able to get away with a decision like that, but the appeal from Mize's decision was decided June 21, 1951. Richard T. Rives of Alabama had been a member of the court for just six weeks, and Dwight Eisenhower was still three years away from making the first of the appointments that would alter permanently the course of justice in the southern United States.

Federal appeals are generally heard by three-judge circuit panels. The judges to whom Chief Judge Joseph C. Hutcheson, Jr., assigned *Peay v. Cox* were distinguished. Louie Willard Strum was graduated at the top of the class at Stetson University's law school. In 1925 he was named a justice of the Florida Supreme Court and in 1931, though a Democrat, was appointed by Republican president Hoover as U.S. district judge for the Southern District of Florida. Strum served as a trial judge until named by President Truman to the "Florida seat" on the Fifth Circuit in September 1950, less than a year before sitting on *Peay v. Cox*.

Also on the panel was the previous chief judge, Samuel Hale Sibley, an honors graduate of the University of Georgia who taught Latin and Greek there while obtaining his law degree. In 1919, President Wilson appointed

Sibley the United States district judge for the Northern District of Georgia. In addition to his own district's work, he often sat by designation with the appellate court. There was little surprise then, despite his also being a Democrat, when President Hoover named him a circuit judge in January 1931. When Sibley left active status in 1949 at the age of seventy-six, Supreme Court justice Benjamin Cardozo praised Sibley as "the soundest and ablest judge on any court in the United States."[34]

After World War II, the flow of the civil rights cases that ultimately defined the circuit's place in history slowly commenced. In 1946 Sibley, writing for the court, struck down Georgia's all-white Democratic primary. It was, obviously enough, "part of the public election machinery."[35]

But two years earlier, Sibley had dissented from the circuit's opinion in *Screws v. United States*, which concerned the death of a handcuffed black man beaten to death by three Georgia law enforcement officers.[36] Though his two colleagues held that federal prosecution was indicated because of the official positions of the defendants, Sibley found no federal law under the color of which the defendants had acted.

Horror at what happened in this case has, I think, interfered with a calm consideration of the law involved. Certainly, if the evidence for the prosecution is credited, the appellants ought to be in the penitentiary. The question is, ought they to be in a penitentiary of the United States?[37]

The Supreme Court reversed the decision 6–3 because of the jury instructions, but agreed with the panel majority that the defendants had acted under color of law and that there was a federal offense.

Hutcheson himself was the *Peay v. Cox* panel's third member. He had been valedictorian of his class at the University of Texas Law School. After seventeen years of private practice, and brief service as city solicitor, Hutcheson was elected mayor of Houston in 1917. Just a year later, however, he left city hall for the federal courthouse when President Wilson appointed him U.S. district judge for the Southern District of Texas. By the time he reached the age of seventy and had to retire as chief judge of the circuit, Hutcheson had written 1,712 opinions during his twenty-eight years on the Court of Appeals.[38] Judge Elbert Tuttle told me that he knew of no civil rights opinion written by Hutcheson, but that Hutcheson did not dissent from pro-civil rights opinions written by others.[39]

The record in *Peay v. Cox* was filed with the circuit court January 22, 1951. Five months later the panel of Hutcheson, Sibley, and Strum rendered their decision. Judge Mize was reversed—with direction—but there was little for the plaintiffs to cheer about. Sibley, writing for the panel, stated: "We think . . . that the remedy by injunction . . . ought not to be had to control the State officer in the conduct of his office even though his conduct may appear to be wrong, until the remedy to correct him provided by the State has been exhausted."[40]

And the remedy: appeal to that *de novo* evidentiary hearing before the board of election commissioners meeting each October. "The commissioners are sworn officers and presumably will give them a fair hearing."[41] And there could, of course, then be judicial appeals.

Naiveté would be the most generous term to apply to Sibley's opinion, but Sibley, Hutcheson, and Strum were far from naive. The gallant early effort of fifteen brave black men and their equally courageous lawyer to overturn an illegal pattern of discrimination by a Forrest County registrar had been deliberately stalled in the very court which eleven years later, under new management, would sound a clear call for justice.

❖❖❖

On January 27, 1997, newspapers throughout the country declared that the files of the Mississippi State Sovereignty Commission would be opened to the public. "Persons who were subject to investigation or surveillance without their knowledge, consent or approval" could now review what the commission's spies had written about them and to request to have it redacted before the records were made public.

I was #2-45-1-85-3-1-1, one of the more than seven hundred "victims" who contacted the Mississippi Department of Archives and History within the allotted time period.[42] Half of us were disappointed to find we hadn't been mentioned. The *Boston Globe* reporter Curtis Wilkie, a white liberal student activist at Ole Miss at the time of James Meredith's entry there, wrote: "For many, it was like being left off President Nixon's enemies list."[43] Revelations about the Sovereignty Commission might appear amusing to some outside of Mississippi decades later, but the intimidation of the commission was deadly serious for those blacks targeted in the late fifties and the sixties.[44]

On May 17, 1954, "Black Monday," as it came to be known in Mississippi, the Supreme Court, in *Brown v. Board of Education*, outlawed official school segregation in the United States. Two days later the phrase was used on the floor of the House of Representatives by Mississippi congressman John Bell Williams. It was, however, a local circuit judge, Tom Brady, who popularized it, first in a talk to the Sons of the American Revolution in Greenwood, then in a pamphlet expanding his remarks.[45] Brady, a graduate of the New Jersey prep school, Lawrenceville, and of Yale, was one of the best-educated men in the state. But that had not improved his racial attitudes: "The social, political, economic and religious preferences of the Negro remain close to the caterpillar and the cockroach . . . A cockroach or caterpillar remains proper food for a chimpanzee."[46]

Citizens' Councils sprang up throughout the state composed of white civic leaders seeking a form of opposition more "respectable" than the violence of the Ku Klux Klan. "White collar Klan" was what Bill Minor called them. Senator Eastland declared the South will not "obey this legislative decision by a political court."[47]

In the 1850s, Senator John C. Calhoun of South Carolina had advocated interposition, placing oneself on behalf of the state to block the national government. It was alive and well in a resolution passed unanimously by both houses of the Mississippi legislature on February 29, 1956.[48]

On March 29, 1956, with the support of the new governor, James P. Coleman, the Mississippi State Sovereignty Commission came into existence.[49] On May 16, 1956, the *Jackson Daily News* reported that the twelve lawyers who constituted the Sovereignty Commission had voted "to employ secret investigators as 'an official arm of state government' who would 'serve as the eyes and ears' in the state's fight against racial integration."[50]

By 1959, the commission had "gone into every county in Mississippi to determine just where NAACP chapters are located, who the negro agitators might be, and where the potential trouble spots in the state might be."[51] The commission gathered information on civil rights activists, real and imagined, investigated meetings and other activities, and made plans to subvert them.[52]

Several times between 1958 and 1960, commission investigators reported that there was "no racial activity" in Forrest County. Still, they collected the names of alleged NAACP members. Spies were paid to infiltrate organizations and voter registration drives,[53] and the commission had black informants.[54] Minutes of the commission reflect that Percy Greene, the editor and publisher of the black weekly, the *Jackson Advocate*, a man scorned in the black community as an "Uncle Tom," was paid $3,230 during 1958 for either "investigations" or "advertisement."[55]

Jackson's biggest newspapers, the *Clarion-Ledger* and the *Daily News*, "regularly killed stories and ran segregationist propaganda at the request of the state Sovereignty Commission in the '50s and '60s."[56] Harassment of Medgar Evers, state field secretary of the NAACP, and the heart and soul of the civil rights movement in Mississippi, was an ongoing commission activity until his murder in June 1963.[57] The financial problems the NAACP had throughout the 1950s did not lessen the threat the commission saw in it.[58]

Applicants for teaching positions or even notary public were investigated as a matter of routine. "Is he NAACP?" was the standard question. Those who applied to teach in the black schools of Forrest County had their references checked by commission investigators, not for their teaching ability, of course, but for possible NAACP ties.[59] This went on until 1973.[60]

Nathaniel Burger, an Alcorn College graduate and principal of Hattiesburg's black high school, recalled that black college presidents had to clear with the State Board of Higher Education the names of any outside speakers they wished to invite to their campuses.[61] On December 11, 1958, Burger himself was visited by Zack Van Landingham, the commission's chief field investigator, about Clyde Kennard, a black former paratrooper and decorated veteran of the Korean War.[62] Kennard had attended the University of Chicago and announced his intention to enroll at Mississippi Southern College. Five days earlier he had stated in a letter to the editor that was published in the Hattiesburg *American*:

> *Although I am an integrationist by choice, I am a segregationist by nature, and I think most Negroes are . . . , but experience has taught us that if we are ever to attain the goal of first class citizenship we must do it through a closer association with the dominant (white) group.*[63]

Burger stated that he was "well acquainted with Kennard, whom he described as intelligent, well educated and a deep thinker."[64] But he denied knowing whether Clyde Kennard was a member of the NAACP or whether there was even a chapter in the nearby Eatonville community, where Kennard had been running a poultry farm since returning from Chicago.

Burger did tell the investigator that he thought "nothing but ill will, dissention and strife would result" from Kennard's attempt, and that he was "willing to work with a committee of Negroes to try to get him to withdraw this application."[65] Burger was one of a number of black leaders interviewed who attempted to trade their efforts to have Clyde Kennard leave Mississippi Southern alone in return for a "badly needed" junior college which "would go a long way toward satisfying the negroes in that area."[66]

Kennard withdrew his application after a two-hour meeting with Governor Coleman and Southern's president, but then resubmitted it following the August 1959 Democratic primary. Blacks rightly feared economic pressure if they attempted voter registration, and there was all the more pressure applied to Kennard because of his integration attempt.

The Forrest County Cooperative foreclosed on his poultry farm and confiscated his stock. The Southern Farm Bureau Insurance Company canceled its liability coverage on his automobile.[67] Sovereignty Commission records reveal various plots considered against Kennard, who it claimed was an NAACP leader and associated with a Jewish "self-confessed Communist."[68] Among the schemes not carried out was attaching dynamite to the starter of Kennard's Mercury.[69]

A nonviolent alternative in this "dry" state was planting whiskey in Kennard's car. This took place on September 15, 1959, minutes after his rejection. A devout Baptist who neither smoked nor drank, Kennard was charged not just with being a bootlegger, but with reckless driving, though his locked car had been parked for half an hour. Two constables claimed they had observed Kennard speeding earlier that morning and had chased him, but lost the car. Van Landingham reported to Governor Coleman what he recognized as "a frame-up with the planting of the evidence in Kennard's car."[70] However, on September 29, 1959, Kennard was found guilty of illegal liquor possession and reckless driving and fined $600.[71]

That conviction was later reversed, with Medgar Evers observing from the segregated balcony, but Kennard was convicted on November 21, 1960, of burglary after a ten-minute deliberation by an all-white jury.[72] Johnny Roberts, a nineteen-year-old black, testified that he had stolen $25 of chicken feed from the same cooperative that had foreclosed on Kennard's farm and that Kennard had bought it despite knowing it was stolen.

Roberts received a suspended sentence. Kennard's sentence was seven years at Parchman, Mississippi's maximum-security facility.[73] No one who knew Mississippi could doubt that Clyde Kennard's real crime was trying to attend Mississippi Southern.

In a press release he issued the next day, Evers called the proceeding "the greatest mockery [to judicial] justice." Evers was then found guilty of contempt, fined $100, and sentenced to serve thirty days in jail.[74] That conviction was reversed on appeal. Kennard's was not.

R. Jess Brown and Jack H. Young, two of the small number of black attorneys in the state, appealed Kennard's conviction to Mississippi's supreme court, on the grounds of the systematic exclusion of Negroes from juries. But the court found "that there were Negroes who were on the jury lists . . . The issue here is not whether some individual or individuals have been denied the right to register."[75] Thurgood Marshall's petition for certiorari to the United States Supreme Court was denied.[76]

A year into his confinement at Parchman, Kennard contracted intestinal cancer. By the time he was granted early release by Governor Ross Barnett, Kennard weighed under a hundred pounds. Taken to Chicago for emergency surgery, he died on Independence Day, 1963.[77]

Four decades later, Judge Barbour wrote:

> *As the secret intelligence arm of the State, the Commission engaged in a wide variety of unlawful activity, thereby depriving the Plaintiffs of their constitutional rights to free speech and association, to personal privacy and to lawful search and seizure . . . through unlawful investigations and through intentional actions designed to harass and stigmatize . . . The avowed intent of the Commission and its co-conspirators was to chill or preclude the Plaintiffs from speech, assembly, association, and the petition of government.[78]*

That was life in Mississippi in the decade before *United States v. Theron Lynd* first came to trial: state-financed investigators, spies, and informers intimidating and punishing any black citizens in the state bold enough to assert their rights, even by trumping up false charges and applying outrageous prison sentences for them.

In 1991 Sovereignty Commission records and the investigative reporting of Jerry Mitchell, working for the new owners of the *Clarion-Ledger*, demonstrated to a public becoming interested in Mississippi's civil rights–era transgressions its abuse of Clyde Kennard. Johnny Roberts recanted his confused perjured testimony. In 1993 the University of Southern Mississippi named its Social Services building for Kennard and retired Alcorn president Walter Washington. While Governor Haley Barbour declined to pardon Kennard posthumously in 2006, he did join with university officials and others in successfully petitioning the court in which Kennard had been convicted to exonerate him.[79]

CHAPTER 2

A CIVIL RIGHTS DIVISION
IN JUSTICE

The alumni of the Justice Department's Civil Rights Division can now indulge in nostalgia about our past. We print up T-shirts with the department seal. But before 1960 it was by no means certain there would be any deeds worth celebrating.

The Civil Rights Division was formally created pursuant to the Civil Rights Act of 1957 by President Eisenhower's second attorney general, William P. Rogers.[1] The United States Department of Justice is composed of offices and divisions, each with its own assistant attorney general and dealing with its own area of the law: for example, antitrust, civil, criminal, lands, tax. Their creation is no casual matter. The new division, however, could build upon a civil rights section established by Attorney General Frank Murphy in 1939 in the Criminal Division under the name Civil Liberties Unit.[2]

President Franklin Roosevelt had been overwhelmingly reelected in 1936 but had backed away from anti-lynching legislation, a severe disappointment to America's black citizens who had said "farewell to the party of Lincoln" and joined Roosevelt's coalition.[3] However, the NAACP's unsuccessful anti-lynching campaign appeared to have some influence in the section's creation, as had labor support from the powerful Congress of Industrial Organizations (CIO).[4]

Once in existence, the unit often seemed to be spinning its wheels, squabbling with the FBI over whether to implement the surviving Reconstruction statutes of the Civil Rights Act of 1866.[5] Enforcement was a problem for the fledging section attempting to prosecute police brutality cases despite the hostility of juries, particularly in the Deep South.

The lawyers also were lodged in an administrative environment of a division that had other important priorities. And FBI director J. Edgar Hoover, whose hostility toward civil rights was well known, had little desire to enter situations in a way that would only harm the bureau's highly cultivated relationship with local police chiefs and sheriffs.[6] While one may sympathize with the legal problems of civil rights enforcement before the 1957 Civil Rights Act, it is still shocking to observe the paper shuffling that went on as a substitute for law enforcement. Forrest County itself is a prime example.

On May 13, 1952, the Criminal Division acknowledged receipt of the nine Forrest County affidavits from Thurgood Marshall.[7] Over the next year memoranda strolled back and forth between the division, the FBI, and the United States Attorney for the Southern District of Mississippi. Finally, the U.S. Attorney met with Luther Cox and Attorney M. M. Roberts, who assured him "that all persons entitled to register would be registered" and that Cox would no longer require interpretations from those who could read.[8] President Eisenhower's first assistant attorney general of the Criminal Division, Warren Olney, then advised Thurgood Marshall that they regarded this assurance as "a satisfactory disposition of the matter, unless we receive valid complaints to the contrary in the future."[9]

In less than two months Thurgood Marshall submitted twenty-four additional affidavits on behalf of blacks rejected in February and March. Only three blacks had been registered. Leading the new affiants was teacher Addie Burger. Also included were the Reverend I. C. Peay, lead plaintiff in the 1950 litigation against Cox; teacher Iva Sandifer; Savannah Davis; local NAACP leaders Vernon Dahmer and B. F. Bourn; druggist Charles W. Smith; Alfonso Clark; and Milton Barnes, who ran the cleaning shop. Bourn, Smith, Clark, and Barnes had also been plaintiffs in *Peay v. Cox*.

The case was reopened.

❖ *May 8, 1953*: The New Orleans office of the Bureau advised that 27 victims had been interviewed. All had either been rejected by Cox personally or told by the female clerks in the office that they would have to see Cox. Almost a month later, Olney drew the obvious conclusion for the U.S. Attorney that Cox, "despite his promise, has deliberately refused to register Negro citizens because of their race."

❖ In mid-June, the U.S. Attorney, still not replaced by the new administration, conceded that Cox "has not carried out the representations and promises made to me and to [Assistant U.S. Attorney Robert Hauberg]," and asked what statute Cox had violated. In July he was instructed to seek a criminal indictment against Cox for violations of Title 18 United States Code sec. 242. Mrs. Burger was the model victim. On the same date, the FBI advised Olney that Hauberg had told a New Orleans agent that no further investigation was necessary and that the grand jury presentation would likely be made in September or November. None was made until April.

◆ *May 6, 1954*: Hauberg, by now promoted to U.S. Attorney, reported that evidence had been presented over two days, but the Grand Jury failed to indict. "There was some discrepancy in the testimony of Addie Burger. Another of the witnesses admitted that he had recently been allowed to register." How about another conference, he urged, perhaps with four or five of the leading attorneys in Forrest County?

A week later, Olney replied that before he would authorize such a conference, he wanted to review a transcript of the grand jury testimony. But there was none. Hauberg didn't have a court reporter at the grand jury session. Eleven weeks then passed before Olney, occupied with other Criminal Division cases, and possibly discouraged, asked Hauberg what was happening with the conference Hauberg had suggested.

◆ *August 30, 1954*: Hauberg reported that he had talked to the Hattiesburg lawyer who would probably represent Cox were he indicted, who "believed such a conference would be beneficial . . . . He stated he would immediately contact Mr. Cox in an effort to advise him that he (Cox) would have to see that qualified persons were permitted to register."

September passed and then the first week of October before Olney sought to find out what, if anything, was occurring in Mississippi. He learned that Hauberg had been busy at the U.S. Attorneys' Conference, and the Hattiesburg meeting would be held the following week.

Two weeks later Olney was advised that Hauberg had met with "four or five of the leading Hattiesburg lawyers and three judges." The president of the Forrest County Bar Association agreed to appoint a committee to determine what could be done upon his taking office the next month. One or two of the lawyers again brought up the failure of the applicants to exhaust their administrative remedies.

Apart from a few plaintive what's happening inquiries by the bureau, there was no action on the matter from November 12, 1954, to February 24, 1955. What passed for action then was Hauberg's forwarding to Arthur B. Caldwell, chief of the Civil Rights Section since 1952, a "Dear Robert" letter he had received from former chancery judge Lester Clark, a member of the committee, endorsing Cox as a "very high class, conscientious public official (who) has always tried to perform his duties . . . to continue the harmony and goodwill between the races." Judge Clark also noted that

"Negro leaders are cooperating with us in a splendid way in bringing better schools, better school buildings and facilities for all our children."[10] Judge Clark concluded that "the best Circuit Clerk we have ever had" would "perform his duties in keeping with (his) solemn oath of office."

Hauberg called the department's attention to new requirements for registration passed by the Mississippi legislature in November. He was busy in Biloxi, but would be "glad to furnish you a copy of it if you so desire."

◆ *March 9, 1955*: Olney to Hauberg: "Although we appreciate very much the services of Judge Clark and his committee, we are, nevertheless, struck by the absence of . . . a statement on the part of Mr. Cox . . . that he intends to afford all qualified citizens an opportunity to register regardless of race or color." In the absence of such a commitment, consideration should be given to filing an information [a prosecution the U.S. Attorney could initiate himself] since you view another Grand Jury presentation as futile.

◆ *April 19, 1955*: Hauberg reported another dilatory conference which included Judge Clark and Senator, later state Judge, Stanton Hall, who said they would take up the Department's request with Cox. A week later Hauberg forwarded a second letter in which Judge Clark stated: "Our Bar Association Committee is convinced that the provisions of the Constitution and of the Election Laws of the State of Mississippi.are being and will be fully complied with." Clark added that Cox already had four opponents in the forthcoming election. The arrival of Theron Lynd on the county political scene was thus noted, though he wasn't singled out.

◆ *May 12, 1955*: Olney noted to both Hauberg and the Bureau that Judge Clark had again failed to set forth any commitment by Cox and requested that the Bureau look at all registration activity since January 1, 1954, white and black. Hauberg was again told to consider filing a criminal information unless the Bureau found no discrimination.

On May 30 the FBI reported that 2,195 whites and five blacks had been registered in Forrest County since January 1, 1954. Finally, eleven months later, another bureau query brought this response from Olney: "No further action is desired in this matter."

That was it. Four years had passed. Multiple memoranda had traveled back and forth, arms-length dealing among the Criminal Division, the United States Attorney in Southern Mississippi, and the FBI, all parts of the Department of Justice. There had been one rejection by the grand jury, two meaningless conferences, and a clear unwillingness to commence a criminal prosecution on the part of the U.S. Attorney. Whatever Hoover's attitude was, many times it was only FBI prodding that caused Justice's Criminal Division to open its file.

◆◆◆

On April 9, 1956, Attorney General Herbert Brownell sent to Congress legislation dealing with the right to vote, creating a Commission on Civil Rights, as well as a Civil Rights Division with its own assistant attorney general, and asserting Justice Department power to intervene in civil rights violations generally. While Senate Democrats such as Thomas Hennings of Missouri branded Brownell's belated arrival on the civil rights scene as blatant election-eve politics,[11] the House passed the voting rights bill in less than three months. Brownell had pushed the legislation despite White House support only for a Civil Rights Commission to educate the public.[12] A negative briefing by the FBI's J. Edgar Hoover at a March cabinet meeting may have reinforced President Eisenhower's "inclination to passivity."[13] The Senate recessed the next day without having considered the House bill.

After the 1956 election the Civil Rights Section asked the FBI to find out how many whites and blacks had voted in the 1952 and 1956 presidential elections in Mississippi and four other southern states. The bureau declined, contending that the request was made to promote civil rights legislation, not to investigate violation of federal statutes within the bureau's jurisdiction.[14]

A Civil Rights Commission was proposed that would fill this gap. It was to be an independent bipartisan agency with no enforcement powers, though it could hold hearings and subpoena witnesses. The mission of the six part-time appointed members would be to investigate and identify instances of discrimination for the Justice Department to act upon.

Brownell's effort for civil rights legislation with the next Congress, still Democratic controlled, began early. He appeared in February 1957 in the friendly confines of Congressman Emmanuel Celler's House Judiciary Committee. Part I of the act established the Civil Rights Commission, Part II a Civil Rights Division within Justice, and Part IV authorized the attorney general to seek injunctions to protect Fifteenth Amendment voting rights. All had been recommended by the President's Committee on Civil Rights.

In Part III, however, Brownell requested authorization for the attorney general to seek injunctions in civil suits designed to protect the wide range of Fourteenth Amendment civil rights violations. The Civil Rights Section attorney Dave Norman considered Part III "a decoy to get voting rights."[15]

The NAACP lobbyist Clarence Mitchell, Jr., and other liberals wanted to rush the bill through the House so there would be enough time to overcome a Senate filibuster. On the Senate side, hearings were held before Senator Hennings's Subcommittee on Constitutional Rights. For three days, Brownell was grilled by North Carolina senator Sam Ervin, Jr., particularly about Part III. Tension was high since the bill was being heard during the highly fraught period of the impending desegregation of Little Rock's Central High School.[16]

Hennings had reported the bill to the full Judiciary Committee the year before and believed his cozy three-member subcommittee could do the same in 1957. He had not counted on Senator Eastland's adding Ervin and three other conservatives to the subcommittee when Judiciary first met. It was two months before the subcommittee's favorable report went to the full committee.

That put the bill overtly in the hands—or satchel—of Senator Eastland, who gave an interview to Tom Wicker, then a twenty-eight-year-old reporter for the *Winston-Salem Journal*. Wicker wrote: "The soft-spoken man propping his gouty foot on the big cluttered desk doesn't seem to mind [that he had become a] byword for prejudice." Eastland told Wicker that liberals planning to move the bill quickly through Judiciary would not find it "as easy as they thought."[17] Eastland simply did not recognize Hennings's attempts to bring his subcommittee's report before the full committee.

On June 18, after a final push by Speaker Sam Rayburn, the House passed the legislation, H.R. 6127, 286 to 126.[18] From then on, Majority Leader Lyndon Johnson, who had preserved the filibuster as a potential tool early in the session, tirelessly worked senator after senator to ensure there be no senate filibuster of the bill. Johnson knew he could only sell legislation securing the right to vote. Support for a long-sought federal dam at Hells Canyon attracted western votes to a version of the bill southerners would not filibuster, and the bill made it to the Senate calendar. Moving it from the calendar to the floor was the next major hurdle.

Intense Senate debate followed, with Part III, the section giving the Justice Department authority to protect a wide range of Fourteenth Amendment rights, under particular attack by Georgia senator Richard Russell. Senator Olin Johnston of South Carolina declared the new Civil Rights Division would be a "new Gestapo."[19] By a vote of 52–38 Part III was eliminated, but the prospect of something passing was preserved.[20] This was largely due to the arm-twisting, in-your-face intense pressure from the towering Senate Majority Leader from Texas, Lyndon Johnson.

No civil rights bill had been passed by Congress since the 1870s.[21] The Fifteenth Amendment to the United States Constitution, enacted then, explicitly forbade the right to vote being denied or abridged because of race or color, but any hope of enforcement died with the disputed election of Rutherford B. Hayes over Samuel J. Tilden in 1876. Now the southern senators who had succeeded in eliminating Part III wanted to add the right to a jury trial in the event the attorney general prosecuted anyone for interfering with the right to vote. A populist Democrat from Wyoming, Joseph O'Mahoney, made their motion. Knowing the practices of all-white southern juries, the reaction of liberals was quick.

An article by Carl Auerbach, later dean of the University of Minnesota Law School, led to the first breakthrough.[22] O'Mahoney's bill envisioned only criminal contempt, which would mandate a jury trial. Auerbach proposed the addition of civil contempt, which need not have a jury.

The final key move toward passage came from Idaho's first-year Democratic senator Frank Church. His contribution to O'Mahoney's amendment repealed the section of the United States Code that restricted federal jury duty to those who met their state's qualifications for its own juries.[23] Thus blacks barred from jury service in their own states, at least in theory, could serve on federal juries, including prosecutions for interference with the right to vote. Church, who had incurred Johnson's wrath after voting against the filibuster at the beginning of the session, had voted with the southerners to eliminate Part III. Now he was rewarded with appointment to two choice committees, Foreign Relations and Senator McClellan's Labor Rackets Committee.[24]

With Church's contribution in place, Senator John F. Kennedy joined the majority that passed the jury trial amendment 51–42, at 12:19 A.M. on August 2, not an easy political decision for a man intent on becoming the next Democratic presidential nominee. Meanwhile, the majority leader from Texas, by putting together and passing the first civil rights legislation of the twentieth century, was increasing his national stature. He also meant to be president of the United States.[25]

Republicans were unhappy in varying degrees about the legislation, as were liberal Democrats, but only Senator Wayne Morse in the liberal camp and no Republican voted against the bill which passed 72–18. Indeed five of the twenty-two southern senators voted for passage. On August 27, the House of Representatives passed the Senate version with just one minor variation, 279–97.[26]

That the Civil Rights Act of 1957 was not a total solution was well recognized. Roy Wilkins, the public face of the NAACP, disparaged the act as "a small crumb from Congress."[27] The same William Rogers who would formally create the Civil Rights Division likened the legislation to "giving a policeman a gun without bullets."[28] They were right, but the important principle of civil rights legislation in the twentieth century had been established, and the 1957 act was just the start.

❖❖❖

So there was a Civil Rights Division, enacted by Congress, approved by the president and proclaimed by the attorney general. Who would head it? Who would staff it? Where would they come from?

Wilson White, the Civil Rights Division's first assistant attorney general, was a bright Philadelphia corporate lawyer who had served as U.S. Attorney there before heading the Justice Department's "intellectual" shop, the Office of Legal Counsel. He had no civil rights background when Attorney General Brownell made him the department's point man in the integration of Little Rock's Central High School, but Brownell remained high on him, as did the president. The Judiciary Committee, however, delayed reporting the nomination to the Senate floor, and White did not take over the division until July 1958.[29] Supportive telegrams that month to committee members from Dr. Martin Luther King, Jr., may have helped finally to move the nomination along.[30]

Arthur Caldwell, who had become White's assistant, considered him "the sweetest guy; the most inoffensive and ineffectual man available," adding, "You've got to be a son-of-a-bitch, a troublemaker. Being in charge of the Civil Rights Division takes courage and guts."[31] Nick Flannery had joined the division after graduating from the University of Pennsylvania Law School in 1958. He recalled White as having "an upper-middle-class orientation. The Division awaited complaints from the victims." There were few investigations and far fewer prosecutions. "Victims of civil rights crimes are not your middle-class politically conscious types," Flannery explained.[32] "Supine" and "reactive" was how he described the Civil Rights Division he joined in the late fifties.[33]

White resigned after a year, in part because of recurring clashes with the Civil Rights Commission. That conflict became only somewhat muted during the Kennedy administration. Dave Norman disliked the commission's "always demanding information from us [which] diverted our energies."[34] Norman, nonetheless, conceded that the department became "sensitive to their prodding."[35]

Joseph M. F. Ryan, White's first assistant as he had been in the Office of Legal Counsel, became acting assistant attorney general upon White's resignation, holding that post for much of the next year. Caldwell, not one to mince words, termed Ryan "a hostile right-wing Catholic."[36] Flannery thought hostility an overstatement,[37] while Norman believed "Ryan didn't seem to want to enforce the law, but this is probably no more than a reflection of the Administration's attitude."[38] Both White and Ryan "appeared more sympathetic to the FBI's desires than to the views of their own subordinates."[39]

Henry Putzel, a division section chief who had spent a decade in the Civil Rights Section, delicately described the Ryan tenure as "a period of cautiously feeling our way, developing techniques."[40] And there was no place in Ryan's "decisions for any influence from the NAACP or other civil rights groups."[41] After the 1959 lynching by the Klan of Mack Charles Parker in Pearl River County, Mississippi, Caldwell was promoted: "I became Assistant to the Assistant Attorney General for Civil Rights. I had a much better office, a secretary, and not a goddam thing to do."[42]

That was the leadership. Who were the troops? Nine of the ten or so lawyers of the Civil Rights Section were transferred to the new division. Also, Norman explained, "The Office of Alien Property was finishing up its post-World War II business, so we got about half-a-dozen lawyers from there . . . Three were real drags."[43] Flannery said: "Out of the twenty lawyers, five or six were real drones, coming from other divisions who were glad to see them leave."[44]

Putzel again put it delicately: "At the beginning, we were all very dedicated people with emotional and intellectual involvement. When the Division was formed, some straight criminal types, not civil rights zealots, found themselves in the Civil Rights Division—to their great surprise and perhaps dismay . . . There was no imaginative, serious effort to use new techniques."[45]

A *New York Times* editorial charged that the division had been "plodding when it should have been imaginative, timid instead of courageous, sluggish when swift action was needed."[46] Administration reaction was not immediate, but change occurred in the Civil Rights Division with the confirmation of Harold Tyler as assistant attorney general on July 14, 1960, and the arrival that month of John Doar as his first assistant. Norman described it:

1960 was an election year. A decision was made high up that we had better do something . . . [Tyler] spent a little time looking around and

decided fairly quickly that he needed a first assistant that could really
go. He knew John Doar from Princeton days. It was a decision to go
and go hard on civil rights.[47]

Harold R. "Ace" Tyler, Jr., was a thirty-eight-year-old New York lawyer
with brief experience as an Assistant U.S. Attorney and some expertise in
tax litigation.[48] His appointment was also delayed eight months by the Judiciary Committee. Once confirmed, Tyler and his first assistant, John Doar,
began to change things.

Doar was an independent-minded Republican who brought great drive
and tenacity to the Civil Rights Division. Born in Minnesota in 1921, John
Doar grew up during the Depression in northwest Wisconsin. His father
was a country lawyer, his mother a teacher who did not think the local
school was good enough for her children. So John and his brother went to
a country day school in St. Paul, living during the week in a rooming house
down the street from the headmaster.

John was as passionate about sports as about his studies. His school had
only an intramural basketball program, but Doar was determined to play
college basketball. Doar went to Princeton, and, hustling and overachiev-
ing, averaged 7.2 points a game during a 14–6 varsity season led by Hall
of Fame coach Butch Van Breda Kolff. In 1943, after his junior year, Doar
left Princeton, training as a bomber pilot, but the war ended before he was
deployed.

Back at Princeton, Doar was a member of Tiger Inn, a club with many
southern members: "good guys," John says, who recognized they had a racial problem, but wanted to fix it themselves without Yankee interference.
During his senior year, the members of Tiger Inn split down the middle on
the question of admitting a black, and nothing came of it. Six decades later,
Doar received the Princeton Varsity Club's Citizen Athlete Award for self-
less and noble contributions to sport and society.[49]

Doar went to law school at Cal-Berkeley and intended to make his for-
tune in the West. He took the Oregon bar exam but had promised his father
he would take the Wisconsin exam, too. With his father seriously ill, John
returned to Wisconsin and joined his brother Tom and his cousin, Warren
Knowles, in a family practice.

But Doar maintained his California ties and was trying a paternity case
there in July 1960 when he received the call from Tyler asking him to become first assistant of the Civil Rights Division. He had not been Tyler's
first choice, but high-powered New York and D.C. lawyers would not take a

nonpresidential appointment for only a few months in office. So John Doar became the number-two man in the Civil Rights Division.[50]

Four new voting rights suits were brought in Harold Tyler's six months—as many as had been brought in the preceding two and a half years.[51] Caldwell didn't like the way Tyler shared Attorney General Rogers's "Don't offend Eastland" attitude and deplored the fact that there was so little progress in the prosecution of police brutality.[52] That would take place years later during the Johnson administration, flowing directly from deaths such as Vernon Dahmer's in Forrest County and those of Freedom Summer workers Goodman, Schwerner, and Chaney. All this related to the right to vote and the civil voting rights litigation authorized by the 1957 act and initiated in meaningful fashion by John Doar.

Doar's first memories of the division were the pile of complaints from over three hundred Negro tenant farmers who had been evicted in Heywood County, Tennessee, and of Henry Putzel fussing over the files.[53] The old division stalwarts considered Doar a mixed blessing. Putzel recognized the "dramatic change when Doar came in. With regard to the racial aspects of voting, he took over the entire operation himself."[54] Caldwell considered Doar "a good man. He just didn't know a damn thing about criminal law. . . . He was the hardest-working person I have ever seen—young and energetic—we didn't get along too well."[55]

Norman noted the internal tensions:

Those cats [Putzel and Caldwell] had been on civil rights business for years. The way you operate in the Criminal Division is to let the U.S. Attorneys do the work. Washington lawyers review and supervise. It was the bureaucratic way. . . John had never been in the bureaucracy . . . Fieldwork . . . They almost thought it was improper.[56]

Things would never be the same in the Civil Rights Division. The days of division lawyers sitting back in Washington and reading FBI reports were over. Southern blacks courageous enough to try to register to vote would meet, not blasé FBI agents, doing their job one day on voting rights as they might the next on the interstate transportation of a stolen motor vehicle, but brash young lawyers from Washington committed to the still-radical idea that no American be excluded from voting.[57]

CHAPTER 3

CIVIL RIGHTS AND THE 1960 CAMPAIGN

In November 1960 the country elected a new president. For the first time a president would be elected who had been born in the twentieth century. For the first time since 1948, Democrats had a chance of winning.

Dwight Eisenhower's post–World War II popularity had been so broad that he probably could have won the presidential nomination of the Democratic Party. Adlai Stevenson's campaigns against him in both 1952 and 1956 had been noble holding actions, giving the Democratic Party a nominee of eloquence and dignity, but one doomed to defeat.

By 1956 John F. Kennedy, a World War II hero, had been in elective politics for a decade, as a Massachusetts congressman for six years and a U.S. senator for four. At the 1956 Democratic Convention Stevenson threw open the nomination for vice president. In an exciting contest with Tennessee senators Estes Kefauver and Albert Gore, Kennedy had gained stature and a new national audience. His loss to Kefauver was a blessing in disguise, for when Stevenson was swamped by President Eisenhower in the election, Kennedy took none of the blame.

Nostalgia, respect, and a powerful nominating speech by Senator Eugene McCarthy of Minnesota led some Democrats to support Stevenson for a third try in 1960, when for the first time he might have had some realistic hope of winning. Other liberals supported McCarthy's Minnesota Senate colleague, Hubert H. Humphrey, a strong influence on the national party since his fervent speech on civil rights at the 1948 convention. And there was the man from Texas who had delivered on civil rights legislation, Majority Leader Lyndon B. Johnson.

Kennedy was fighting not only his youth but also the prevailing belief, since Al Smith's defeat in 1928, that no Roman Catholic could be elected president. Kennedy's primary victory over Humphrey in heavily Protestant

West Virginia helped his cause, but West Virginia had only a small black population. The New Deal had brought blacks into the Democratic coalition.[1] For Kennedy to defeat Richard Nixon in November, he would need a large turnout of black voters in the key industrial states, and he would need to receive the overwhelming majority of those black votes.

Harris Wofford had corresponded with Kennedy after the senator's stirring speeches in Poland and about Algeria in 1957. Wofford, a Notre Dame professor and counsel to the Civil Rights Commission in 1959, became a civil rights advisor to Kennedy. He found Kennedy "had no entrenched positions at all in this area, but he was learning, and he was offended by the discrimination."[2]

Robert Kennedy said of his brother:

He voted in favor of the jury trial amendment (to the 1957 Act), so there were some reservations about him on that. Nixon didn't have a bad record as far as Negroes were concerned, so they were reasonably interested in him. . . . The Negro vote in the 1960 election was there to be won or lost.[3]

Party platforms are generally read only by members of platform committees, opposition researchers, and some of the media. But what is written about them can have great effect. The Democratic Platform Committee chairman in 1960 was a respected party elder statesman, former congressman and ambassador to India Chester Bowles of Connecticut.

Federal fair employment practices (FEP) legislation was frequently talked about at this time but generally dismissed out of hand because of hard-core southern opposition. Bowles assumed there would be some watering-down of his civil rights plank to placate the South and went all the way, including FEP legislation in what would be "the strongest platform ever adopted by the Democratic Party."[4]

Political campaigns are generally chaotic. During national conventions, the left and right hands may lose touch. Such a breakdown occurred here. Robert Kennedy, managing his brother's campaign, did not realize that the platform proposed to the delegates was not the more moderate version that Bowles had envisioned would be adopted, but rather the hard-line first version.

The word was passed, and Kennedy delegates resisted any attempt to amend the report of the Platform Committee.[5] Included in the platform was endorsement of the "peaceful demonstrations for first-class citizenship which have recently taken place in many parts of the country" and of "whatever action is necessary to eliminate literacy tests and the payment of poll taxes as requirements for voting."[6] Thus the broad civil injunctive power to deal with civil rights violations, sunk by Congress during debate on the 1957 act, resurfaced in the platform.[7]

Five months remained before a new president would take office, but an impression of John F. Kennedy had already taken hold among the white power structure in Forrest County, Mississippi. M. M. Roberts, the key lawyer for Luther Cox and Theron Lynd, advised another local lawyer: "Protestants and other conservatives alike are against Kennedy and his gang of liberals, who are socialists, not Democrats."[8]

The Montgomery bus boycott, which began in December 1955, had made national figures of Rosa Parks, the forty-three-year-old tailor's assistant who had refused to give up her seat for a white man, and the twenty-six-year-old Atlanta-born minister of the Dexter Avenue Baptist Church who coordinated the boycott, the Reverend Martin Luther King, Jr. By 1960 Dr. King and his Southern Christian Leadership Conference were approaching the top of the American civil rights firmament where Roy Wilkins and the NAACP had long been and James Farmer and the Congress of Racial Equality would soon arrive. King had returned to Atlanta from Alabama and had been sentenced to twelve months at hard labor—for driving on his Alabama license more than sixty days after having moved back to Georgia.

The sentence was suspended, but it still hung over King as the wave of student sit-ins moved into Atlanta. Rich's, Atlanta's premier department store, was the target. King's relationship with student activists was often tenuous. By the midsixties, after Stokely Carmichael's ascendancy in SNCC, King would be mocked as "Da Lawd." The year 1960 was a simpler time, but King understandably felt he must join the student protest. Upon his arrest at Rich's on October 19, King was imprisoned to serve his sentence and was soon transferred to a rural penitentiary some two hundred miles away.

Three events of moment to the presidential campaign occurred. At O'Hare Airport in Chicago, Sargent Shriver, Kennedy's brother-in-law, suggested that Kennedy call Coretta Scott King, Dr. King's wife, to express his sympathy and concern.[9] Shriver gave Kennedy the telephone number; a ninety-second call was placed and later widely publicized.[10]

Atlanta mayor William Hartsfield was visited by Morris Abrams, a noted Atlanta lawyer friendly to Kennedy. Abrams expressed Kennedy's concern about King's situation. Hartsfield told Abrams, "I'm giving him the election on a silver platter."[11] The mayor then announced Kennedy's intervention on King's behalf. Decades later Harvard professor Henry Louis Gates, Jr., described the call as "the moment when the Republican Party lost black America."[12]

Despite his apparent annoyance over the political fallout, Robert Kennedy then called Georgia judge J. Oscar Mitchell of the DeKalb County Court. Kennedy attributed the suggestion of the phone call to Judge Mitchell's close friend, Georgia governor Ernest Vandiver, who thought Kennedy could achieve King's release.[13] From a pay phone on Long Island, the future attorney general placed the call. King was released on bail.

The calls were effectively used by Louis Martin and others to get out black voters, notably in Cleveland, Philadelphia, Detroit, Chicago, and New York.[14] And there was the little blue pamphlet, *The Case of "No Comment Nixon" versus the Candidate with a Heart, Senator Kennedy*, printed for distribution in front of every black church the Sunday before the election.[15] Those whom M. M. Roberts feared the most were on their way to the White House.

The black vote was crucial for JFK in the big industrial states as he very narrowly won the total popular vote 49.7 percent to Nixon's 49.6 percent.[16] In Mississippi only 25.6 percent of the eligible voters—almost all white— voted.[17] The state's eight electoral votes were won by unpledged electors who later cast their votes in the electoral college for Virginia senator Harry F. Byrd.[18] A statewide telecast expressing nominal support by Senator Eastland for the Kennedy-Johnson ticket accomplished little.[19]

As 1961 began with Kennedy's inauguration, black voters had a right to expect quickening federal action to secure civil rights. But as the outcome in *Peay v. Cox* had illustrated, all the activity in the world would fail if the federal judges in the south did not enforce the law. Kennedy and his brother, the new attorney general, had a major opportunity with the new judgeships that they would fill. But control over the confirmation of judges was still exercised by Senator James Eastland.

The senator was expected to be more lenient with executive branch appointments. Burke Marshall, like John Doar, was part of John Kennedy's generation. Born in 1922, he was a graduate of Phillips Exeter Academy, Yale College, and Yale Law School. Marshall had joined Covington and Burling, one of Washington's most noted law firms, upon his graduation from law school. He had never been active politically, and his legal expertise was antitrust law, representing clients such as Standard Oil.[20]

He never really knew why Robert Kennedy selected him to run the Civil Rights Division, though he thought it likely due in part to the recommendations of Deputy Attorney General Byron White or presidential civil rights advisor Harris Wofford. Wofford had, in fact, been interested in the job himself and had submitted a letter of support from Marshall, his former Covington and Burling colleague.[21]

Marshall knew exactly why he accepted, however:

It was President Kennedy, (his) personal attraction, and then the subject matter of civil rights and bringing to bear the processes of the law. . . . That was going to be the most interesting lawyer's work going on in the country. . . . [I]n his inaugural address itself . . . the movement of generations . . . he put into words the things that attracted people of my age and experiences and interests into his Administration.[22]

The *Washington Post* later described Marshall:

Bespectacled, soft-spoken and slight of stature, Marshall was undramatic, with an aversion for the spotlight. He . . . had an analytic and incisive mind and a calm, cool demeanor, which was an asset in dealing with the burning passions of the period and such polar opposites as the Rev. Martin Luther King, Jr. and segregationist governors Ross Barnett of Mississippi and George Wallace of Alabama.[2]

Robert Kennedy saw that Burke Marshall was dedicated to civil rights, but not controversial.[24] Wofford has said that Robert Kennedy "was, by the time he was killed, more deeply committed to the whole black problem than anybody else in the United States, I would guess. And Burke played a crucial, crucial role in that."[25]

One of the cases brought during the last year of the Eisenhower administration was *United States v. Deal*, involving East Carroll Parish, Louisiana, a redneck area on the Arkansas border where, one morning a few years later, I emerged from a motel to find the tires slashed on my rental car, a silent warning to a young northern lawyer. John Doar had become acting assistant attorney general on Inauguration Day 1961, serving until Marshall's confirmation in March. The *Deal* case had problems that Robert Kennedy wanted resolved. Doar flew to Jackson, Mississippi, that same afternoon and was in Lake Providence, the parish seat, by 4 A.M. That was the kind of quick action and energy the Kennedys had promised to bring to government. Even though John Doar had arrived in the dying days of the Eisenhower administration, he was going to stay.

Civil Rights Division appellate lawyer Howard Glickstein observed the transition from Tyler to Marshall: "Marshall didn't roam the hall, slap you on the back, and come in and chat like Tyler did. He was a man of few words. He asked you a question and got your answer . . . He and Doar really hit it off together."[26]

Frank Dunbaugh, who led the division's efforts in Louisiana, considered Burke "very much a listener . . . He allowed us the luxury of thinking that Doar was running the government. Marshall was a thinker, long-range, where are we going . . . Kennedy to Marshall to Doar was a very effective chain of command . . . Kennedy made the policy; Marshall thought it out; Doar put it to work."[27] Marshall described the Civil Rights Division he inherited as very small and not very efficient [or] very active.

What we tried to do was recruit young lawyers that would travel and work very hard, and we were pretty successful in doing that. A large part of that building up of the division was moving people out of it that had been put in it when the division was created because they were . . . surplus from the other divisions.[28]

The lawyers Marshall and Doar recruited for the division were those willing to work "sixteen hours a day, seven days a week, without ever giving up on the situation. Good sense and effective decision-making. Those are rare qualities."[29] Those lawyers, plus holdovers they felt had the same qualities, were assigned to Doar.

Doar's lawyers came at last to Forrest County. Registrar Luther Cox had died, but his successor was no improvement.

CHAPTER 4

THERON LYND
AND THE END OF AN ERA

Change was also coming to Forrest County—or was it? The first stirrings actually occurred during the 1955 campaign for county office. A new face presented himself to the white electorate. What was Theron Lynd thinking? Why did he want to do it?

Ever since high school, Lynd had worked in his father's business as a wholesale distributor of petroleum products. It seemed like a good job. He had started as a service station operator, then moved to truck delivery salesman and, for twelve years, office and bulk plant manager.

Then, in March 1955, Lynd made public on the front page of the *Hattiesburg American* his puzzling decision to run in the August primary against Luther Cox, the longtime circuit clerk of Forrest County. Cox had served in World War I as a combat infantryman in France. He was an Elk, a 32d degree Mason, a noted pitcher on his college baseball team, a tennis player, and a golfer.[1] Most important to the white electorate, Cox had blocked all but a dozen blacks from the registration rolls.

Born in Moss Point on Mississippi's Gulf Coast in 1920, Lynd had come with his parents to Hattiesburg at the age of three months and been raised there. He was thirty-five, six feet, two and a half inches tall, and he asserted his good health despite his weight, which fluctuated between 320 and 350 pounds. He had played right tackle for his school football teams. As he later recalled: "I won no conference honors, but lettered two years. I filled quite a large hole in the line, whether I was standing, sitting or bottom side up."[2] Lynd was popular at school and served as vice president of his high school senior class.

Lynd attended Mississippi Southern in Hattiesburg, but transferred to Mississippi State's School of Business and Industry, where he received a B.S. degree in 1943. Like Cox, Lynd was both a Mason and a member of

Broad Street Methodist Church. He was also on various boards. Fishing was his only hobby.

Lynd ran on a platform of banalities: "This important county office should have a man of high moral character, honest, courteous, efficient, capable, active and sober, and a man who will protect the best interests of our citizens." There was no public sign that Theron Lynd understood that his main task as circuit clerk would be to deny black people the right to vote.

Eight years later, when Lynd had moved from a quixotic challenger to an incumbent under attack from the United States Department of Justice, the *American* paid more than its earlier nominal attention to him:

Speaking softly, he never seemed angry or off balance when cross-examined, rather he was easy going and composed . . . At times his voice drops almost to a purr . . . He wears specially-made clothing and special-order shoes. His white short-sleeved sports shirts seem roughly the size of a pup-tent and he fills a king-size chair to overflowing. When he carries the big courtroom ledgers they look little larger than classroom notebooks.[3]

As it turned out, Lynd was not the only opponent for Cox, but it was Lynd who made it to the runoff with him. He lost that election, but was ready when Luther Cox died three years later, on December 13, 1958. In the best tradition of the time, Mrs. Cox was handed her husband's job. But she was only willing to serve until a special election was conducted on February 10, 1959.

In Alabama, the rising star of the federal trial judiciary, Frank M. Johnson, Jr., had ordered voter registration records of three Alabama counties made available to the staff of the U.S. Commission on Civil Rights. In Forrest County, the white electorate had to decide whether Lynd's having put himself forward in 1955 was a plus or a minus.

Seven others paid the $5 filing fee and become candidates for the $44,000 a year position of circuit clerk: six men and one woman; four Baptists, two Methodists, and a Presbyterian. Three of them forthrightly addressed their announcements of candidacy "TO THE WHITE DEMOCRATIC VOTERS OF FORREST COUNTY." All of them expressed the same basic intention: "to continue the policies that have been in force in this office since its establishment."[4]

The one woman in the race was thirty-nine-year-old Helen Andrews Autry, deputy circuit clerk under Cox for sixteen years until going to work for a life insurance company three years earlier. She was as emphatic as the men:

> *Because of recent Civil Rights litigation, the office of Circuit Clerk has become one of the most important administrative offices in the State. . . . I am thoroughly familiar with the methods and policies in conducting the affairs of the office and . . . promise to keep (them) in effect.*[5]

There was one major change from Lynd's 1955 campaign. His admiration seemed to have grown for the "former Circuit Clerk who served us so well. He did an outstanding job." Lynd, too, made it clear that, if elected, he would carry on the affairs of the office just as Luther Cox did.[6]

And Lynd was elected. He trailed Mrs. Autry in the preliminary election, but decisively defeated her in the runoff. Defendant Theron Lynd would be in Judge Harold Cox's courtroom when the trial began on March 5, 1962.

CHAPTER 5

PREPARING FOR TRIAL

In July 1961, I was twenty-seven, a year out of New York University Law School, married, with a one-year-old daughter. I was an active Democrat, back in Boston in private practice. My wife, Stephanie, and I had enthusiastically supported John F. Kennedy's nomination and election. We took Constance, not yet three months old, to the polls with us, wearing her "Youth for Kennedy" pin.

With each passing month, I was more eager to be part of this new administration, of the energy that had replaced the lethargy of the Eisenhower years. President Kennedy had urged the nation: "Ask not what your country can do for you, ask what you can do for your country." What could I do for my country?

That July the Department of Justice filed its first voting rights cases against Mississippi counties where witnesses had been found to document the denial of the right to vote to black citizens. That same month I was interviewed by the leaders of Robert Kennedy's Civil Rights Division, Burke Marshall and John Doar, for a position on the small trial staff that would prosecute these cases.[1]

By mid-fall, the FBI had determined that I was neither a communist nor any other kind of security risk, and the IRS had confirmed that I paid my taxes. Stephanie, Constance, and I moved to a new apartment building on Naylor Road in southeast Washington, with a handy bus stop for travel to the department when I was in the District. On November 13, 1961, I was sworn in.

By February 1962, I was in Mississippi to help prepare for trial the government's case for injunctive relief against Theron Lynd, the man in charge of preserving Forrest County's virtually all-white electorate. In 1962 and 1963 I also worked on various matters in forty-four of Mississippi's eighty-two counties.

Emmett Till, a visiting black Chicago fourteen-year-old, had been murdered in the "wolf whistle" case in the Delta nearly a decade before. It was still two years before Freedom Summer workers Michael Schwerner, Andrew Goodman, and James Chaney would be killed after being "released" from custody by Neshoba County deputy sheriff Cecil Price, part of a plot with Sam Bowers, imperial wizard of the White Knights of the Ku Klux Klan, and his henchman, "Kleagle" Edgar Ray Killen, who would be convicted in 2005.[2]

One summer Friday in 1963, before Neshoba County became known for the brutal law-enforcement-aided terrorism that occurred there, I was the first Justice Department attorney to investigate that county in the heart of central Mississippi's "Bible Belt." An intern and I developed black contacts for future follow-up. Black ministers and undertakers, both independent of the white community, were likely prospects.

Catholics at that time were not allowed to eat meat on Fridays. At lunchtime I scrutinized the menu of a small restaurant in Philadelphia, the county seat, looking for some nonmeat dish. Finally I asked the waitress, who smiled at me and said: "Why, you must be a Catholic." I ate quickly and left, regretting having called attention to myself.

In 1963 I had a brief change from voting rights cases. I was the only Justice Department lawyer assigned to a small Department of Defense team investigating on-base discrimination against black servicemen and their dependents on southern air bases, including Columbus, Greenville, and Biloxi, Mississippi.

In Washington, the Bay of Pigs invasion of Cuba that President Kennedy had inherited and mistakenly authorized had proved a disaster, but he was still popular in the country at large, if not with Congress. At the Justice Department, Attorney General Robert Kennedy continued to pursue Jimmy Hoffa and labor racketeering, as he had done while staffing the McClellan Committee in the Senate in the 1950s, but the Kennedy Justice Department had a major civil rights goal, too: delivering the right to vote to disfranchised black Americans in the Deep South. Senator Eastland had been gently told that Mississippi would no longer be exempt from civil rights actions.[3]

In the fall of 1962, Governor Ross Barnett was preparing to defend the pride of Mississippi higher education, "Ole Miss." The Fifth Circuit had ordered integration in the person of African American air force veteran James Meredith. Lieutenant Governor Paul Johnson, Jr., meant to run to succeed Barnett as governor in 1963. Each candidate in that race would promise the almost all-white electorate that he was the one most qualified to maintain Mississippi's "way of life."

In the Civil Rights Division, there was both the fresh face of Burke Marshall, calm, bright, and methodical, and continuity in the person of the Wisconsin trial lawyer, Republican John Doar, energetic, tenacious, and intense, who had brought life to the division in July 1960. By the time my interview with Marshall and Doar was winding down, they felt sufficiently sure I would be joining them to caution me never to say, when told to leave for the South on a Friday afternoon, that I had personal plans for the weekend.

Field operatives of the Civil Rights Division spent the full workweek in Washington, analyzing registration and poll tax records from those southern counties where we had them or otherwise developing investigations or preparing cases. I sat before a microfilm machine, getting a headache looking at thousands of pages photographed by the FBI on murky microfilm, in those days before high-quality reproduction and personal computers. We also read, not just the *Washington Post*, but also the *New York Times*. We knew when the *Times'* courageous civil rights reporter Claude Sitton came upon a new incident of southern violence it could affect where we went and when.[4]

Six or eight of us would fly south Friday afternoon for stays as long as three weeks, locating black registrants in counties we hadn't visited, driving unannounced to visit contacts in other counties, and preparing witnesses where cases were close to trial. None of us ever said we couldn't go, that we had plans for the weekend. Constance's first sentence was, "Daddy go bye-bye plane."

What made me interested in the grueling work of the Civil Rights Division as the start of my legal career?

I became a Democrat despite trudging daily to school in the fall of 1944 by the local Republican headquarters proclaiming, "Win the war quicker with Dewey and Bricker." My mother had died when I was six, and my father had agreed that I be raised by her older sister, Lillian Hennessy, in West Roxbury, an outlying part of Boston. Aunt Lillian was determined that I get the best possible education.

She wanted me to go to Roxbury Latin School, a distinguished nearby independent secondary school, if I could. My elementary schoolteachers were able and caring. When my sixth-grade teacher, Evelyn Houghton, learned that I was applying to Roxbury Latin, she stayed after school with me to go over extra material that would be on the entrance exam, and I was accepted.

At Roxbury Latin, in my senior year the moral lessons four classmates and I learned from Dr. Van Courtlandt Elliott as we sat with him in the second-floor classical study and read the classics in Greek became a bedrock of my life. Firmly engrained was the idea that some things were right and some were wrong, and good people had a duty to change what was wrong.

At Harvard, where nine of our fifteen graduates matriculated, I majored in Government, did some acting, and became president, first of the Harvard Young Democrats, then of the New England Intercollegiate Young Democrats, meeting my wife, Stephanie, when I recruited her to start a Radcliffe Young Democratic Club. I lived in the same entry of Adams House, known as Harvard's "Gold Coast," where Franklin Delano Roosevelt had lived as an undergraduate.

As a senior I was fortunate enough to have as advisor on my honors thesis the legendary political scientist V. O. Key, witty and perceptive, whose 1949 book on southern politics remains the standard by which later works are judged. Key understood life for blacks in the South, and termed literacy tests "cloaks for the arbitrary exclusion of voters . . . If any tests of understanding were applied at all to any substantial number of citizens of status, the registrars would be hanged to the nearest lamp-post and no Grand Jury could be found that would return a true bill."[5]

I was enthralled by two diverse courses: Oscar Handlin's American Social History and Arthur M. Schlesinger, Jr.'s American Intellectual History. Schlesinger was the model of an academic who was also a political activist. He ridiculed the vagaries of American Protestantism in his course, ignored Catholicism, and invited me to his home when he had Senator Hubert H. Humphrey over after a speech.

I went down to the senior tutor Zeph Stewart's Adams House office as I was applying to law schools. He was the brother of U.S. Supreme Court justice Potter Stewart and the son of the chief justice of the Ohio Supreme Court. Zeph gave me the sound practical advice to remember that I had no money, to forget Harvard, Yale, and Columbia, and to accept the country's largest law school scholarship, the Root-Tilden at New York University School of Law.

Periodically, we Roots would mutter about wishing we had gone to Yale, which we considered more social-science oriented, but we had made no mistake. NYU was on its way to becoming one of the country's top law schools. One of my activities was serving as president of the Catholic student group, the St. Thomas More Society. When the saintly Catholic activist for the poor, Dorothy Day, accepted an invitation to speak to the society, she first had a glass of sherry with Stephanie and me in our dormitory apartment. Needless to say, we were in awe.

After graduating and passing the Massachusetts bar exam, I was ready to embark on a legal career. Government and public service had been my goal since I was at Roxbury Latin, and the Root-Tilden program reinforced this objective. Idealism was bubbling up in me.

I had seen firsthand Boston's residential segregation, but I knew the single greatest social wrong in my country was the denial of the right to vote to black people in much of the South. I was going to have the chance to help address it.

On Friday afternoon, February 16, 1962, after putting in a full workweek in wintry Washington, I followed the regular division schedule flying south. My flight was to Georgia, home of my father's family. In addition to my grandmother in Bainbridge, near the Florida border, I had aunts and uncles in Decatur and Dublin. Aunt Doris had come to my Harvard graduation with her younger sister Grace. At our wedding, though it was her first integrated social event, Doris had not hesitated to take the arm of my law school classmate Dawnald Henderson, an usher who was African American.

Doris took my new occupation in stride: "Gordon," she told me, "you are always welcome here unless you are on official business." Official business would take me to two Georgia counties for the first time: "bloody" Terrell County[6] and Daugherty County, where the city of Albany was gaining notoriety.

Five months later, I was the only Justice Department lawyer in Albany when Dr. Martin Luther King, Jr., was arrested for the second time by the force of Police Chief Laurie Pritchett. I was accused at a press conference by Albany mayor Asa D. Kelley, Jr., of "fomenting disorder" on behalf of Robert Kennedy, whom I still hadn't met,[7] as well as "conspiring with the leaders of the Albany Movement and the outside agitators . . . to violate city ordinances and . . . disrupt the peace."[8]

But in the Civil Rights Division of 1962, five months was an eternity. This was still February and, as to Georgia, simply a quick trip to maintain contact with black sources of information there. The main event on the department's civil rights calendar was preparing for the trial of the department's first big effort in the state of Mississippi, the preliminary injunction being sought against Forrest County registrar Theron Lynd, whose records we had been barred from seeing.

I was accompanying my section chief, D. Robert Owen, a thirty-two-year-old graduate of Princeton. Princeton, the southernmost of the Ivy League schools, retained a southern presence that Harvard and Yale never had. A son of Mississippi senator John Stennis was just one example. But the dedication of Princetonians Doar and Owen to the cause of civil rights was extraordinary.

Bob was described by his Princeton classmate, *Washington Post* reporter Don Oberdorfer, as having come out of Albany, Texas, and three years at Connecticut's Choate School with "that ruddy complexion, the big wide grin nearly as big as all of Texas, and the ready laugh, almost a guffaw."[9] But behind the guffaw was resolute tenacity. Bob was a junior varsity football player who stayed with it and made Princeton's varsity as a senior. He was also president of the Presbyterian Club and a leader of the campaign to make the eating clubs, the heart of Princeton's social life, open to all of its students. After two years of army service, part of it in Korea, and a year teaching at Choate, Owen attended the University of Texas Law School, finishing at the top of his class.

In the late fifties, he was selected for the Justice Department's honors program and joined the division almost at its inception. John Doar described Owen as "an essential part of the mind of the division, but the dead center of its soul."[10] Writing for Princeton's tenth reunion publication at the time of our trip south, Bob described his occupation as being a Civil Rights Division trial attorney "selling an unwanted product mostly in Mississippi."[11]

Bob and I flew from Georgia to Mobile, Alabama, where we rented a sedan. Soon I was in Mississippi for the first time, about to help sell that unwanted product. Having an out-of-state license plate was certainly not desirable, but, with Mississippi plates bearing the county name, a Hinds County car from the Jackson airport would have attracted about as much attention.

That first visit remains vivid. We drove in thick humid air forty miles northwest of Mobile on two-lane Route 98, where the small, rolling hills and scrubby terrain of Rocky Creek, Mississippi, gave way on the right to a large truck stop where the diner proclaimed in large block letters its right to refuse to serve whomever it wished.

Next was Lucedale, the little county seat of George County. Only seven of the county's 580 black residents were registered to vote. Between May

21, 1960, and April 24, 1962, when we obtained a temporary restraining order against the registrar, Eldred Green, 283 whites and 16 blacks filled out application forms. All but one white was registered. Not one black was registered. Two-thirds of the whites were asked to interpret Section 30, one of the easier sections of the Mississippi Constitution: "There shall be no imprisonment for debt."

One of those white applicants was John Cecil McMillan, a forty-two-year-old white farmer. His interpretation of Section 30 was: "I thank that a nearger Should have 2 years in college Be for voting. Be cause he don't under Stand."[12] McMillan joined the other white applicants as a registered voter. Five, or 31 percent, of the black applicants received Section 30. Among the rejected blacks were high school and college graduates and teachers, one the holder of a master's degree from Northwestern University.[13]

But George County, as yet, meant nothing to me. Later, I was eating in a Lucedale restaurant on a Friday night when performers gathered after their annual minstrel show. After everyone had arrived, still in blackface, the local white funeral director, who headed the event, rose and gave his financial accounting, reminding all loudly that a few dollars must be deducted for the "nigger stuff" they were wearing.

From Lucedale, we continued up Route 98, by Camp Shelby, an army base, and into Hattiesburg. Bob and I were joined for a few days by another division attorney, Carl Gabel, who worked mostly on Alabama cases, but helped us there. Carl was an able, large, gregarious man, whose undergraduate and law school years at the University of Illinois had been interrupted by two years in the army. He had joined the division a month after I did.

The *Lynd* case had been scheduled for trial in Jackson in January, when a severe ice storm blanketed that part of Mississippi. Lynd and his lawyers never appeared, but fifteen of our sixteen black witnesses made it through the ice and snow, only to find the trial postponed. Delay was rarely welcome in the Justice Department as it fought the racial disfranchisement that had endured since the end of Reconstruction, but nature's continuance in January had given us the chance to rethink our approach to the case.

We had been prepared to present our case solely through the testimony of those black witnesses, who would now have to travel to Jackson again. They were a diverse, impressive group. Five were teachers, three men: Jesse Stegall, David Roberson, and Chuck Lewis, and two women: Addie Burger and Eloise Hopson, all with master's degrees awarded or in process from prestigious northern universities. There were six workers from Hercules, Hattiesburg's major factory: the Reverend Sam Hall, T. F. Williams, Sherman Jackson, Willie Thigpen, Willie Simpson, and John Mosley. They ultimately filled skilled jobs once reserved for whites. Two were full-time ministers: the Reverend James C. Chandler, a Baptist, and the Reverend Wendell Phillips Taylor, a Methodist. The Reverend Wayne Pittman was both a minister and an interior decorator. Finally, there were B. F. Bourn and Vernon Dahmer, lay leaders of the black community.

Now we planned to add to their testimony that of Forrest County whites for each general time period when one of our black witnesses was either rejected or not permitted to take the state's literacy test. We were not seeking converts to the cause of black voting rights. We just wanted a "control group" of white people who would testify honestly that they were registered upon making just one visit to Theron Lynd's office, and that, if they had to fill out an application at all, they were assisted by Lynd's staff, and given one of the easier sections of the Mississippi Constitution to interpret.

Judge Harold Cox had handled the case since its filing in July 1961, the month he was sworn in as a judge. Cox had barred our presenting any testimony dealing with voting discrimination prior to the February 1959 day Theron Lynd took office. Thus, we had to focus on recent applicants for registration, the vast majority of whom would have just turned twenty-one, then the voting age.

Cox had also dismissed the August 1960 demand the U.S. Attorney General had made for Forrest County's voting records pursuant to the 1960 Civil Rights Act, saying we had abandoned that action when we brought the basic voting rights discrimination suit under the 1957 act eleven months later. There was no legal basis for his outrageous dismissal of our records demand. Nor was there any sound basis for his ignoring our discovery motion in the new case to review Lynd's records.

There was a time when all civil litigation was a "play your cards close to the vest" affair. You tried to surprise your opponent. The Federal Rules of Civil Procedure had ended that in U.S. District Courts generally well before I was in law school, but not, I learned, in civil rights cases in the Southern District of Mississippi. We were confronted with what Judge Elbert Tuttle would term the "well-nigh impossible task" of proving voting discrimination by Theron Lynd without access to any of his records.[14]

I spent my first week in Hattiesburg getting to know our black witnesses and preparing them for that second trip to Jackson. The staff of the chamber of commerce never asked who I was or why I wanted a map. They just provided me with a large-scale map of the city. With some trepidation, I also looked in on the registrar's office to get a direct sense of the physical layout where our witnesses had been turned away.

I soon was able to write Stephanie: "I now know Hattiesburg better than any city except Boston. I know it by sections like Glendale Community (white), Kelly Settlement (Negro), and East Jerusalem Quarters (Negro) just the way I know Roxbury and Jamaica Plain in Boston." I also noted that I had survived my first Mississippi haircut, one dollar in cost. The fact that I got a haircut there suggests I was still a bit naive about the dangers.

Bob, Carl, and I were in fact leading double lives in Hattiesburg, spending much of our time in the black community with our prospective witnesses, but going to a white barbershop, eating at a delicious whites-only ribs restaurant, and staying at the whites-only Dumas Motel just south of downtown on Route 11. Indeed, all of the lawyers then working the South for the Civil Rights Division were white. Unlike other divisions of the Justice Department, the Civil Rights Division had actively and successfully recruited black clerical staff from area business schools, and there were a few black lawyers who did not travel and remained in Washington. But it was not until later that year that Thelton Henderson, later a distinguished federal judge in California, became the first African American in the field for the division.

There was a reason for the racial makeup of the voting rights trial staff, apart from the fact that America's law schools were graduating few black lawyers. This was still more than two years before the public accommodations provisions of the Civil Rights Act of 1964 would bar racial discrimination in hotels, motels, and restaurants. With few exceptions, a black lawyer in the Deep South had no public place to stay or eat.

Yes, one of our black witnesses might take him in—and we were all men, with America's law schools also turning out very few women lawyers. But that could endanger both the witness and the lawyer. There were risks for white lawyers, but at least we had the motels frequented by traveling salesmen where we could sleep and restaurants where we could eat.

Thelton Henderson was recruited by John Doar from Doar's legal alma mater, Boalt Hall at the University of California. Doar felt strongly that, despite those difficulties, we should add a black presence to the trial staff. Upon joining the division, Henderson was constantly on the road and had persistent lodging problems.

In Birmingham, he could stay at the A. G. Gaston Motel owned by a wealthy black, where Dr. King and the other leaders of the Southern Christian Leadership Conference stayed. In Selma, there was Craig Air Force Base. Greenville Air Force Base, which I had inspected for discrimination against black servicemen and their dependents, was a good location if he was working in the Delta. But in Jackson, Mississippi's capital, there was only a former funeral home where Thelton stayed, never to forget the harsh smell of formaldehyde.[15]

The days were flying by as I continued to talk to our black witnesses. I learned that a little dirty pool had been played at the Hercules Powder Company by M. M. Roberts, Registrar Lynd's principal trial attorney. With the obvious cooperation of local Hercules management, Roberts had gone on February 20 to the plant, accompanied by Hattiesburg's chief of police.

Two of our witnesses, T. F. Williams and Reverend Hall, were called up to the office to be interviewed by Roberts, along with seven other black employees. Roberts took statements from all nine. The chief was not in uniform, and was not introduced in his official capacity, but every southern black in 1962 recognized his chief of police. That morning Assistant Attorney General Dugas Shands had reminded Roberts that "instead of the lawsuit" they would be trying our witnesses and those who had encouraged them to attempt registration.[16]

The notion of Roberts conducting interviews was not unethical, even allowing for the tape recorder he brought with him, as long as that was in full view. But it was blatant intimidation to have them summoned by their employer from their workstations to the interviews, with the police chief in attendance. The only two we intended to call, Williams and Hall, did not succumb to the intimidation, despite Roberts making clear that "trouble" was being stirred up.[17]

One afternoon the city police barged into the home of one of our prospective black witnesses, executing a search warrant as we were interviewing the witness there. The police never asked who we were. We assumed that they knew. Apparently the police were looking for hard liquor, then illegal in Mississippi, though prevalent in Gulfport on the coast, where the man worked.

I was struck by the humidity as I set off to meet Reverend Hall when he emerged from his shift at Hercules at 3 P.M. Hall had been working for Hercules since 1939, had become a lead man in their lab and, more important, had achieved what he really wanted: to preach. Every Sunday he made a thirty-eight-mile round trip to Mount Hebron Baptist Church in Sumrall. We went to his home and reviewed together his attempts to register. Reverend Hall was ready to testify.

Judge Cox's adroit exclusion of testimony about Lynd's predecessors had at least targeted the white populace we had to reach: those who had reached the voting age of twenty-one in the last three years. I went first to the local library to check the yearbooks of Hattiesburg High School and of the county high school. Bob and I were in and out of the Hattiesburg library for much of three weeks, searching out newspapers, yearbooks, city directories, and other documents to identify and locate whites who might recently have been placed on the rolls by Forrest County's registrars.

I also thought of my own church. Mississippi wasn't settled by Catholics, and Klan activity made it a none-too-congenial environment for them. In 1962, of 2.25 million Mississippians, there were only some 71,000 Catholics, slightly more than 3 percent. This broke down to 6 percent of the white population and half of 1 percent of the blacks. Richard O. Gerow, a seventy-six- year-old native of Mobile, had been bishop of the state's only diocese, Natchez-Jackson, for thirty-seven years, a longer period as bishop than any other Catholic prelate in the United States.

Two-thirds of the diocesan priests had been born and educated in Ireland. Only a handful of the American-born priests were native Mississippians. The state's few black Catholics were cared for by orders that focused on that work: the Josephites and the Society of the Divine Word.

The foreign-born priest insulated himself from questions of race, and I learned that Bishop Gerow had barred priests from preaching on civil rights. The church's position in the state was precarious, its still Latin ritual foreign to the fundamentalist beliefs of most of the state's citizens.

One example of an anti-Catholic whispering campaign occurred in July 1961 after the state's Board of Trustees of State Institutions of Higher Learning confirmed the appointment of a new dean of education for Mississippi State University—a Catholic. Dean W. Colvard, the university's new president, learned that "a former officer of the university had quietly raised the question as to whether this new dean might join with other Catholics in favoring racial integration."[18]

In fact, any white Mississippian not a Baptist had cause for concern. For only white Baptists were certain to reflect the soundly racist position of white Mississippi, and Baptist candidates for office never hesitated to trumpet their religion. Methodists, the second largest denomination in the state, were becoming suspect. Early in 1963, a declaration of religious principles by a number of white Methodist ministers that moderately spoke of racial tolerance was widely publicized in the state. Many of them lost their pulpits as a result.

I went to see what help I could get at Sacred Heart Parish, the stately brick church attended by most of the small number of white Catholics in Forrest County.[19] I was in luck when I visited Sacred Heart. The priest who greeted me warmly was Father John Izral, raised in a very religious Polish-American family in Wisconsin, who had attended an independent seminary in Ohio. After his ordination as a priest, he'd been able to choose among several dioceses interested in him.[20]

I was fortunate that he had chosen Mississippi. Father Izral believed in what I was doing and understood both our need for white witnesses and the time frame to which we were restricted. He went to the church's baptismal and marriage records and quickly found me the name of Helen Marie Coughlin, daughter of the local florist, as well as those of other young Sacred Heart adults. My unofficial designation as division point man dealing with Catholic parishes in Mississippi and Louisiana was thus established.

With Father Izral's names, and those of many more from the high school yearbooks, we were ready to bring on special agents from the New Orleans office of the FBI. It was a sensible division of labor. The FBI would get on better doing cold interviews of white southerners; we certainly did better with blacks.

Henry Putzell, back in Washington, described FBI reports as "something of a mixed bag—sometimes good, sometimes bad. They needed a lot of direction. You'd have to dot every 'i' and cross every 't.'"[21] With the bureau director J. Edgar Hoover no enthusiast for our work, we set forth the exact language of every question we wanted asked, in the order we wanted them asked, from name and address to precisely what was said to and by the women who serviced Theron Lynd's registration counter. And that was what we did in a lengthy memorandum to "Director, FBI," from John Doar.[22] Much of the bureau's New Orleans regional office was soon working the white residences of Forrest County, asking those questions about their registration experience, in order, in our words.

I worked with Don Steinmeyer, one of the special agents conducting our interviews, in a number of Mississippi counties. Don had grown up in a small Minnesota town. He'd soon realized that blacks in the Deep South "were being had," while "all kinds of illiterate whites were being registered." He considered one circuit clerk he encountered "mean, an out and out Klansman."[23]

After we reviewed the reports of the bureau interviews, I did some follow-up visits to whites we expected to call. About 7 one evening I was interviewing a twenty-five-year-old man when his father marched into the living room and ordered me out of their house in no uncertain terms. You did not delay in that situation, but I decided to make one final stop and drove to the outskirts of Hattiesburg to see a young man whom Carl Gabel had talked to briefly before leaving for Selma.

I was greeted by the Arnolds, angry parents in their fifties. They accused four FBI agents of having harassed their son, also twenty-five, several times throughout the day. It took an hour, but finally the Arnolds conceded that the agents had not intended to gang up on their son.

Bureau agents always worked in pairs, as we also were supposed to. The FBI had mistakenly sent two pairs of agents to the Arnold house, the first in the morning, and two other agents in the afternoon. By the time I had agreed that all of the Arnolds were "100% Americans" and certainly not "outlaws," I had been invited to stay for dinner, which I politely declined, and to "come back and shoot a bird sometime."

I gave them a brief pep talk about sticking up for their stated belief that qualified blacks should be able to vote. That belief may not have been shared by the younger Mrs. Arnold, an attractive nineteen-year-old grand-niece of Mississippi's late racist governor and senator, Theodore Bilbo. In 1946, Bilbo had "called on every red-blooded white man to use any means to keep the Niggers away from the polls."[24]

I didn't ordinarily give sales pitches to southern whites, but by then, we were getting on well. Mr. Arnold also appeared to be impressed that, in contrast to the FBI agents, I had come to their house alone. I was lucky to have had the time to win them over and to have emerged unscathed on that and other occasions when I did make calls alone. I could have encountered a shoot-first, talk-later couple. By 11 P.M., Bob and I went to sleep, exhausted and feeling under the weather.

But the next day I was ready to visit 123 Reader Street and meet John Dennis Bennett, a twenty-four-year-old roofer's helper at Burkett's Sheet Metal Works, whose FBI interview I had read. I also met his twenty-two-year-old brother James. The Bennetts were clean-cut impressive young men, and I put them on our subpoena list. I thought they would testify clearly that they were registered promptly without being required to take any literacy test.

That, however, illustrated the problem of being forced to prepare for trial without records. In fact, John had filled out an application form in March 1961, interpreting section 118, that the governor's compensation not be changed during his term of office, a not overly taxing section. Deputy Clerk Wilma Walley registered him, filling in the precinct on his form.

James Bennett had told me he had no memory of filling out anything except his registration card when he went to the office in September 1961. But he had interpreted section 128, that the lieutenant governor was elected for the same term as the governor. At least both were clear on the fact that the woman who registered them had written in their precinct. This was significant because many of our black witnesses had been rejected for not knowing the name of their precinct.

Our thirty-two subpoenas, typed for security reasons ninety miles away at the Jackson office of the U.S. Attorney, were served on the afternoon of Wednesday, February 28. White Hattiesburg was shaken. One local lawyer, whose wife we excused because of recent childbirth, told me he had never seen such furor at the county courthouse that lodged the office of Theron Lynd.

John Doar joined us Friday night by way of Biloxi and New Orleans, and ready for action. He would try the case in Jackson the next week. We would lead with what we considered our greatest strength, the black teachers, starting with an elementary school principal followed by the wife of the high school principal.

CHAPTER 6

THE NEW JUDGE IN THE SOUTHERN DISTRICT OF MISSISSIPPI

Just who was Judge Cox? How did he get there? For answers we must first turn to a meeting in the spring of 1961 between Robert Kennedy and William Harold Cox.

The meeting took place in the U.S. attorney general's massive office between Constitution and Pennsylvania Avenues. Robert Kennedy, brash and intense, the harasser of corrupt labor leader Jimmy Hoffa, was the campaign manager who had gotten his older brother elected president. Now Robert Kennedy was thirty-six years old. He was attorney general of the United States.

William Harold Cox (no relation to Luther Cox) was about as different from Robert Kennedy as he could be. Cox was deeply rooted in Mississippi, the son of the two-time sheriff of Sunflower County in the Delta. More important, Cox was a longtime friend and supporter of the powerful chairman of the Senate Judiciary Committee, James Eastland.[1] Cox was rated "exceptionally well qualified" to become a federal judge by the American Bar Association. But Cox was a racist.

Robert Kennedy and Harold Cox both spoke the English language, though Kennedy's clipped accent was a world away from Cox's slow drawl. Kennedy recalled the meeting:

I said that the great reservation that I had was whether he'd enforce the law and whether he'd live up to the Constitution, and the laws, and the interpretation of the Constitution by the Supreme Court . . . He assured me that he would. He was really, I think, the only judge whom I've had that kind of conversation with. He was very gracious. He said that there wouldn't be any problem about that, that he felt he could accomplish a great deal, and that this would not be a problem to him.[2]

They heard each other, but never was there a greater absence of understanding.

The Kennedys were often criticized by northerners, sometimes correctly, as excessively cautious in moving ahead on civil rights. Yet most white southerners viewed the brothers as arrogant, aggressive enemies, using every tool in the federal arsenal to bring down the southern way of life. Robert Kennedy's laws and Constitution were radically different from Harold Cox's.

Cox, however, said all the right things. His FBI background check had turned up nothing untoward, and he had that ABA rating. Burke Marshall considered both checks "by and large worthless," since the investigators generally spoke to lawyers who would practice before the nominee and found superlatives the tactful response. "The FBI would not normally go and interview black people . . . the black people wouldn't talk to them . . . certainly wouldn't talk candidly to them."[3]

Yet Cox was "one of the very few lawyers in Mississippi who had not joined the White Citizens' Council." The Kennedys thus had no evidence against Cox except his relationship with Eastland. Neither Kennedy could tell Senator Eastland that association with Eastland was fatal to a man's chance to become a judge. And so William Harold Cox became President Kennedy's first judicial appointee.

The victor in the 1960 election had seventy-three judgeships to fill—judgeships created by an omnibus judiciary bill. But the presidential power to appoint was far from unfettered. The powerful tradition of senatorial courtesy meant that a state's senior senator controlled the selection of that state's judicial nominees when the president was of the same party. And if the senator was James Eastland, chairman of the committee that passed on every judicial nomination, senatorial courtesy was senatorial command. "The Senator no doubt had many virtues," Marshall recalled, "but he was a very tough cookie to deal with, and so the possibility of a logjam [of Kennedy judicial nominees] was very real."[4]

Judge Elbert Tuttle understood what happened in the attorney general's office:

They were talking different languages. When Bobby asked if he would uphold the law of the land, he was thinking about Brown v. Board of Education. When Cox said yes, he was thinking about lynching. When Cox said he believed Negroes should have the vote, he meant two Negroes.[5]

Liberals might get Thurgood Marshall as circuit judge for New York, Connecticut, and Vermont, but the Southern District of Mississippi would get Harold Cox. Senator Eastland had been told by Robert Kennedy that there would be no hands-off policy for Mississippi. Eastland had responded with his own hands-on policy. Cox would have a whole new range of cases to deal with: actions brought by the Civil Rights Division of the United States Department of Justice. The judicial hands on *United States v. Lynd* would be those of William Harold Cox.[6]

William Harold Cox was born in June 1901 to Adam Charles and Lillie Emma Ray Cox in Indianola, the Sunflower County seat in the center of the Mississippi Delta.[7] A. C. Cox was serving the first of two widely separated terms as sheriff of Sunflower County. In 1900, the ratio of African Americans to whites in the county was 3–1, a legacy of large slave plantations that stood in the county forty years before. The black to white margin rose to 4–1 by the time young Cox was ready for college in 1919. While growing up, Cox encountered a boy three years younger, James Eastland, son of a lawyer and a wealthy planter in nearby Doddsville, who, of course, knew the sheriff.

We know a great deal about the environment in which Cox was raised because Indianola, home of the first White Citizens' Council, under pseudonyms such as "Southerntown" and "Cottonville," became the subject of intense psychological—anthropological research in the late 1930s by both Yale's John Dollard and Hortense Powdermaker of Queens College. Dollard found that "Caste has replaced slavery as a means of maintaining the essence of the old status order in the South."[8]

Powdermaker also described the caste-like social system and asked seventy-one detailed questions about the racial attitudes of the community's white citizens. Two hundred fifty-six responded, including members of the chamber of commerce and the Rotary Club and adherents of Methodist, Baptist, and Presbyterian Churches and a nearby Jewish Sisterhood. Most of the respondents were junior college students, possibly doing it as an assignment. Among the questions and responses were:

Negroes are all right as long as they stay in their places, True 96%, False 2%;

The Negro should be granted full political equality, True 5%, False 94%;

The Negroes' place is in manual work, True 79%, False 17%;

Negroes are inferior to white people in innate capacity, True 84%, False 13%.[9]

❖❖❖

In 1924, Harold Cox received both a bachelor of science degree and the basic law degree from the state's premier higher education institution "Ole Miss," the University of Mississippi in Oxford. That same year he was admitted to the Mississippi Bar and began practice in Jackson, the state capital.

In 1932, Cox was admitted to the Bar of the United States Court of Appeals for the Fifth Circuit, the court that thirty years later would regularly reverse him. Cox received the "av," rating, the highest possible, denoting both ability and integrity, in the Martindale-Hubbell national law directory. A general civil practitioner, he handled 108 cases before the Mississippi Supreme Court during the twenty years before his appointment to the federal bench.

At the time of his nomination, Cox was still practicing in Jackson's Deposit Guarantee Bank Building, by then with another "av" rated lawyer, Vardaman S. Dunn. He and Mrs. Cox belonged to the First Baptist Church in Jackson. He enjoyed hunting and fishing and spent many Saturdays on his skeet-shooting range.[10]

Rare is the federal judge appointed without political connections or participation. Cox had both: his early ties to Senator Eastland, and, most important, his membership in the Hinds County Democratic Executive Committee beginning in 1950, and serving as chairman for four terms. It is said that when Eastland first ran for the Senate in 1942, Cox showed him his checkbook, told him what he needed to live on, and declared the rest to be Eastland's for the campaign.

In 1955, the Eisenhower administration had slotted a Fifth Circuit seat for Mississippi and asked Eastland for suggestions. The two names he put forth to Deputy Attorney General William Rogers had been District Judge Sidney Mize and Harold Cox. Victor Navasky reports that Rogers "literally laughed." He "considered the idea so implausible because of what he understood to be Cox's segregationist reputation that he neither ordered a preliminary investigation within the Justice Department nor asked the Bar Association Committee to check him out."[11]

Two weeks later, Rogers accepted Eastland's selection of Meridian railroad lawyer Benjamin Franklin Cameron, which was also supported by Fifth Circuit judge John Minor Wisdom, with whom Cameron would have constant strife in the future. Cameron was as staunch and ornery a segregationist as Cox, but, like Cox, was on his best behavior during the interview process and had not joined the White Citizens' Councils.[12] Appointed United States Attorney by Republican Herbert Hoover, Cameron had remained at least a nominal Republican.[13]

During the administration of Dwight Eisenhower, the American Bar Association's Standing Committee on the Federal Judiciary made itself a key player in the process of selecting federal judges, a role that continued until the arrival of George W. Bush in 2001.[14] Truman's deputy attorney general, Ross Malone, a member of the ABA Board of Governors who had returned to private practice, established with the Justice Department a procedure whereby the ABA committee could rate a prospective candidate before the nomination was made.[15]

In the last two years of the Eisenhower administration, the ABA committee had "virtual veto power," with only those candidates rated at least "qualified" going forward to the Senate as nominees.[16] The committee was a rotating group of older big-city lawyers, one to a circuit. From 1953 on, its major player was Bernard Segal, the first Jewish chancellor of the Philadelphia Bar (1952–1953), and the first Jewish president of the ABA (1969–1970).[17] In 1959, Deputy Attorney General Lawrence Walsh advised the ABA's House of Delegates that Bernard Segal had become "next to the Attorney General himself . . . my most intimate associate in Washington."[18]

The ABA continued its influence during the Kennedy administration, despite Segal's having co-chaired a Citizens for Nixon Committee. But the ABA Committee's great clout did not survive the election of 1960. Thirty-two of President Kennedy's first thirty-three judicial nominees had ABA ratings. Six, one of them Harold Cox, were considered Exceptionally Well Qualified, seventeen Well Qualified, eight Qualified, and one Not Qualified.[19] In all, however, President Kennedy appointed seven judges rated Not Qualified by the ABA.[20] Could they have been worse than the "extremely well qualified" William Harold Cox?

John Seigenthaler, a key aide to Robert Kennedy in the Justice Department, used to see Senator Eastland at social functions: "The banter was always light, but he would inevitably during the course of an evening, get it across that his . . . lifelong friend was going to be a great district judge."[21] Eastland had also reminded Deputy Attorney General Byron White, the official charged with managing judicial appointments, "I told you I was going to mention this matter to you every time I saw you."[22]

Leon Jaworski, a distinguished Houston lawyer, and a personal friend of Lyndon Johnson, was the ABA Committee's review chairman for Cox.[23] Two dozen Mississippi lawyers and judges whom Jaworski respected assured him that Cox would be fair. But Segal remained wary and flew to Jackson to have lunch with Cox. He remained sufficiently concerned about Cox's racial attitudes to "express deep concern" to Robert Kennedy.[24] Thus the conversation on the attorney general's sofa described earlier took place: would Cox enforce the Constitution of the United States as the Supreme Court (and the Fifth Circuit) interpreted it?

On June 27, 1961, William Harold Cox was confirmed and prepared to move over to the federal courthouse. Vardaman Dunn replaced him with William H., Jr., down from Ole Miss with his newly earned law degree, and Charles Clark, an able lawyer who represented Governor Barnett at the time of James Meredith's entry into Ole Miss and later served on the Fifth Circuit. Clark became the first chief judge of the smaller court after the circuit was divided.[25]

Cox took the oath of office in July, just short of his sixtieth birthday. One month later, he stopped hearings in four Department of Justice actions that demanded the voting records of Forrest, Clarke, Jefferson Davis, and Walthall counties under the straightforward provisions of the Civil Rights Act of 1960. My mentor, Bob Owen, was the division attorney frustrated by the court.

It was a fraud case, though a vague and premature one, Assistant Attorney General Dugas Shands argued for the state. And Cox agreed: "A gross willful, deliberate discrimination is involved. When you don't let a colored person vote with the same qualifications of a white man who votes, I can't, to save my life, consider that as anything but fraud."[26] It was fine philosophy, but not honored by Cox later. He lectured Owen: "I don't approach a civil rights case any differently from that of any other kind."[27]

On September 6, the hearings resumed with further dilatory requests made for "more definite statements" by the state. The department asserted that none of Clarke County's three thousand Negroes of voting age was registered to vote. However, Cox made clear that the fact that none was registered meant "nothing to (him). I don't know how many wanted to register or tried to register."[28] At the same time, he was making it impossible for the government to provide him with that information.

On October 21, 1961, the Justice Department complied with Cox's order that the names of those blacks discriminated against in Forrest County be filed with the court. The *Jackson Daily News* chose to print only the names of Clyde Kennard, whose attempt to enroll at Mississippi Southern had led to a seven-year prison term on a trumped-up charge, and the Reverend W. D. Ridgeway, who, testifying before a U.S. Senate committee, was one of the first persons to state publicly that Circuit Clerk Luther Cox was asking black vote applicants: "How many bubbles in a bar of soap?"[29]

The new year arrived with Cox dismissing as "abandoned" our records demand cases for Forrest and Clarke counties.[30] He would be duly reversed and lectured by Circuit Judge John Brown: "We emphasize again that the filing of the application by the Attorney General is not the commencement of an ordinary civil action with all its trappings. . . . There is no place for a motion for a bill of particulars or for a more definite statement."[31] With "no indication that this interminable proceeding would ever come to an end . . . the District Court effectually denied the Attorney General's application."[32]

How did it happen that state attorney generals were representing these four county registrars? In a June 1962 letter to all eighty-two registrars Attorney General Joe T. Patterson set forth these alternatives:

> *More than likely you will . . . be visited by representatives of the Attorney General of the United States with the request that you permit them to inspect and reproduce all voting and registration records. . . .*
> *1) You may choose to allow [this inspection]. . . .*
> *2) It is your privilege and right to decline to make the records available for inspection and reproduction, in which event the Attorney General of the United States will in all probability attempt to obtain a federal court order.*

Patterson stated that this decision was "solely and completely within the power and decision of the Circuit Clerk." However, he went on to say, "I, along with the entire staff of this office, stand ready to render to you any assistance and service that this office can render."[33] His office was already representing the clerks in the four Mississippi counties sued prior to his letter.

Judge Cox had even worked on an August Saturday, ruling that Mississippi's Breach of the Peace law under which two hundred Freedom Riders were arrested for refusing to leave a segregated bus terminal was

> *a perfectly natural and necessary exercise by the state of well-known and well-recognized police power . . . this court may not be regarded as any haven for any counterfeit citizens from other states deliberately*

seeking to cause trouble here. Their status as interstate passengers is extremely doubtful—their destination was Jackson but their objective trouble. . . . They had no civil right to . . . provoke mob violence.[34]

Cox charged Freedom Rider attorney William Kunstler with attempting to convert the law into a segregation statute.[35] The word about Cox had certainly reached Kunstler, a renowned civil liberties litigator, who was seeking a route to the Fifth Circuit.

On September 7, 1961, John Hardy, a twenty-one-year-old Negro from Nashville, was struck on the back of the head with a pistol wielded by John Wood, circuit clerk of Walthall County. Hardy was leaving the clerk's office in Tylertown, the county seat, with two black registration applicants who had been turned away by Wood. In an affidavit, Wood said he hit Hardy because he had refused to leave his office when ordered and had a "contemptuous glare" on his face.[36]

Hardy had completed his sophomore year at Tennessee Agricultural and Industrial State College and had come to Walthall County with several other black students to conduct a voter registration school for SNCC. Classes had begun August 18 with attendance varying from twenty-five to fifty each evening. On the day he was attacked, Hardy had gone to the circuit clerk's office with Lucius Wilson, sixty-two, and Edith Simmons Peters, sixty-three, both farm owners in the county. Mrs. Peters had an eighth-grade education, all that was then available for blacks in the part of Mississippi where she was raised.

Hardy waited just outside as Wilson and Peters entered the office. When Mrs. Peters advised Wood that they wanted to register, he replied: "I am not registering anyone now. You all have got me in court, and I refuse to register anyone else until this court is cleared up." Wood presumably was referring to our Walthall County records demand, one of the four Judge Cox was delaying.

Hearing this, Hardy entered the office. He had given Wood only his name when Wood said: "Do you see that door, John? You get out of it." Hardy turned to go, but Wood struck him on the back of the head, saying: "Get out of here you damn son-of-a-bitch—and don't come back in here."

Wilson and Mrs. Peters helped Hardy out of the building. He went first to the office of the *Tylertown Times*, whose editor had written about him a week before. The editor told him to seek medical attention, but Hardy wanted to see the sheriff, Edd Craft, whom Hardy had met the first day he accompanied blacks to the office. Craft, not surprisingly, was far from sympathetic, telling Hardy he had no business there and placing him under arrest "for disturbing the peace and bringing an uprising among the people." The sheriff also told Hardy that any comments from him would cause Craft to "beat [him] within an inch of [his] life."[37]

The Department of Justice, concerned over how unusual it was to seek to block a state court prosecution, did not move with the speed of some later cases. Hardy's trial was scheduled for September 22 before a justice of the peace. The department's suit, seeking first a temporary restraining order to bar Hardy's prosecution, was filed on the twentieth. At 5 P.M. on the twenty-first Judge Cox denied the order and refused to sign a certificate allowing the government to appeal what was an interlocutory or preliminary order.

The government contended that the prosecution of Hardy, regardless of its outcome, would intimidate blacks from exercising their right to vote, in violation of the Civil Rights Act of 1957. Thus, while what Cox had issued seemed, on its face, merely an interlocutory order, it was really a final order depriving the government, and the voting age blacks of Walthall County, of the relief sought. John Doar and assistant Mississippi attorney general Ed Cates appeared before Cox. The judge declared that "the Government's contention 'that the trial of that case tomorrow will irreparably damage the United States in deterring colored people in Walthall County from registering . . . is without any substantial support . . . and appears as a non sequitur.'"[38]

Doar and Cates flew that evening to Montgomery, Alabama, where at 10:30 P.M., they were received by Circuit Judge Richard Rives in his home. Doar presented Rives with a petition to stay the state prosecution pending appeal of Cox's decision. Judge Ben Cameron muttered in his later dissent that "the whole procedure was in keeping with the government's practice of demanding and, and most often receiving, special treatment."[39] Cates agreed to continue Hardy's prosecution pending disposition of the government's appeal,[40] and Rives scheduled an expedited appeal for October 3. Judge John Brown joined Rives and Cameron on the panel. Burke Marshall argued the case for the United States, a 2–1 victory for the United States, correct on its merits, and also predictable, because two of the judges were Brown and Rives.

On October 27 the court held that the 1957 statute required that the district judge grant the restraining order and hold a full hearing with witnesses. Rives declared: "The foundation of our form of government is the consent of the governed. Whenever any person interferes with the right of any other person to vote . . . he acts like a political termite to destroy a part of that foundation."[41] The decision was applauded in the *New York Times* and the *Washington Post*.[42]

Cameron was left in his dissent to deplore the "enthusiastic write-up with photographs in its issue of December 5, 1960, page 14" given six of his colleagues by *Time* Magazine. One could understand his dislike for an article entitled "Trail-Blazers on the Bench—South's U.S. Judges Lead a Civil Rights Offensive."[43] Matters were not helped in Cameron's mind by Hardy's having told the editor of the Tylertown paper that he was skeptical "about the existence of God" and "did not believe in service in the armed forces."[44] But the heart of Cameron's dissent was a plaintive cry to leave his way of life alone:

> *At a time when the daily press is filled with stories of racial strife from every corner of the globe, men of good will have, for more than a century, avoided such strife and have advanced together in a spirit of brotherhood with a speed which those who take the trouble to learn the facts think is phenomenal.*

That "spirit of brotherhood" had not allowed a single black man or woman to vote in Walthall County.

It would be nice to say that the division always confronted intimidation so well and so successfully. That would not be accurate, however. "We could have done more," John Doar concedes today.[45] Marshall and Doar always had in mind that there was no federal police force. They wanted to make local law enforcement do its job. They felt that the insertion of federal forces that ultimately would have to be removed would leave situations back where they were before their arrival. The historian Michael Belknap has pointed out that their approach ultimately worked, that "by the late 1960s most of those responsible for law enforcement in Mississippi and the rest of the South were committed to combatting racist violence."[46]

Where federal force was necessary to enforce court orders, such as the enrollment of James Meredith at Ole Miss, force was, of course, used.[47] But no one in the administration forgot that two deaths occurred there, and they were grateful that such force was avoided at the University of Alabama[48] and elsewhere.

We did not expect violence in Hattiesburg in March 1962. We were ready to put before Judge Cox, among other witnesses, five black teachers with master's degrees who had been rejected by Theron Lynd. Our task under the 1957 Civil Rights Act was to prove a pattern of racial discrimination. I hoped Lynd's systematic rejection of obviously qualified teachers would make that burden easy.

CHAPTER 7

THE FIRST WITNESS,
JESSE STEGALL

In any multiple witness trial, a significant strategic decision for a lawyer is choosing the first witness. The first witness will likely get the longest, toughest, possibly nastiest cross-examination. The first witness will set the tone of the case, impressing or not impressing opposing counsel and, more important, the judge.

You don't want a witness you must protect excessively with objections, sound or not. That will only annoy the judge. You must keep in mind that one of your tasks is building the record for an appeal, here to the far more receptive arena of the United States Court of Appeals for the Fifth Circuit.

For us the choice to lead off was not that hard. Jesse Stegall was an elementary school principal, married, a father, a man with a lot to lose in publicly seeking to vote in hostile Forrest County.[1] My friend Jim Groh found him.

◈◈◈

Every one of the small group of lawyers who made up the southern trial staff of the Civil Rights Division had certain landmark events in his career. Jim Groh had worked on the Tennessee sharecropper cases with John Doar when John first became first assistant. Jim was also proud of being the first division lawyer to talk with Jesse Stegall.

Groh grew up on a farm near Richland Center, Wisconsin. After majoring in history at Ripon College, he briefly taught high school history and German before attending Marquette Law School in Milwaukee. Jim joined the Civil Rights Division right out of law school in 1960. He was, as he put it, a "less than closet Republican."[2]

In late September 1961, Jim, then twenty-seven, was "sent down to cruise Forrest County and make cold calls on possible sources/witnesses":

We were still feeling our way around in Mississippi, having spent most of 1960 in Tennessee and then focusing on the Middle District of Alabama . . . with time out for the Freedom Riders for most of May 1961 . . . Hattiesburg was obviously a gold mine, and Jesse was obviously the key to the mine.

By that time I had probably visited fifty or so counties full of frightened, intimidated, and often very marginally educated people. To find a school principal and other teachers—people with graduate degrees—who were willing to try to register and to testify was like finding the Holy Grail. I also believe that Hattiesburg was the largest town we had tackled to date . . . Forrest County immediately became a hot prospect. I don't think it is any secret that the Kennedy Administration at the time was interested in early, dramatic and successful results, and I suspect that is why Forrest was put on the front burner.[3]

Because of the Berlin crisis, Jim was recalled to active army duty from October 1961 until August 1962. But he had made a contribution in Forrest County, just as he had in Tennessee and in Alabama. Fresh out of the army, he grabbed a suitcase and left for Oxford, Mississippi, where he helped safeguard James Meredith, serving as one of his dormitory roommates during the battle to achieve Meredith's entry into Ole Miss. Jim would not be in court in Jackson with us on March 5, but Jesse Stegall would.

Who was Jesse Stegall? What gave him the necessary courage to step forward?

Stegall was born in Charleston, Tallahatchie County, Mississippi, in 1931. His father, James Willie Stegall, was a hard worker and devout Baptist, who moved his family to Laurel when Jesse was three. Bruce Lumber Co., his father's new employer, had family housing for its workers called "Bruce's Quarters." The Stegalls lived there until 1940, when his father obtained an apartment at the Maple Street government projects. Public housing would be home until Jesse finished Oak Park High School in 1950.

I knew just one of my grandparents, my father's father, Willie Stegall. He worked in Memphis at the York Arms Company, which was like a sporting goods company. And he would send us boxes of balls and bats, damaged products that we could play with. I once asked him how we got the Stegall name. It came from the German Jew who lived on the Tennessee-Mississippi line, our master in the slave period. I was concerned about it. You don't find too many black people named Stegall, you see.

Jesse's father quoted the Bible to him. He measured and cut lumber for the Bruce Company. Jesse's mother had died when he was six months old, and he was raised by his father and his stepmother, whom his father married after moving to Laurel.

Jesse's father and stepmother had no children together. Mother, as he called her, had worked with preschool children in Laurel, and Jesse learned from her about the need to help undernourished young children.

We were God-fearing Baptists. About the only thing I knew as a boy coming up, was going to church, working, and going to school. I remember being baptized at the age of five at the Union Baptist Church up at Bruce's Quarters. I sang in the choir in church. I went to prayer meetings on Thursday nights, and I went to the Baptist Young Peoples' Union in the afternoon. My life growing up was really so highly religious that you get those kinds of things in you that you never lose.

Jesse was the youngest of seven children born to the first Mrs. Stegall. Most of them went in different directions—from Memphis to New York. The only other Mississippi voter applicant among Jesse's siblings was Annie Kathryn, the only black registered nurse of her day at Hattiesburg's Forrest General Hospital.

When I was coming up, you could get on the free lunch program at school. But we were not poor enough. We were the working poor. My father and mother knew how to make ends meet, how to sacrifice, and we never went hungry or anything like that. They instilled in us those attributes. So when I look back, I had a happy life. I didn't get to play high school football, because I had a job after school, but I did end up one of the cheerleaders.

The Stegalls subscribed to the local paper, the *Laurel Leader-Call*. Mrs. McKenzie, the black editor for the *Leader-Call*, wrote about their local community activities: the social lives, the academic side, the organizations. The Stegalls also read the leading black press, the *Pittsburgh Courier* and the *Chicago Defender*. Through them African Americans learned what black people were doing in sports, education, and the rest of American life, and were exposed to outspoken coverage of American racism, on both the news and editorial pages.

> *We were under these laws, and therefore we took the position that whites were over there, and we were over here. We had pride in ourselves. We felt, even when we got ready to go to college, that it wasn't just for the sake of prestige. We wanted to go, and when we got there, we wanted to accomplish something.*

Of the fifty-four in Jesse's graduating class at Oak Park High School, over half went on to college.

> *Ten went with me to Jackson State and five or six to Alcorn. Willie Brown went right to Maharrie Medical School. He is a doctor in L.A. Lewis Brown went to a school in California and is an attorney in Anaheim. King George went to Wilberforce. He's an art teacher in L.A. Charles Walker got his degree in pharmacy from Xavier in New Orleans. Then he was stationed in California in the service and established his pharmacy practice there. Charles tried to get me to come out, but I just felt like staying here in Mississippi.*
>
> *The teacher that really was most responsible for me being where I am today was Mrs. Hattie V. J. McInnis, my high school music and choral teacher. She thought enough of me to recommend me to the music people at Jackson State and take me over there to try for a music scholarship.*
>
> *Mrs. McInnis was Leontyne Price's music teacher. When I was in the sixth grade, Leontyne was in twelfth, but she and my sister were very close. She lived just a block from the projects. I played ball with her brother George, who became a general. Mrs. McInnis would have Leontyne's golden voice singing in Christmas cantatas.[4]*

Willis Perkins was the only white person to influence Jesse's early life. Perkins had been in the service. On the Fourth of July when Jesse was a junior and senior in high school, Jesse camped out with the Perkins family around the Tombigbee River.

> *I worked downtown in Laurel at the Roth Stores from the time I was 10 or 12 until I finished high school, sometimes a salesman, sometimes a custodian, whatever the need would be. I worked with Mr. Perkins, the*

manager. And, would you believe: when I finished high school, he took
me to Jackson State, to go to college.

When Jesse was a student there, Jackson State's majors were limited to
elementary education, language arts, physical education, or music. Jesse
had a music scholarship, but he did not want to be a music teacher. He
settled on language arts, was an honor student, and sang with the college
choir in black churches in Detroit, Chicago, and Birmingham, as well at
the old chapel at Fisk University and an integrated church in Evanston,
Illinois.

When I was working on the college's 75th Diamond Jubilee Anniversary
in 1950, I met Langston Hughes, who was a member of my fraternity,
Omega Psi Phi . . . He autographed a number of his books for me, in-
cluding Simple Speaks His Mind. He said we've got to wake up people.
Later, I would read it to my own students, to show the writing that one
of our own was doing, and interpret it, and have them also do research
on Hughes. Langston Hughes impressed me not knowing how great he
was. He was just a normal, down-to-earth person who enjoyed being
around students. When I began teaching black history, we celebrated
a Hughes February.

I also met Zora Neale Hurston, who did Jonas Gourdvine. I hadn't
known the caliber of writers that we had among the Negro race. Dr.
Margaret Walker Alexander, who wrote Jubilee, taught me "The Bible
as Literature" in my junior year.

Dr. Jacob L. Reddix, our president, said: "You can lead a horse to
water, but you can't make him drink. But you can get his mouth wet."
People called him a dictator, but he and I were very good friends.

Besides working on campus, Jesse was vice president of the Student
Council and business manager for the choir. He also managed his fraternity
house. At the time he became a "Q," it was very selective: a B average was
required, as was persevering and helping the less fortunate. At a fraternity
dance, Jesse won a membership in the NAACP.

Jesse's first job was teaching Language Arts to grades seven through
twelve at a small school about five miles south of Columbia and about thirty miles from Hattiesburg, where his wife was from. The future Mrs. Stegall
had arrived at Jackson during his junior year. They married secretly a year
later in 1953. She dropped out and worked until Jesse finished college. Their
first child was born in 1957.

The Stegalls lived with her grandmother in Hattiesburg, so there was a lot of commuting, but the next year Nathaniel Burger, the principal of Hattiesburg's Broad Street High School, which became Rowan High, hired him. Jesse recalled that "Mr. Burger was a fine person, very academic and smart, a very strong administrator and good supervisor I liked to emulate. He stood behind you and encouraged you. We walked together, about five miles every afternoon."

Jesse never aspired to be a principal. He was happy teaching at Rowan and helping Mr. Burger operate a school for veterans at night. But when the principal of the Bethune Elementary School retired, the superintendent asked Mr. Burger to recommend a replacement. Jesse was his choice.

Summer study was the only way he could earn a master's degree. Jesse selected the University of Wisconsin, which offered tuition and room and board at a reasonable price. He studied in Madison summers from 1960 through 1963.

Brown v. Board of Education was decided by the Supreme Court at the end of Jesse's senior year in college, May 1954.[5] He and his friends considered it a historic moment in their lives as future teachers, but it would be a long time before Mississippi integrated schools. Not even the staffs of Jackson's schools were integrated until 1970. When the Supreme Court in the second *Brown* decision in 1955 urged "all deliberate speed,"[6] Jesse thought that would mean prompt action. He learned otherwise.

Jesse and his friends always wanted to vote. They didn't like paying two dollars a year poll tax just to be eligible to vote, but blacks who applied were able to vote in Jones County, and Jesse didn't think he would have a problem—until he arrived in Hattiesburg. Hattiesburg and Laurel are about thirty miles apart and similar in size, but Jesse felt Laurel had better race relations.

You didn't have the fear of being black. I never was intimidated; I was accepted as just another person. It never struck me, when I moved to Hattiesburg, the difficulty we would have, even to register, till I got there and found out there were so very few blacks who could vote.

Jesse did not attempt to register to vote when Luther Cox was circuit clerk. His first try was with Theron Lynd. Mr. Burger was already registered, as was old Dr. Charles Smith and his brother, pharmacist Hammond Smith. But there were few others. The teachers at Rowan discussed it: Stegall, Chuck Lewis, David Roberson, Iva Sandifer, and Eleanor Harris, and they swore to affidavits before a notary public to let the Justice Department know that they had gone and been refused. Stegall, Lewis, and Roberson told a meeting of the Hattiesburg Teachers Association what they were doing.

> *But when we had gone so many times and when Mr. Groh and all at the Justice Department had become aware of our predicament, and more pressure was being applied from the Justice Department on the Circuit Clerk's office, someone called Mr. Burger to have him tell those of us who had gone down to come back, and they would let us register. This was all before we testified.*
>
> *We refused. I said, "No, it's too late now." We were not going down to be troublemakers. We were going down to get our right to vote. And when you were going down to register to vote, and these barricades are placed before you, you get frustrated, until it really angers you. And you say, "Well, I'm going on," even though people talked to Superintendent S. H. Blair about me. I would tell him: "I need to go to court," and he would tell me to go ahead. Mr. Blair was white, but he never tried in any way to hinder any of us, going to court. In fact, the business, to him seemed to be, "This is your right. Good luck."*

Stegall was married and had a child. He knew he had a lot to lose, but he had told his wife that he was going to go all the way. It was just not right, he felt, for him not to be able to vote. He told himself he was not afraid, that it was an experience.

The January 1962 ice storm caused the first scheduled hearing not to go forward.

John Doar visited Jesse before his second trip to Jackson. Jesse remembers it this way:

> *John told me: "I think I'll put you on first." He said: "What do you think about it?" I said: "Well, okay."*

We were not about to change our minds. Jesse Stegall would be first up on March 5 in the Jackson courtroom of William Harold Cox.

◆◆◆

Our other witnesses were waiting outside Judge Cox's spacious high-ceilinged courtroom. Inside, John Doar took Stegall through general background information, then through his education over Shands's objection.

q. Now are you registered to vote in Forrest County, Mississippi?

a: No, sir, I am not.

Dugas Shands objected that our case was based solely on voting, the Fifteenth Amendment, and evidence of Fourteenth Amendment equal protection violations was not admissible. The judge overruled the objection.

q: Mr. Stegall, have you ever since February 26, 1959, gone to the circuit clerk's office and made application to register in Forrest County?

Stegall described attempting to register with Roberson and Lewis in the fall of 1960. Chuck had been back for a full year by that time from Oregon State where he had been doing graduate study. The three Young Turks, as they thought of themselves, came in the rear door to Theron Lynd's office in the courthouse about 4:15 P.M. A woman asked what they wanted and said they would have to see Mr. Lynd, and he was out. They received no reply to Roberson's question: "Is Mr. Lynd the only one that registers you?"

Stegall looked up to the wall above Judge Cox. He saw images of cotton pickers that he found "really depressing." Stretching across the back courtroom wall was a chilling mural of "happy plantation life." At the left, slaves dutifully picked cotton, while other slaves carried the cotton away on their backs and another played the banjo in the background. In the center, three generations of white plantation owners appeared before their four-columned brick mansion. Then there was a white clergyman holding his Bible and another white man evaluating blueprints or other plans, while a helpful black looked over his shoulder. The family dog was nearby.[7] The fond message of "the good old days" was not lost upon Stegall.

Stegall testified that he returned to the registrar's office just before 5 P.M. and again was told Lynd was not in. They were back again after school on a November 1960 day just after 4 P.M.

Mr. Lynd came to the counter where Mr. Roberson and I had walked, and asked: "What do you boys want?" I stated: "I came to find out procedures on which to register." He said: "What is your name?" I told him my name. He asked what did I do. I told him my occupation. He asked where I lived. I told him that also.

And then he said: "No, I can't register you," [H]e said he did not have the time. . . . I asked, when would it be possible for me to see him when he had the time. He said he did not know.

Stegall laughed to himself when Doar asked him to identify Lynd. He didn't find it too difficult with Lynd weighing well over three hundred pounds.

The three teachers did not return until September 29, 1961, again just after 4 P.M. They were by then well aware that there was a new president and a new Justice Department trying to get people registered to vote.

Lynd asked Stegall all the same questions again, then said:

> "I can not . . . handle all of you, at the same time, you will have some papers to fill out," and Mr. Lewis asked him what type papers were they to be filled, and also how long probably it would take. Mr. Lynd stated: "If you do not finish by five o'clock you will have to begin all over." . . . So we decided to leave.

M. M. Roberts objected to John Doar's "leading the witness," and Judge Cox told Doar: Yes, Counsel, this man is certainly literate, and I think he's able to answer your questions, so don't lead him. Jesse Stegall's literacy was obvious to all, and, whether Judge Cox realized it or not, he had come very close to saying Stegall was qualified to vote.

The three Young Turks were back again the next afternoon, a bit earlier this time, about 3:35. Lynd came to the counter and told Stegall to follow him into the upper end of the office. He gave him an application form and two index cards with section 178 of the Mississippi Constitution to interpret, dealing with the power of the state legislature to charter corporations. It took Stegall about thirty-five minutes to fill out the form. Lewis would follow him, but there was no time for Roberson.

Shands objected at length that Stegall could have memorized the section between the time he applied and the day he testified and made the mistake of bringing up the best evidence rule.

THE COURT: Do you have the evidence?
SHANDS: It's in the office.
THE COURT: You don't have it here?
SHANDS: I have a copy here.
THE COURT: All right, you want to let him have the copy?

We were delighted with a copy and quickly agreed in exchange to provide Shands with any FBI reports we might have for our witnesses. It was the first time we had seen a Forrest County voting form.

Shands asked if he could have a continuing objection to Stegall's testimony.

THE COURT: Yes, sir.

SHANDS: And an added ground to that objection is that as against the State of Mississippi this evidence is not admissible. That applies to every bit of his testimony.

THE COURT: All right, sir.

Even Judge Cox was getting tired of Shands by this time, and it was just midmorning of the first day.

Stegall's answer on his September 29 form read:

The legislature has the power to establish corporations. The legislature also has the power to abolish such corporations provided that no injustices are done to its stockholders. Under this section of the Constitution of Mississippi, no charter shall be issued to corporations for capital gain more than a period of ninety-nine years. The property and franchise of corporations having charters exceeding ninety-nine years shall be assessed for taxes and subject to the right of surrendering excess length of time over the ninety-nine years' duration.

As to the duties of citizenship, Stegall wrote:

Each citizen under a constitutional form of government has the duties and obligations of: 1, Upholding the laws of the government; 2, Abiding by the laws of the government; 3, Respecting the rights and properties of fellow citizens; 4, Working faithfully to free the government of all subjects who attempt to overthrow the government or try to retard its functions as a constitutional government.

A week later Stegall returned to Lynd's office to find out if he would be allowed to vote. Lynd told him: "No." When asked what part of the application was failed. Lynd said he could not divulge that information. When asked when it would be possible to fill out another application form, Lynd said it would be, "according to law, six months." Stegall left the office. It was clear to him that, even if he had a Ph.D., being black, he was not going to pass, not under Theron Lynd.

THE COURT: How many times did you attempt to register?

THE WITNESS: Six times, sir.

Then Dugas Shands cross-examined:

Q: Did you ask Mr. Lynd for any help?

A: Yes, sir.

Q: What did you ask him to help you on?

A: I wanted to ask him a question in regard to a statement that was on the form, not as . . .

Q: You mean you didn't know how to fill out the form?

A: No, no, not necessarily that, sir. . . . It was something pertaining to a minister, a minister plea, which I could not quite understand, sir . . .

Q: You did not understand that question dealing with the kind of oath you were required to take, is that correct?

A: Could I quite—I'm trying to follow you, sir, you—you—

THE COURT: He doesn't understand the question. Ask it again.

Stegall got the impression that Judge Cox thought Stegall was imposing on his time, that he didn't seem to have much concern whether blacks got to vote or not. Stegall's foregone conclusion was that Cox was going to rule against them.

Fear had not affected Stegall's willingness to testify and, in fact, be our leadoff witness. However, he would not have been human if he were not nervous. Dugas Shands tried hard to suggest that Stegall's request for clarification from Lynd showed he was unfit to vote. A stubborn clash between Shands and Stegall over information versus clarification seemed interminable.

Finally Shands moved on:

Q: Do you swear that you signed that application?

A: Yes, sir.

Q: You filled it out completely?

A: Yes, sir.

Q: Would you be surprised to know that you did not sign that application?

Shands had still not shared Stegall's application with him, or us, but pressed him to explain why he hadn't signed it. Stegall, of course, thought he had signed it. This was all a new experience for Stegall who had never been in any court before coming to Jackson to testify. He was not likely to forget the interrogation of Dugas Shands, but he kept remembering what we had told him: "Be sure, whatever you do, to tell the truth."

Q: Now, how many times have you read Section 178 of the Constitution since that day? How many times have you read that section?

A: I can't recall, sir, to tell you the truth.

Q: You've read it a great deal, haven't you?

A: No, sir, I have not . . .

Q: How many times have you read it, Jesse?[8]

A: Sir, to be frank with you, I do not know.

Q: All right. Have you read it more than five?

A: No, sir.

Q: More than three?

A: No, sir.

Q: More than two?

A: Maybe approximately two.

Q: Uh-huh. You haven't talked to the Department of Justice lawyers about it?

A: I have sir.

Q: How many times have you been over it with them?

A: Once, sir.

Q: Did you complain to the Department of Justice and file a complaint, Jesse? . . .

A: Sir?

Q: Can you hear me?

A: Yes, sir, I can.

Q: Well, what are you delaying about?

A: Well, I'm trying to get the implication of your question.

By worrying about the implications of Shands's questions instead of just answering them, Stegall was hedging his answers more than an effective witness should. Shands and Stegall then fenced about whether Stegall had filed a written complaint with the Justice Department. Stegall had orally complained to Jim Groh, his first visitor from the Civil Rights Division. Jim's visit had given the Young Turks feelings of hope and of confidence that the Justice Department was at work in Hattiesburg, trying to help them.

Stegall told Groh he had just been to register a few days before he came, and, when the time came, he'd go back. Groh told him not to wait the six months Lynd had decreed and to write a narrative report of what happened and forward it to them. Stegall felt he had a direct line to the Justice Department.

Shands continued:

Q: Who brought the Department of Justice men to you, Jesse?

A: They came to me, sir, on their own . . .

Q: How did they get your name?

A: I do not know, sir.

Q: Uh-huh. You didn't ask them how they got your name?

A: No, sir. I only answered the questions that they asked me.

Stegall did not know who had suggested his name. He had a feeling it was Mr. Burger, because Burger was a key person in the black community whom everyone knew and respected. Stegall was not, however, about to volunteer that thought to Shands.

Q: How many times had they been to you before you filled out the application?

A: Mr. Groh came to me before that time approximately three times.

Q: Did Mr. Groh tell you that you ought to go back and try to fill out an application?

A: He told me to try again, yes, sir.

Q: And did you try again as he directed you to do?

A: I told him . . . after filling out the application I could not go back, according to the ruling of Mr. Lynd, in six months.

Q: Mr. Lynd told you that?

A: Yes, sir.

Q: You knew better than that, didn't you?

A: No, sir.

Q: Uh-huh. Now, when was it Mr. Lynd told you that?

A: On October 6th, 1961.

Q: Do you understand, Jesse, that you are under oath here?

A: Yes, sir . . .

Q: You understand that you are sworn to tell the truth, the whole truth, and nothing but the truth?

A: Yes, sir.

Q: And you say that Mr. Lynd told you that you could not come back for six months?

A: Yes, sir.

Shands concluded with a series of repetitive questions about whether or not Stegall signed his application. On re-direct, John did get the copy of Stegall's application into evidence and pointed out that Stegall had signed it on the third page.

John then asked Judge Cox if Stegall could leave. Shands told the judge that they wanted Stegall to stay in a room incommunicado, for further questioning. Stegall considered that a ploy to punish him because they could not upset his testimony. He was there until evening, when Judge Cox released him. He was not permitted to listen to the other testimony and couldn't even go out for food.

But our strategy in beginning with Jesse Stegall had, on the whole, been successful. His testimony had demonstrated Theron Lynd's consistent pattern of refusing to permit black applicants to register to vote. It had also made clear that Stegall was an educated, thoughtful man whose only agenda was to exercise his constitutional right to vote, against all odds. Addie Burger would be next.

CHAPTER 8

FOR THE DEFENDANTS

Dugas Shands and M. M. Roberts

Amazing as it might seem, the job title for Dugas Shands was head of the Mississippi attorney general's Civil Rights Division. "God, what a racist he was" was the way Bill Minor described Jesse Stegall's antagonist.[1] A different Jackson reporter wrote: "A white-haired, slow-speaking lawyer stands between Mississippi and racial integration."[2] They were really saying the same thing.

Shands was born in Panola County in the northern part of the state in 1906, and moved to Cleveland in the Delta at an early age. His bachelor of arts degree was from Vanderbilt, and he attended the first year of law school there. But his law degree came from Ole Miss, where in 1929 he served as the first student editor of the *Mississippi Law Journal*.[3] He was also a member of a national fraternity chosen on the basis of literary ability. Not just in Shands's law school class, but appearing on his page in the 1929 annual, were John C. Satterfield, the 1961–1962 president of the American Bar Association, and Allen Thompson, later mayor of Jackson.

In 1950, Shands moved to Jackson and represented various public agencies and utilities. At one point Senator Eastland brought him to Washington to serve on the staff of the Senate Judiciary Committee. Mississippi's then attorney general J. P. Coleman appointed Shands an assistant attorney general in 1954. In 1959, Joe Patterson, who succeeded Coleman when the latter became governor, picked Shands to be the first chief of his Civil Rights Division.

He was the second Garvin Dugas Shands. His grandfather and namesake, born in Spartanburg, South Carolina, in 1844, fought in the Civil War, first as a private, then a sergeant of the Second South Carolina Cavalry. For ten years after the war, he practiced law in Senatobia, Mississippi, serving from 1871 to 1875 as the area's state representative. Shands was lieutenant governor from 1882 until 1890 and in 1894 joined the law faculty of the University of Mississippi, becoming the Law Department's first dean in 1897.[4] In 1906, he became the first president of the newly created Mississippi State Bar Association.[5]

A student said Shands had "the most inexhaustible supply of words" he had "ever heard from a man's mouth."[6] His grandson took after him. A century later, the younger Dugas Shands was still fighting what his grandfather considered the "War of Northern Aggression."

James Meredith had his own thoughts about the Dugas Shands he encountered. Meredith's legal route to becoming the first African American undergraduate at Ole Miss was tortuous despite his having the superb representation of the litigating leaders of the NAACP Legal Defense Fund, Constance Baker Motley and Jack Greenberg.[7] A plaque at the National Civil Rights Museum, located at the site of Memphis's former Lorraine Motel where Dr. Martin Luther King, Jr., was assassinated in 1968, sets forth Meredith's view about the manner in which the second Dugas Shands deposed him June 8, 1961:

> *[Shands's] pattern was crystal clear. It is what I always refer to as the "Nigger Treatment," the most common and basic system used in dealing with Negroes in the Mississippi courts. The tactic is used to provoke the Negro, to frighten him, and then to break him down and cross him up. The aim is to imply that the Negro is dishonest, immoral, a thief by nature, and generally unworthy of being considered fully human.*

Meredith, an air force veteran who had attended Jackson State and found it inadequate, had to wait until February 3, 1962, for his case to be decided in federal district court, where Judge Sidney Mize famously ruled that the "University (of Mississippi) is not a racially segregated institution."[8]

On June 25, 1962, Judge John Minor Wisdom of New Orleans, appointed to the United States Court of Appeals for the Fifth Circuit by President Eisenhower, emphatically rejected that absurd conclusion on behalf of his court. That fall, Shands advised Governor Ross Barnett on how to resist Meredith's entry into Ole Miss.

Before appearing in the Forrest County case, Shands represented the state in a case involving Freedom Riders who hoped to end segregation in transportation facilities. While preparing the case, Shands was hospitalized for exhaustion. By a 2–1 vote the state's request for a month's delay was granted. On an August Friday in 1961, Judge Mize adjusted his schedule to accommodate Shands's caseload and health. Just a few days earlier, Shands had clutched at a railing in Mize's courtroom to prevent falling.

The belief was that Shands had suffered a heart attack, and when he made his debut on August 12 before the new judge in the Southern District, Harold Cox advised him to sit if he wished. Before Cox was a motion involving both Forrest and Clarke counties and lots of what Cox called "wailing and carrying on."[9] That aptly described Shands's mode of litigating, which annoyed even Judge Cox, who agreed with his positions. Shands chose to stand as he decried the Department of Justice lawyers who had termed his motion trifling and preposterous.[10] The hearing continued two days later, consuming some four and one-half hours.

Shands may have appeared pale and worn in the summer of 1961, but by late December he was busily playing games in the Oxford courtroom of Judge Claude Clayton of the state's Northern District. Justice Department lawyers believed they would suffer fewer difficulties there than in the Southern District, since the week before the hearing Judge Clayton had ordered the sheriff and the circuit clerk of nearby Tallahatchie County to turn over to the government poll tax and voter registration records. Tallahatchie County had 6,483 black residents descended from slaves, and none permitted to pay their poll tax or register to vote.

Although fortunate to have that county's records, the department lawyers found many similarities to the situation they would encounter just two months later in Forrest County. Tallahatchie sheriff E. R. Dorgan, like Theron Lynd, had just taken office in 1959. Like Theron Lynd, Dorgan would not permit his subordinates to wait upon blacks. Dorgan's office deputies testified that they were under orders to refer to Dorgan any African American who wanted to pay the poll tax. They had never personally accepted a poll tax payment from them. Some Mississippi counties did accept poll tax money from African Americans while not permitting them to vote. Tallahatchie County was consistent in neither taking their money nor letting them vote.[11]

On a dark forbidding night, November 14, 1961, John Doar came to the Tallahatchie hill country, looking for the small homes of four potential black witnesses. Wary of retaliation, each was reluctant to sign an affidavit setting forth the number of times over the years he or she had been rebuffed in trying to pay the poll tax. One refused, but Sylvan Drake, Grafton Gray, and Birdia Kegler agreed to go the next morning to the federal courthouse in Oxford for their affidavits to be executed and witnessed.

Mrs. Kegler lived in her own home, a house made of concrete blocks outside Charleston, the county seat. It was across a bridge and a railroad track and about two miles down a dirt road. When Doar reached her home the next morning, her son Robert, protective of his mother, said she was sick in bed. A skeptical Doar asked to see her, and found Mrs. Kegler, a small woman wearing her nightcap, in a double bed under three or four quilts. She had obviously passed a very anxious night. Doar sat by her bed, and, after they talked for a bit, he told her that he was going to get Drake and Gray and expected her to be ready upon his return. When Doar returned and knocked on the door on Mrs. Kegler's rickety porch that rainy morning, she was wearing her Sunday best.[12]

Birdia Kegler, fifty-three, managed a funeral home for blacks. In late 1959 or early 1960, she had been turned down in her first attempt to pay her poll tax. A year later, she encountered Dorgan on the street and asked when Negroes would be allowed to pay poll taxes. "He said he didn't know."[13]

At a subsequent hearing, Dugas Shands started to cross-examine Mrs. Kegler in his usual grueling, condescending manner, but he had a little surprise for her. Rising to his full height, Shands declared: "Since you were at the sheriff's office . . . do you know that Sheriff Dorgan found that you were qualified and that a poll tax receipt has been issued you, and all it lacks is a date and two dollars?"[14]

Mrs. Kegler obviously did not know, and Doar said she would pay the two dollars that she had been trying to pay for ten years. Shands may have made a tactical decision to give Judge Clayton some ammunition for a ruling in their favor. Mrs. Kegler paid her poll tax and voted during the next four years.

But about 6 P.M. on January 11, 1966, Mrs. Kegler was returning home by car from a civil rights meeting in Jackson. She and another black woman died in an automobile crash believed caused by a white driver under circumstances long considered suspicious. However, a 2009 investigation by the Civil Rights and Restorative Justice Project of Northeastern University School of Law located a credible witness and determined her death had been an accident.[15]

For some time Shands assumed that Burke Marshall was black. He clarified that for M. M. Roberts, writing: "I have met Mr. Marshall, and he is not a negro, tho he is certainly doing all he can for them."[16]

As the *Lynd* injunction trial began, Dugas Shands would be the lead lawyer cross-examining our witnesses, but, working in Jackson, he had been removed from the daily fray in Hattiesburg. For Theron Lynd, as it was for Luther Cox, ongoing legal guidance came from M. M. Roberts.

We had scarcely sat down in Judge Cox's courtroom on March 5, 1962, when M. M. Roberts painted for the court his picture of our trial preparation: "Swarms of federal government employees, they go in the nighttime to see them, everybody in the nighttime under cover of night, without a moon."[17] We were not foolish enough to do that, however. We generally worked from early morning to early evening. Nighttime was reserved for dinner and planning the next day.

What did the great judges of the U.S. Court of Appeals for the Fifth Circuit think of M. M. Roberts? John R. Brown told me he would never forget Roberts:

He was a real busybody—a fairly competent lawyer. Had a tremendous practice, apparently for a lot of insurance companies, and he had ten or fifteen secretaries. He was always flitting from one place to another; I'd meet him here, meet him there, but he was not a real good scholar. He just talked all the time, so you couldn't really tell what he was saying. He was the idol of the old Mississippi who wanted to keep things like they had always been, and he'd always been successful in doing that. We had to adjust our schedule to his sometimes. . . . Lynd was a tool, that's all. I don't think he had a real idea about what he ought to do. He was just in the complete control of M. M. Roberts.

Brown continued:

You know that football stadium at the University of Southern Mississippi is named for Roberts. Now that they have a mostly black team, he's turning over in his grave a hundred times. He was a typical Mississippian with a typical Mississippi attitude toward blacks. No place for them in the government.

John Minor Wisdom called Roberts "completely ineffective" and "a babbler."[18] Dugas Shands considered Roberts a useful Hattiesburg accomplice. I found Roberts effectively evil.

Malcomb Mettie Roberts, the man who controlled Theron Lynd, was born in 1895 in a two-room log house in a remote area of Jackson County near Mississippi's Gulf Coast. At the age of three, M. M. fell ill. A doctor summoned from Lucedale, twenty-five miles away, painted M. M. with a black substance. The little boy was "fearful that (his) skin would thereafter be black."[19]

Roberts's mother, Nellie Bond, had served as a washerwoman for a wealthy family nearby and had been tutored by a Scottish missionary who worked with an Indian tribe. Armed with only an eighth-grade education, she had gone some forty-five miles from her home to teach school, boarding with the parents of Malcolm Jerome Roberts, who eventually became her husband. Both of M. M.'s grandfathers had fought for the Confederacy, and his mother's father had been shot in the chest at close range by a Union soldier.

For his first eight grades, Roberts attended the local one- teacher school, named the Roberts School since only Roberts's children attended it. In honor of M. M., the structure has been transported to the vestibule of the Education and Psychology Building at the University of Southern Mississippi.[20] He enrolled at USM when it was still known as Mississippi Normal College, played left end on the football team, and graduated in 1917, despite spending his senior year among the "cow punchers," as Mississippi A&M students were called.

World War I was underway, and Roberts entered the U.S. Navy, becoming a wireless operator. The law did not immediately summon M. M. upon his release from the navy. He spent the next three years as an entomologist with the U.S. Department of Agriculture, then became a teacher and the principal at the Greene County Agricultural High School.

Fifty years later members of the graduating classes in 1922, 1923, and 1924 joined in a letter expressing their "deep and abiding love and gratitude for the dedicated and inspiring service which (he) rendered to the school and to (them)."[21] Roberts had upgraded the staff and the curriculum, enabling the school to be the only one in the area fully accredited.

He was also a coach, and, on weekends, superintendent of the Sunday School. He played the piano in the local Methodist Church. Essie Dean, a graduate of Mississippi College for Women, taught home economics at the high school, and in 1922 she and M. M. were married.

Why did the beloved young teacher forsake education for the law? County superintendent of education was an elective post, and the superintendent did not trust Roberts because M. M. was a friend of the man the superintendent had defeated in the election.[22] Roberts thus departed for Ole Miss and intense work at its law school, delaying a master's degree in education until 1931.

At the law school, Roberts kept his nose to the grindstone. The yearbook said of him: "Mine epitaph shall be mine name alone. Ole Miss lawyers will not soon forget Roberts. Large was his bounty and his soul sincere."[23] Writing years later to a young friend who wanted an automobile, Roberts described that period of his life:

I drove my automobile down to my father's home and jacked up the wheels on blocks in the old buggy shed and went away to school for more than two years where I knew I must save all I could. I walked 1 1/2

*miles each way to school each day and worked as a college law librar-
ian for $15 per month and refused to buy even the Sunday paper.*[24]

In June 1926, Roberts was awarded his degree entitling him to practice
law in Mississippi. He had $600 left over from law school which he used to
set up a small office on the Gulf Coast with William Colmer, the Jackson
County attorney who went on to serve in Congress for forty years.

Roberts soon moved to Hattiesburg. When, in 1951, the impressive array
of disfranchised black men filed a complaint against Registrar Luther Cox,
Roberts was the lead attorney among the many local lawyers who signed
Cox's brief. In 1952, he was elected president of the Forrest County Bar Association. In 1956, it was the presidency of the State Bar Association. With
white, wavy hair and black-rimmed glasses, intense in everything he did,
M. M. still sometimes found time for golf. He played alone, covering the
course at a fast walk or trot.[25]

Before Hurricane Katrina erased a seventy-mile stretch of coastline in
August 2005,[26] you could drive along Biloxi's U.S. 90 on the Gulf Coast and
at Veterans Avenue come to a deserted one-story building with an imposing bell tower. Easy to overlook among the glitzy high-rises housing the
gambling casinos of the coast, that simple building was the place to be on
the coast in mid-twentieth century, before the state bar association began
to ignore its own resorts and moved its annual meeting to Destin, Florida.
"The old Buena Vista Hotel was the most popular sleeper on the Coast."[27]

The 1957 annual meeting presided over by Roberts had to be held there,
and the president always made an address. M. M.'s remarks are remembered
for one thing. Three or four black lawyers were in attendance. To general
embarrassment, Roberts told the group he did not like blacks and did not
want them as members. A prominent Mississippi litigator in attendance,
aware of the USM football stadium's later having been named for Roberts,
told me with disgust that he wouldn't name a toilet for Roberts.[28]

When during the Barnett years a vacancy arose on the state Board of
Trustees of the Institutions of Higher Learning, who was more congenial
a selection than M. M. Roberts? Barnett and Roberts had worked together
in the Ole Miss law library, and Roberts quickly became Barnett's principal ally on the board.[29] Roberts served as chairman of a special committee
dealing with the tenure of faculty members rash enough to openly question
segregation.[30]

In 1963, Dean Colvard, president of Mississippi State University, broke
the state's unwritten law by permitting his men's basketball team, champi-
ons of the Southeastern Conference, to enter the racially integrated NCAA

basketball tournament. Roberts led the call for a special meeting of the board to try to prevent this. Happily, sports had its own constituency, and Roberts's motion won only two other votes. Eight were opposed, and his subsequent motion that President Colvard resign died for want of a second.[31]

Roberts did not give up easily. Two weeks later, he and three other trustees tried to get all controversial matters referred to the board.[32] Roberts's caustic criticism of university actions that he felt favored blacks continued after Colvard left. Roberts objected to Colvard's successor permitting speakers on campus who did not stick to the segregationist script. In 1970, Roberts wrote to the other trustees that he wanted to "clean house" of "those who do not understand Mississippi and its way of life."[33]

Roberts had been instrumental in the selection in 1963 of a friend, Josh Morse, as dean of Ole Miss Law School.[34] As integration slowly evolved, and students began to participate in a legal services office in Oxford, the dean came under attack. In December 1966, the *Clarion-Ledger* columnist Tom Ethridge wrote that some felt Morse had made the law school "a tool of the leftist Ford Foundation, the Negro revolution and the politically minded U. S. Justice Department's efforts to 'change Mississippi.'"[35] Roberts felt "embarrassed" by his law school which he also felt was "being ruined" by too many out-of-state students.[36]

In September 1960, Roberts had suffered a heart attack while advising the registrar of voters of Bolivar County and was hospitalized in Greenville, but he was well enough to represent Theron Lynd. On April 28, 1961, Roberts had written Harold Cox, copying Senator Eastland: "Please know that I would prefer you be named (to the court) rather than any other person who has been mentioned to me. . . . I want to assure you that I shall always want to be co-operative and helpful as a trial lawyer in your court."[37]

In July 1961 Roberts wrote to Lynd and his co-counsel Francis Zachary that the case would become a full-time operation, that he and Zach would be able to make "a career of it," but we're "serving Mississippi and our way of life."[38] Roberts also cheerily advised Lynd not to hesitate to make a brief trip out of town: "If there is need for occupying a jail cell while you are gone, I'm sure Mr. Z will be willing to take your place."[39]

A month later, while urging Dugas Shands to take care of his health, Roberts wrote that there was no greater tragedy than John F. Kennedy being president. He mentioned that he had tried to convince some students that President Franklin Roosevelt was a "skunk."[40]

Roberts's mistrust went well beyond the Kennedy administration to Washington in general. This he vividly expressed in a letter to Peter

Stockett, youngest of the state assistant attorney generals he was working with on Lynd's subsequent petition for certiorari to the Supreme Court:

I have so little confidence in the [Supreme] Court and so little respect for it, that I cannot get up much hope . . . That is a negro court and the nation is doing a "negroidly" job in its plan for total integration and the ultimate amalgamation of the races.[41]

Two weeks before the trial, the pressure was getting to both sides. On February 20, 1962, the same day that Roberts and the police chief went to the Hercules Powder Company to interview black employees who Roberts thought might testify for us, he and Shands did some trial preparation. Shands told him: "I'm getting you what you ought to have." Roberts sadly admitted: "I cannot read these 40 cases to save my soul."[42] He found time, however, to be a source for Sovereignty Commission investigators looking into individuals believed to have Hattiesburg connections.[43]

But the young lawyers working for Burke Marshall and John Doar could take some satisfaction from Roberts's exclamation when Theron Lynd was first cited for contempt on April 30, 1962: "You don't know what the United States Government by the Civil Rights Division will do for one Negro voter against a million whites through this business."[44]

Then there was Theron Lynd's quite different co-counsel, Francis Zachary, who had handled various personal matters for Lynd. All the sharp edges in Lynd's personal defense team belonged to M. M. Roberts. Nasty confrontations were not Francis Zachary's cup of tea. His son Tom, Forrest County's attorney in the 1990s, told me: "My daddy always said, 'Stay out of church and school fights.'"

United States v. Theron Lynd was a racial confrontation. The white community was united in support of the status quo, not divided as it might have been in a school fight or the schism of one of its many Baptist churches. And Zachary was Lynd's personal attorney. Corporate and insurance defense work were the heart of his practice, with some representation of Sears Roebuck and the railroad and occasional judicial patronage from old Judge Wellburn. Zachary had to be there with Lynd. But Dugas Shands and M. M. Roberts would wield the sword.

CHAPTER 9

THE BURGERS OF HATTIESBURG

As a lawyer, if you are pleased with your first witness, you want to avoid a letdown with the second. If the leadoff witness was mediocre, you can't wait to get your case on track. Regardless of how one had viewed Jesse Stegall's testimony, Addie Burger, wife of the respected principal of the black high school, was a solid follow up and unafraid to create waves.[1]

Addie Burger was born in 1914 at Alcorn College in Lorman in Claiborne County. Her father, William S. Nelson, was superintendent of the laundry, and also taught laundrying because Alcorn was then a mechanical college where various trades were taught. Her parents were natives of Nashville where her father had owned a laundry.

> *My father met President Martin of Alcorn at Tuskegee, Alabama, where my father worked for three years and installed the early laundry. President Martin just insisted that he come to Alcorn.*
>
> *My father was about fifteen years older than my mother. I was 14 when he died. My mother, Addie Rutherford, died in 1940. They are buried on the campus behind one of the dormitories. My half-brother, Carol L. Cannon, took over as superintendent of the Alcorn laundry. He had been at A&T College in North Carolina. Instead of moving us to him when my father died, he came to Alcorn and remained until all of us went on to college. His holding that job helped support my going through college. There's no other way that I would have gone through. We maintained the same home provided by the school. We didn't even have to pay rent.*

Addie went straight through from first grade through college right on the Alcorn campus. She felt she had a strong religious life, though Alcorn was nondenominational, and enjoyed the chaplain, Reverend Craig, who also taught shoemaking.

When my husband was principal of Hattiesburg's black high school, he pushed for it to be named for the Alcorn president who followed President Martin, Leroy J. Rowan. I didn't have any sense then as to whether Alcorn had the resources that it needed to do a good job. I thought we were getting a good education, and I still think so, because the teachers were just good dedicated teachers.

Addie's husband-to-be, Nathaniel R. Burger, was born in Brookhaven, Mississippi, in 1909. His family moved to Hattiesburg when he was six. In 1928, Nathaniel Burger came to Alcorn. By Christmas, they had met and had started to court. She was just a fourteen-year-old in the tenth grade, and he was a college freshman. "He just started picking at me," Addie says.

Nathaniel Burger described the Hattiesburg of his youth this way:

There were no paved streets in the black community . . . You had dirt roads . . . when [an automobile] did go through, you knew it because of the big . . . cloud of dust. So that's in the black community. The town proper had paved streets . . . going north you had curbs and gutters, and I don't think anything east of Main Street had. That's where the black community started, just across the Illinois Central tracks.[2]

He had different jobs at Alcorn. Keeping the auditorium clean was one. Later on he drove for President Rowan. Just about everyone at Alcorn worked.[3] The flooding of the Mississippi River in 1927 had wiped out the state's cotton crop, and the Depression also set in. Alcorn students were affected like everyone else. As Burger put it: "The Depression got me." He went home to Hattiesburg for two years, chauffeured for a wealthy man he worked for in high school, and did construction.

Addie caught up a little bit in school at that time. Because of his two-year break, they were only a year apart when they got their degrees. In the 1934–1935 academic year, Addie taught at a high school up in Covington County, then came back, spent the last quarter at school, and marched with the class at graduation. Nathaniel taught math and coached football at Pike County training school in Magnolia. His team had "an almost perfect record, at the zero end."[4] They married just after she graduated in 1935.

Addie and Nathaniel's three sons all attended college. Leroy, the youngest, attended Morehouse College for one year and then was graduated from the University of Southern Mississippi in 1969, majoring in computer science. He became a senior program analyst for General Electric in Pennsylvania. Morehouse, a pillar of Atlanta's great private educational complex for

African Americans, provided the youngest Burger with quality education in an exciting environment, but it was neither cheap nor near Hattiesburg.

However, by the time Leroy was in college, change had come to USM, and, unlike his older brothers, he was able to transfer to the previously all-white state-supported university right in his home community. His parents' courage in persisting in their quest to vote contributed to his ability to transfer to USM, without being subjected to the harassment and trumped up charges that had greeted Clyde Kennard, when he attempted to integrate the university a decade earlier.

After marrying, Addie taught home economics for six years at Hopewell School in Covington County toward Jackson. During her fifth year, Nathaniel became principal of the school. He tells us:

> [Before 1954] white schools were consolidated into districts with buses, but black schools remained little separate schools far apart. I always boast about [one of my former students] who now has his PhD. He . . . always walked about five miles to get to school. I imagine two, three or four white buses passed him on the road.[5]

In 1940, Nathaniel Burger was appointed principal of Eureka, Hattiesburg's black high school. As World War II approached and nearby Camp Shelby was activated, he was confronted with overcrowding caused by a huge influx of children. Band-aid solutions dealt with the overcrowding. However, there was another more difficult problem the Burgers were going to have to deal with. The war had subsided when the first stirrings about black voting occurred. In Hattiesburg, blacks just didn't register.[6]

Neither Burger registered to vote when they were in Covington County, but Nathaniel Burger did register in Forrest County in 1952, the year that Dwight Eisenhower first ran for president. How it happened remained vivid to him.

Finally, he found a way to get through to the circuit clerk, Luther Cox:

> I told him I knew of no other way that I could be accepted as a citizen of this country, other than through registration, and that he really made me a free agent if he closed the door of democracy in my face. If I did decide to ally with some other group then he was the cause of it. I wasn't near about ready to become a Communist . . . After a few minutes . . . he called his secretary and told her to bring the book over and I got registered that day. I don't know, I just confronted him.[7]

Nathaniel Burger actually voted. He wasn't just on the books.

The Burgers liked Superintendant Blair, who ran a good system and had picked Mr. Burger to be the principal at Eureka, but neither Burger was naïve about the facts of segregated life in Mississippi. Mr. Burger was particularly blunt:

> *The black teachers and a black principal worked for what he could get. It's just that simple. . . . You hate to mention the type of salaries offered the black teacher . . . In the rural areas, especially, you didn't get paid every month. You would probably get paid those first four months with a check coming out of the chancery clerk's office, signed by the county superintendent of education. After that, in many counties, you took a yellow sheet, a voucher, and if you got any money you had to cash this voucher at a discount. Now this wasn't altogether limited to blacks, but most of the blacks, this is the way they survived. About four months of the year they got the little twenty-five, thirty, forty dollars a month. Then after that they got that voucher . . . If it was forty dollars it was discounted to twenty-five dollars because the one who cashed it was going to get twenty percent of it. The vouchers were issued through the county superintendent of education's office and you could cash it with any of the merchants . . . You had little recourse to fight back, so you took what you got.[8]*

Mr. Burger remembered that in the late fifties or early sixties, "They came up with an instrument that black teachers had to sign when they got their contract. You had to name at least five organizations that you belonged to."[9] This was, as he well knew, simply a way of finding out who belonged to the NAACP. Teachers who listed the NAACP were in trouble, and, if they were members and neglected to say so, they were also taking a risk.

Burger was one of the hundred black leaders invited to the state capital by the governor of Mississippi just after the Supreme Court rendered its 1954 decision in *Brown v. Board of Education*. Governor White asked them to accept voluntary segregation. They had not expected that, but Burger reports the governor's request was rejected:

> *Dr. [Arenia C.] Mallory, the president of Saints Industrial Institute in Lexington, Mississippi stood on the floor that morning and told the governor that no one, white or black, could be caught violating the*

law of the land. The Supreme Court had spoken . . . Now, that was one side of it. However, those who went down there went down ready to tell them that this change is overdue. For a long time, even though the blacks probably didn't vocally ask, they sought equalization under the state law.[10]

Mrs. Burger went to New York University for her master's degree. She, of course, could not attend any of the white universities in Mississippi, and the black colleges lacked graduate programs. Her friend, Iva Sandifer, had already spent two summers at NYU and was delighted to have company. The state did help finance some of the cost. Addie enjoyed Washington Square, watching the people of all nationalities coming and going.[11] She also visited her brother and sister in New York. The family had gone to Cornell every summer Mr. Burger studied there, but their children were small, and Addie was mostly taking care of them, though she did receive some credits there.

Mr. Burger was stuck on Cornell. We went up one summer just to visit friends. After that, he transferred to Cornell to complete his graduate work. He had been to Atlanta University one or two summers, and Fisk one summer before going to Cornell. Cornell did become a school that attracted Black Mississippians to attend. We sort of influenced one another.

I belong to the Delta Sigma Theta Sorority, just a civic-minded group of ladies. We try to do things for the uplift of the community. I joined the graduate chapter in 1949. Alcorn didn't have sororities.

Mrs. Burger became a United Methodist after visiting various churches in Hattiesburg. She liked the organization and the service of the Methodist Church as well as serving as a delegate to its annual conference.

Years ago we belonged to the NAACP, but nobody knew it. We had our card, but it stayed in our purses. I don't think we attended meetings. Now my husband was a lot more pushy. He just wasn't afraid of things like that.

Well, I finally got interested in voting . . . several of us in the White Rose Federated Club, like Miss Sandifer and Miss Hopson. It's a very active club interested in the home, mother, and the child in our community. I was once the state president. We would get together for civic meetings.

Mr. Burger encouraged me to go whenever I gave the desire. None of my friends attempted to discourage me. Some people said, "Oh, she's going to lose her job." I just didn't have that feel. Mr. Burger did tell me that he discussed it with the superintendent. The superintendent told him, "Let her just keep going." I was just dedicated to what I was trying to do.

Mrs. Burger chuckled at David Roberson having told me, "When the principal's wife went, that was a big deal because the principal's wife wasn't supposed to be rocking the boat." She chuckled again as she recalled lawyers from the Civil Rights Division coming to her dormitory at New York University one summer looking for her. "Something was going on, and they wanted me to be a part of it."

I went to Jackson to testify. I wasn't scared. When we went first in January, we really put our lives on the line, because the roads to Jackson were just iced. Because we were subpoenaed, we felt that we had to go. We didn't know that the whites weren't going.

But on March 5, 1962, Addie Burger was the second witness for the United States. Her testimony and her application form with its elegant penmanship may not have rocked Theron Lynd's boat, but they certainly put it in motion.

"My full name is Mrs. Addie N. Burger. I am forty-eight years old. I have lived in Hattiesburg since 1935 and have been teaching there since 1942."

With that we had moved to a witness who would have an easier time than Jesse Stegall. She was not leading off, and she showed more poise. She was not only a woman, but also the principal's wife. Shands clearly knew who her husband was. On cross-examination he inquired about him and how long he had been registered to vote. Shands objected to Mrs. Burger's testifying that she had already achieved twenty-seven of the thirty-four points required for an NYU master's degree, but after that was admitted, her testimony moved along.

I went to the circuit clerk's office during the fall of 1959, and at that time Mr. Lynd was in the office, and I told him that I would like to register. He said that I would have to come back, that he did not have his feet on the ground, and of course I answered back . . . saying that he had campaigned for the office to accept the responsibilities of registering persons in the county, and . . . was it that he had not registered anyone at that time?

Lynd just repeated that she would have to come back. It was not until April 8, 1961, that Mrs. Burger returned to the circuit clerk's office. This time the lone person in the office was a female clerk. "Well, I asked her if I may register, and so she went to her desk or her files and brought me an application form and two sharpened pencils, too, and then she went to another filing cabinet and gave me a section of the Constitution that I was to interpret on this application."

Maybe the clerk was new on the job, or maybe she felt another woman need not be put through the "See Mr. Lynd" routine. However, she gave Mrs. Burger the type of section of the constitution that Lynd's staff reserved for blacks. The 3-by-5 cards handed to her set forth section 211, an intricate outline of the legislative power concerning title and leasing of "Sixteenth Section lands in this state or lands granted in lieu thereof in the Choctaw purchase." It did not faze Mrs. Burger:

> *Well, it was really self-explanatory because it was very lengthy, . . . but it was giving the power to the legislature to decide on the administration of it, and . . . the term of the lease ninety-nine years in a municipality, and outside of a municipality ten years, . . . the funds were to be used for township schools.*

Mrs. Burger went on for an extra page to complete a strong answer. She also wrote her signature in a place Shands could not object to and gave this statement of the duties and obligations of citizenship:

> *Citizenship responsibilities include one's duty and loyalty to the constitution of the state and nation. One should be law-abiding and make a contribution in all ways possible to the progress of the community and state. The constitution being one for the people that the people should share in having the right kind of representation in its government.*

The following week Mrs. Burger returned to the office to learn the result. The first time Lynd wasn't there, but a few days later she found him in.

> *I told him that I had come to see what the result was of the application that I had made on April the 8th, and he asked me my name and went to the file and pulled the file out and just pushed it back, and*

*said that I did not qualify, and then I asked him on what basis . . . was
I disqualified, and he just continued to walk in the next office, did not
answer me at all.*

Mrs. Burger filled out another form on October 9, 1961, but Judge Cox
excluded it because it did not appear in the amended complaint he had ordered us to submit a month before the trial, in response to one of the many
defense motions for more definite statement. Before Lynd gave her that application, he had said, "You were up here not so long ago." He provided her
the form only when he learned six months had passed since her previous
effort.

Inexperienced trial lawyers are taught not to ask a question unless they
know the answer. Dugas Shands proved the wisdom of that instruction:

"Have you made a complaint to anyone about being mistreated down
there by Mr. Lynd? You haven't claimed to have been mistreated, have
you?"

Mrs. Burger replied, "Well, I think it's a right that I be registered as a
citizen and with the right to vote . . ."

Unlike those black witnesses who had applied only to Theron Lynd, Mrs.
Burger had been interviewed by the FBI back when she had been turned
away by Luther Cox. As noted previously, the grand jury then declined to
indict Cox. The bureau's form "302," the notes of that interview, was turned
over to Shands.

While muttering about that "cloud of witnesses" he had seen, Judge Cox
nonetheless gave Shands the hour and one-half luncheon recess to study
it. At 1:30, Shands was wise enough to have no further questions for Mrs.
Burger. We would present three more teachers as witnesses.

CHAPTER 10

THE OTHER YOUNG TURKS

David Roberson and Chuck Lewis

David Roberson and Robert "Chuck" Lewis were younger than Jesse Stegall, and unlike him they were single, but the three were close friends, worked at Rowan High School, and were dedicated to changing things in Forrest County—to becoming voters.

Roberson was the only one of our black witnesses who would later leave Mississippi.[1] What had made him one of those with the courage to stand up for his rights when others were afraid to? For Roberson, the last of N. R. Burger's bright young men at Rowan High School to testify, there does not appear to have been a single answer. His early years were, however, distinctive: growing up in an all-black rural Alabama farming community of no more than 150 people some sixty miles north of Mobile and fifteen miles outside Evergreen and Interstate 65. Nichburg was named for his mother's forebears, the Nicholsons, who settled there in the postslavery period. There was no electricity and lots of hard work.

David's maternal great-grandparents, his grandparents, and his mother all grew up on their more than a thousand acres in Nichburg. David was the fifth of eleven children, educated until almost age fourteen in the local two-room schoolhouse. At home, there were prayers and Bible reading each night before he and three of his brothers staked out their places in the one bed they shared. His sisters were at the other end of the room.

All-black settlements like Nichburg were common in the Deep South when David was growing up. Nichburg wasn't as commercial as Mound Bayou in the Delta, and lacked its governmental structure and recognition. It was just a farm community, recognized by the state of Alabama only on the map.

The Nicholsons were progressive and good at crafts, and they cared about education. They were the blacksmith, the carpenter—skilled tradesmen, as well as skilled farmers. It may have derived from slavery. The first thing that David remembered was hard farm work, without modern machinery.

As soon as you became large enough, you had something to do, and as you got older, your responsibility became increasingly more demanding. I was always kind of large for my age. So when I was five years old, I carried water to the field, tried to feed the pigs, and do things with the cows.

It was just the immediate family in our house, but my grandmother and grandfather lived a short distance away, and one great-grandmother lived to be about 115. So we heard some slavery stories, and I got to know some of the other older people who'd been through slavery. What disturbed them most was the breakup of the family. That's what they'd sit around and talk about more than anything else. Their parents were separated in many cases, but they were very concerned about their sisters and brothers who were sent in various directions, sold to different slave owners.

When the old people died, we youngsters, even five and younger, would have to dress up and go and sit at the wakes and funerals. You remember having to sit through church when it was very hot and uncomfortable in the summer, and you wanted to be outside. Sometimes we'd be there until 11 or 12 at night.

Nichburg Baptist Church was small and wooden. It had a piano, but no electricity. Electricity still hadn't reached Nichburg when the Robersons moved in 1948.

Small churches in the south, out in the country haven't changed much. Many of them still look like they did when I was growing up. Reverend Brown, the first minister I remember, came in once a month. That was typical in the south; individual churches weren't large enough to support a minister, so he moved between churches.

My parents were very religious Baptists throughout their lives, very. At an early age, sitting around home, we would sing, and they would read the Bible. And once we children learned to read, everybody had to read it. When it got dark, and we stopped doing our outside chores, we'd sit around. Even out there, my mother had newspapers out of Mobile, and we got black papers from Chicago and Pittsburgh. Before we children learned to read, they would read to us, and talk about things we were supposed to remember, and we'd sit around the fire if it's the wintertime, and eat and talk. The ones of school age would do homework.

Nichburg might be poor and isolated, but the family had the two major national publications for blacks, the *Chicago Defender* and the *Pittsburgh Courier*, to acquaint them with news of interest to blacks. And there were no white people around to impose upon David and his siblings the mores of segregation in the Deep South. With the papers came job opportunity. David recalls selling newspapers that he requested through the mail, including the *Defender*, the *Courier*, and the Kansas City paper. They would send fifteen or twenty-five copies to sell, with no money up front.

David's father worked as a professional cook at a lumber camp that moved around in southern Alabama where there was still virgin timber to be cut. He'd come home on weekends and would always read the Bible while he was there. If he wasn't there, David's mother read. As the children got older, they all shared the responsibility. David told me: "The prayers were left up to you, based upon maybe something related to what you read in the Bible or being healthy and hoping that your relatives and friends and other people in the world were getting along well. It was a spontaneous prayer: if there was too much rain, and it was time to get the crops out of the field, we would pray for the rain to stop; or if it was too dry early in the season, you would be praying for rain."

The Mobile paper only wrote negative news about black people—crimes allegedly committed—but the *Defender* and the *Courier* made David aware of what was going on with blacks in different parts of the South.

Things were a lot worse in a lot of places. We were very lucky we weren't sharecroppers dealing with big landowners in places like the Delta in Mississippi, or Black Delta, Alabama, or parts of North and South Carolina. Growing up, we were lucky that we were only exposed to that in the newspapers. The people in Nichburg owned their own land.

We'd take cotton and peanuts to sell in Belleville, where the cotton mill and the cotton gin were. We kept some corn. My grandmother, Eliza Randall, had a mill for making syrup and made syrup for the whole community. We had to get white people involved in the handling of cotton. We sold what little we had to them.

Roberson went through the eighth grade in Nichburg's two-room, two-teacher school. In that agricultural community, the school year started in September and ended in April. Older children would have to miss some time in the early part of the school year to go out and get the fields ready for planting or harvest. David always liked school. He wanted to know things. He had an early interest in biology, which he would later teach, and he recognized that there was "applied biology all the time out there on the farm."

Things changed abruptly for David when the family moved to Moss Point on the Gulf Coast. His father got a job at the International Paper Company where his uncle had been working. David and his brothers were the targets of cruel jokes, of the condescension of the local black children.

I was almost 14; my older brother was almost 16. You're not very so-phisticated, and you go to town, and these town kids are real mean to you. You've gone most of your life when the weather was nice without shoes. There are just certain things you are unaware of, and they make fun of you.

David's father was a laborer for the paper company, and eventually be-came a fireman. There were still certain jobs blacks couldn't have. For the most part, what blacks did was very physically demanding, sometimes de-humanizing. There was no union then.

For the family, it was a real improvement to go from two rooms in the house to five. The four boys now had their own room. David observed wry-ly, "There was not a lot of privacy going on in Nichburg."

David worked hard in school and made better grades than the town kids. By the fall of the year, he had a job at a nursery, doing landscaping, land-scape maintenance, and greenhouse work. He did that for his four years of high school. "Now I hadn't learned how to dance, and my parents didn't go for dancing anyway. They thought it was pretty sinful. They didn't let me go to dances at school, but you can kind of be creative when you're a teenager, and at least look in."

Moss Point had a population of about 5,000, two-thirds white. There were, of course, two high schools, Moss Point High School for the whites and Magnolia High School, actually a 1-12 school, for the blacks. There were twenty-seven in David's graduating class. He had a good principal at Magnolia, a progressive man named W. H. Whisenton, who insisted that the students work hard and study. He maximized the few resources that he had and fought the local school board all the time, trying to get as much as he could from them.

David also admired Mr. McInnis, his boss at work.

Mr. McInnis was white. He was looking for someone who knew how to plow. You've got a weed problem in the south, so you've got to do some plowing. We hadn't been in town that long, but people knew we were from a farm, so . . .

Mr. McInnis was a very nice person, a Mississippi State University graduate, with an engineering degree. He'd been in the Army, and he was very fair. For the four years I was there, I was his only black employee. I had lots of contact with whites on the jobs I went on. He hired a few more blacks as his business got larger.

David's oldest sister Gurtha was very bright. Their parents had not gone beyond the seventh grade, but their mother was an avid reader, and their father valued education also. They decided to see if they could work out Gurtha's going on to college, but they couldn't afford it, and she had to leave Alabama State in Montgomery after one semester.

The elder Robersons registered to vote in Moss Point soon after they got into town in 1948. That was the first time either of them had voted. As far as David was aware, no blacks voted in Alabama, and in such rural areas, there was a sense of being outside the political system. He doesn't recall ever hearing it discussed. Everybody was busy just trying to survive. Basic human needs had to be met first. Voting had to wait.

But the job at International Paper changed things. David's uncle, Justice Roberson, had worked there some time before his father started. He was a voter in Moss Point, as were other blacks David came to know later. So it was kind of the thing to do, and Justice encouraged them to vote. Gurtha was old enough, and she registered, too.

◆◆◆

David chose Alcorn A&M for college because it was affordable. Also, after working at the nursery, he really wanted to be a landscapist. He didn't want any of the hard, manual jobs that blacks were doing. Alcorn didn't have a landscaping major as such, but it did have an agriculture school. Although, once there, David shifted to the sciences.

Alcorn was a necessary choice because of my high school background. I wouldn't have survived in a real tough school. They did the best they could at Magnolia, but they had limited money to work with.

*Equipment was lacking, and the course work wasn't extremely de-
manding. But if it had been demanding, most of the students probably
wouldn't have passed.*

The local kids at Magnolia knew things, but not academic things. The
situation just wasn't designed for David to become strong academically.
Seven in all from Magnolia's Class of 1952 went to Alcorn. One went up
to Fisk in Nashville, and a couple to what is now Jackson State.

Alcorn University was established in 1871 for young African American
men in Lorman, just south of the Delta, and named for Governor James L.
Alcorn. The federal government had authorized states to sell up to 30,000
acres of federal land within their borders to endow "land grant" colleges.
Sixty percent of the proceeds in Mississippi went to Alcorn. Until 1940,
it would be the state's only public four-year college for blacks. Women,
who now constitute a majority of the students, began being admitted in
1884.[2]

Initial state financial support voted by the legislature was significant,
$50,000 in cash for ten years to help establish an endowment. Besides
agriculture and industrial arts courses, Alcorn offered teacher training.
Hiram Revels, Mississippi's first black United States senator, resigned his
seat to become Alcorn's president, but Revels was the wrong man for the
job, at least during Reconstruction. He appeared too accommodating to
whites and out of tune with the rising aspirations of his students. By 1874,
there was enough unrest to cause legislative intervention and the dismissal of Revels and the school's trustees.

In 1876, Revels made a brief comeback when the Republican Reconstruction government was ousted, but within two years Alcorn's educational role
was radically reduced and the school renamed Alcorn Agricultural & Mechanical College. With the reduction in its mission came drastic funding
cuts. Nadine Cohodas quotes Governor James K. Vardaman's emphatic approval of more blows to Alcorn's budget: "I am not anxious even to see the
Negro turned into a skilled mechanic. God Almighty intended him to till
the soil under the direction of the white man, and that is what we are going
to teach him down there at Alcorn College."[3]

In 1925, a northern foundation offered Alcorn $100,000 conditioned on
the state appropriating an additional $200,000. The legislature declined
the offer, though it accepted when the offer was renewed three years later.
Cohodas also quotes Charles Evers's harsh appraisal of his education there
as "the equivalent of a good eighth grade education—maybe."[4]

Alcorn had been designated Mississippi's land grant university under the federal Morrill Act, but with the end of Reconstruction, the state's new officials began diverting the federal largesse from African Americans. The Agricultural and Mechanical College of Mississippi was established in Starkville in 1878 "for white male students only." Once derided as the cowpunchers, Mississippi State University grew rapidly. Its plant and equipment now dwarf those of Alcorn. Mississippi State owns 4,200 acres, enrolls close to 18,000 students, and offers a myriad of degrees, from bachelors to doctorates. Alcorn State University has a simple principal campus of 1,700 acres, about 3,200 students, and awards only bachelor's and master's degrees.[5]

Alcorn had dorms, and that's where we lived. They had separate dorms for girls: oh, very separate. I'd never been away from home for any period of time, and I was meeting a lot of kids, a cross-section from Mississippi, and a few from Louisiana, Arkansas and Alabama. I pretty much covered the cost of college myself. I saved some money from the $500 I'd made working for Mr. McInnis for four years, and I had gotten a little scholarship and also a job. I did janitorial work, making $12 a month for one year. Then the second year I serviced vending machines. I was up to $15. The last two years I did the preparation for general chemistry and organic chemistry. I learned to make solutions and set up labs. I got a $5 raise to $20 a month for that one.

My boss in the Alcorn chemistry lab, R. C. Jones, taught me a lot. I was good in science and had not found the adjustment to Alcorn difficult. I did pretty well academically right from the start and had been a student of his before he hired me to be his lab assistant. Alcorn faculty members didn't talk about voting, but he had been part of a suit which had been filed in Forrest County earlier in the '50s. They still hadn't permitted him to register.

They talked about his case, and, when Jones later found out Rowan teachers were pursuing it, he encouraged them to keep going. "Alcorn had all the regular black fraternities and sororities. I became an Alpha in 1954. They were good to me, but there weren't fraternity houses; nobody could afford it. The Alphas were considered to be the scholars, the academic people, not easy-going, fun guys like the Kappas." It was at Alcorn that Roberson first got to know Chuck Lewis, whose place he would take at Rowan High School while Lewis was doing graduate work at Oregon State.

David entered the army right after college. He had been deferred annually by the draft board down in Pascagoula, thus missing the Korean War.

I started out at Fort Chaffee, Arkansas, for basic training, then went to Fort Sill, Oklahoma, for meteorology school; and finally Korea. Basic training was eight weeks: things you see in movies about hard-nosed sergeants, drilling and conditioning, rifle ranges, all of that. Everybody had to do it, so it didn't bother me.

Truman had gotten rid of segregation in the armed forces, but it took a while before it filtered down. When I reported in Jackson, they kept whites and blacks separate, but I was only in Jackson overnight before getting put on a bus and shipped off to basic training, which was all integrated.

Fort Chaffee was Roberson's first experience with white contemporaries. It took some adjustment. "When you grow up in the South as I did, there's a psychological barrier you have to overcome. You got the feeling that you're kind of second class. You almost have to re-program yourself in a way. But I really got going in the right direction in the army. The army was good for me."

Much of the southeast was assigned to Fort Chaffee, along with Louisiana, Arkansas, Oklahoma, and Mississippi. David didn't have any problem getting on with the others. They were kept so busy that when they finally got a break, they just wanted to rest. The few times he went to town David found arcades that were not segregated, though bars and dance halls were. But both whites and blacks piled on the same commercial bus that picked them up just outside the gate. At Fort Sill, David had a twelve-week course on the collection of weather data, meteorological work that could be applied for ballistic purposes for artillery units. Fort Lewis, near Seattle, Washington, was his first time outside the south.

After a week, I got on a ship and spent seventeen days going to Korea. When I got there in January 1957, it was about fifteen below zero. I was in Korea for eighteen months without any return to the United States, a typical tour of duty. Korea was considered a hardship assignment, and there were no families. I was at a place above the 38th parallel, called Camp Santa Barbara, right at the DMZ, in the observation battalion, not more than fifty people. We had sounding equipment, provided weather data and were also surveyors. You have a lot of time to think when you're in Korea.

The observation unit was easily three-fourths white, with only about ten blacks. Most of the Americans were from outside of the South. Only David and one other were not regular army. David considered it "good duty, not like infantry or artillery, kind of like a white-collar outfit of the army: clean—a certain high education level—technical."

What I got most out of that period was the reading that most people do when they're in high school. I got a chance to catch up on a lot of novels and other books. I started listening to classical music and reading about it, also. There were records and books available right at Camp Santa Barbara. Oh, yes, they had a good library system there. Korean military were integrated with the American military in the unit in Santa Barbara, very nice people. They slept in the same Quonset huts that we did. We all got on pretty well, our white and black soldiers, and the Koreans.

David was discharged in late May 1958 and went back to Moss Point. He needed a job.

I guess I always wanted to teach in some ways. In the South then, the schooling limited a black's options to do something professionally. But teaching was an option. It was decided for me in a sense. I kind of knew that after a semester when Alcorn didn't have courses like landscape architecture.

After graduating from college, you just had to submit your transcripts to have a certificate to teach. I took a job at a local seafood processing place for the summer, and I must have sent twenty-five letters to places, and talked to people I knew. They told me about the job up in Hattiesburg.

My interview for the job was in early August, almost the start of the school year. Rowan High School had at the most 500 students in grades 9 through 12. Mr. Burger, the principal, was a real progressive guy, way ahead in that area because he had gone up to Cornell and got a master's. We hit it off real well right away. He liked my background, looked up my records and, before I left, told me I had the job.

David had lots of interviews, but no other offers. However, Hattiesburg was a desirable situation, more progressive and higher paying. At that time, it was second or third in pay among the state's public schools. David started at $3,150 per year.

Mr. Burger didn't bug me. He let me do my job. He was probably in his early 50s then. Rowan had some real good students and had good staff, also. And all of it came straight from him, reflected his philosophy about education, the things that he had started there. Rowan's facilities were superior to other black schools, except some that I later visited in Jackson.

David's completion of army duty and arrival in Hattiesburg coincided with two significant events in his life, one religious, the other romantic. The first was that he no longer considered himself a Baptist. He joined the Methodist church.

Methodists are a little more sophisticated in the way they conduct their services, a milder tone of religion, without so much fire and damnation. And if you're looking for something less directed, Methodists provide that. That was the reason that I switched, this fear that was projected in the Baptist Church. And the services were too long like those wakes I went to as a child.

The second was the acceleration of a relationship with Angieline Smith from Brookhaven, which had begun when she was a freshman and he was a senior at Alcorn. They had stayed in touch while he was in the service and she was finishing college. They were married the month David first testified for the United States, March 1962.

I first began thinking about getting myself registered to vote after the Brown decision in '54. That was a real turning point in a lot of thinking in young blacks. Those of us at Alcorn would sit around and talk, not just the Alpha Fraternity but generally, and voting would always come up. None of us were registered. Then once I got out of the Army, I felt like, well, I just spent a couple of years there and should have the right to vote. And you start teaching and become aware of some whites who are voting whose academic background, and understanding of what citizenship is all about, is no better than yours, and in most cases not as good.

You should be able to vote; it's a right guaranteed by the Constitution. So we decided, Stegall, Lewis and myself, to try and do something about it. Chuck Lewis was on sabbatical leave the year I came to Rowan. That's his job I took, and he got to be one of my best friends. Jesse Stegall taught English at Rowan my first year there. We were close, the three of us, very close.

Chuck Lewis was the fourth of seven children in a family from Monticello, a small community twenty-one miles from Brookhaven. He was an entrepreneur at Alcorn, and he would be that, as well as an excellent teacher, in Hattiesburg. His business card in later years featured a hand with a finger pointing at the holder saying: "It's YOU we're looking out for! Income Tax Service: Individual—Farm—Business," with a reference to his special tax training at the National Tax Training School. He did not cash checks he received from those he felt could not afford to pay his bill. His office was at another of his operations, Ashford Street Self-Laundry, the first black-owned washeteria, but he wasn't too busy to join the usher board at Sweet Pilgrim Baptist Church, and he was even designated a lifetime Boy Scout.

Lewis paid for his mother to attend beautician school after he moved to Hattiesburg. His eldest sister Genevieve ran his flower shop and raised chinchillas for him in the back of the shop until her death. His younger sister Erlexia lived with him for a time after she finished college and went with him to try to register the month after he testified in Jackson. He was close to his four nieces. The youngest, Ginger Smith, named her son after him. She said he was secretive about what he was doing, read a lot, and didn't need much sleep. He was, Ginger told me, "the type of person who believes in making money."[6]

Lewis had rental property in Hattiesburg, as well as his businesses. He owned land in Costa Rica, condos in Gulf Shores, Alabama, and a beauty shop in Birmingham where he experimented with beauty supplies for people of color. Shirley Mays told me she felt more like a sister than a niece to her favorite uncle, who was a "wheeler-dealer, a gift-giver and a good man."[7]

The black community of Hattiesburg as a whole became aware of Chuck Lewis. From her newsstand at the corner of Sixth and Mobile, Lillie McLaurin knew Lewis as a very busy customer who was active in real estate. She knew he brought his family in to work at his various Hattiesburg businesses.[8]

David Roberson recalled:

> When Chuck got back from Oregon State, we talked a lot about voting in that winter of '59. There was talk about it on a national level also, but the real turning point was during the Kennedy campaign for the presidency. It seemed we were finally going to have some breakthroughs. That was the catalyst which encouraged us to start going down and trying to do something about it. Kennedy sounded so different from all the others who campaigned for president. You got a feeling

that he was going to include all of the citizens of the country, rather than just the white leadership. I guess it really started with Truman desegregating the armed forces beginning in 1948. Blacks felt real good about that. Then with Eisenhower, things seemed to just revert back for the most part to the way things were before Truman.

But David sensed that John Kennedy's election would bring real progress:

I always remember Kennedy's inauguration when he saw the color guards pass by, and there were no blacks. His statement that he wanted blacks in the color guard was publicized. That had a tremendous impression on blacks that I knew: this guy was going to be okay. And that encouraged people who might have been kind of tentative about trying to register or going against maybe the established systems that existed in the South to go out and try to do something. The first step was paying your poll tax. They'll take your money. I first paid in 1960. It was understood that to be able to register you had to have a receipt that you'd paid it.

Stegall had a family, and a house, couple of kids. Chuck and I didn't have anything to lose; just us, that's it. So we didn't even think about our livelihood, anything like that. But Stegall hung in there with us; every time we went together. You tried not to think about violence.

When CBS News became interested in the Forrest County voting situation in September 1962, David was an obvious person to be interviewed. He was blunt:

To look at the overall picture at the school where I work, Rowan High School, you have some 27 teachers there. Of the 27, ten or eleven hold master's degrees from eastern or midwestern universities, and out of this number we have . . . a very small percentage voting. Civics and government is taught at Rowan High School and we have voteless people teaching those courses. So this question we asked ourselves: how can we be qualified to teach, yet we're not qualified to vote?[9]

❖❖❖

David felt that the women in the registrar's office really didn't know how to react when he, Stegall, and Lewis arrived at the office after school in October 1960. He didn't think they made decisions. He wondered if their jobs might be in the balance. How they felt philosophically, he couldn't tell. One woman said Mr. Lynd was the only one who could register them. When they went back a second time that afternoon, Lynd still wasn't in.

Lewis kept a record of their attempts. He sent it to Jim Groh at the Department of Justice. Lewis and Stegall kept the Hattiesburg Teachers Association informed. They were leaders in the association, which had been discussing creating a credit union for employees of the city and county public schools. Their ambitions included creating a co-op for merchandise and groceries, but they didn't get that far.

On March 2, 1961, Roberson was finally permitted to fill out an application form. He interpreted section 273 on the amendment process to the state constitution. Then, for the duties and obligations of citizenship under a constitutional form of government, he wrote:

> *As a citizen under a constitutional form of government, it is my first duty to be of service to the government. This includes civic duties, upholding the law, being fair and honest in all dealings and believing so strongly in our form of government that I would give my life to help and protect our constitutional form of government.*

David was never told whether anything was right or wrong with his answers. He'd have to go back later to determine the results, but it would always be that he didn't pass, without comments. He could not register.

> *Mr. Lynd was obese and had a real sour personality—sour in the kind of stare that he gave you when you walked in: what are you doing here? You have no right to even request to register to vote. Without words, that was the feeling you got. If you took it seriously, you would be intimidated.*
>
> *I remember a state of euphoria kind of set in the three of us, when Bob Owen came to see us for the Justice Department. He explained that he was in the area because of the things we had attempted to do, and he asked us if we would participate in a lawsuit against Mr. Lynd. We really couldn't believe it, because in our whole lives, none of us had ever experienced any kind of thing like that from the government— where the results might be some positive advance for blacks; unbelievable, really*

Bob Owen struck Roberson as very professional.

He was in our same general age range and seemed very compassionate and competent, very efficient, very caring. He made us feel very comfortable, and we needed that. The different attorneys from the Civil Rights Division kept us informed about what was going on. They also recommended to us how to keep good records, and, later, before going to testify, to review and make sure that we had our facts together so that the defense attorney wouldn't really rattle us. Most of us were for the first time in serious court. We didn't know what was going on, and we were a bit rattled by the defense attorneys, but the Justice Department prepared us well.

Before that, however, the Young Turks were back at Lynd's office September 28, 1961. This time Lynd was there to ask: "What do you boys want?" However, when Lynd told them there was only time for one of them to apply, they left.

They returned the next day as early as they possibly could, and two of them did get to fill out forms. Lewis followed Stegall and was given section 121 of the state constitution to interpret, the power of the governor to call the legislature into special session. That wasn't as easy as section 30, "There shall be no imprisonment for debt," the favorite section for those whites required to fill out a form, but not a problem for Lewis, who also capably listed various duties and obligations of citizenship.

When Stegall and Lewis returned on October 6 to get their results, Lynd just told them that they had not qualified and he could not tell them why. "Six months" was Lynd's reply when Lewis asked when they could try again. At the trial, Lewis testified to this familiar sequence of events.

This time Shands's cross-examination was brief: Didn't Lewis know what time the office closed? Lewis also hadn't included the election district and county name and had only signed the general oath, not the final signature line. On re-cross there were Shands's usual questions about contacts with division lawyers and the FBI.

Roberson testified as to his early registration attempts when he took the witness stand. He was twenty-seven, and, National Science Foundation Fellowship or not, he was nervous and had to be reminded to keep his voice up. Ed Cates of the state attorney general's office contended that since the trial was underway, Judge Cox could not grant our pretrial discovery motion and order the defendants to give us Roberson's application forms, nor should he permit John Doar's oral motion to amend the complaint. Cox was plainly annoyed: "It looks like we are doing a lot of horsing around in this case, and I'm getting pretty tired of it."

Cox did admit David's second application form dated October 12, 1961, letting us see one of his forms for the first time. Roberson's interpretation of intricate legislative procedure required an extra page to get it all in, just as Addie Burger's had. His direct testimony concluded with his stating that Lynd told him on his return trip that he had not passed and then walked away when David asked what he had done wrong. The defendants reserved cross-examination until after a thirty-day continuance they were seeking from Judge Cox.

I had never been in court before, and on this first time I ever testified, I was in this strange swivel chair. You'd lean, and it wouldn't support you. It would have been nice just to hold onto something that didn't move.

When I saw Judge Cox, I had the same feeling I got from Lynd, his posture, his personality. It was a federal court, but we heard he had a reputation for not being very fair. Angieline was up in Laurel where she taught, but she was in favor of us registering, though she didn't try herself. I didn't encounter any blacks who didn't think it was the right thing to do. Things had happened, like Little Rock. People were ready to do something, but they didn't know what to do. Many blacks just accepted the fact that they couldn't register and didn't go down there, but you learn how to live and how to avoid real violence, so you don't think about it. You avoid it. There were some basic rules. You knew how to survive.

And our teacher-witnesses had survived. The last to testify was Eloise Hopson.

CHAPTER 11

ELOISE HOPSON

"I'd Like to See Them Make Me Change Anything I Want to Say"

Eloise Hopson, daughter of Nelson Toole, a Methodist minister born in slavery, was vigorous and blunt, feisty and irreverent.[1] She was born May 16, 1913, in Enterprise, a little rural community in Clarke County, just south of Meridian, Mississippi.

Reverend Toole had grown up in Alabama and was basically self-taught. He told his children stories about his slave childhood, among them recollections of slave children eating with their hands at a trough, the way pigs might today.

> *I can recall my father going to his churches on Saturday. There were four of them. So he would leave on Saturday afternoon and spend that night among the members and preach on Sunday, and come back home on Monday. I heard him preach a few times, but we stayed at home and went to our own church. My mother, Irene Adams Toole, was an elementary school teacher, but she taught in different schools, so she never taught me except at home. I had one sister and three brothers.*

Her mother taught Eloise the piano and had private piano students, as Eloise did later. Eloise was brought up learning Methodist hymns and the life of John Wesley. "I am a United Methodist. The Methodist Church certainly during my lifetime has been a much more progressive church than the Baptist Church, though it had fewer adherents among the blacks in Mississippi." There was no electricity in her childhood home, but there were always books, always newspapers, always musical instruments. "I don't remember being unable to read. I read John Bunyan's *Pilgrim's Progress*, childhood version, and *Romeo and Juliet* and *Moby Dick* and *Tom Sawyer*, books like that. I think your values and concepts and your way of dealing with life are learned at home if you have thoughtful parents and caring parents."

Eloise attended a local two-teacher school through the sixth grade, but, with her mother teaching and her two younger brothers in the hands of a babysitter, Eloise was sent to a co-ed Methodist boarding school in nearby Meridian for grades 7-9, and then to a smaller Episcopal boarding school for the rest of her high school years. Her education was a far cry from the mere eight grades offered Mississippi blacks except in the larger cities. By the time she was graduated from high school, her Meridian Methodist school had added a two-year teaching program that Eloise attended. This enabled her to become a certified teacher in Mississippi's black schools. She was the first person in the history of her family to achieve any level of higher education. "I guess I always wanted to be a teacher from the time I was a little girl and lined up my dolls on my mother's front porch and played school with them."

Her first teaching position was in her own Clarke County. She boarded with a family there for two years, just twelve miles from where she had grown up. "Black people weren't allowed to vote in Clarke County. My parents didn't vote, and black people in general in Mississippi were not voting at that time. This business of blacks having the vote is post-Civil Rights struggle."

After two years in Clarke County schools, Eloise taught the second and third grades for five years in Jefferson Davis County fifty miles from Hattiesburg. When the Japanese bombed Pearl Harbor in December 1941, she was teaching in the public schools of Grenada in the Mississippi Delta.

I helped to register men for the draft in Grenada County after the bombing. We were complacent and had no idea anything like that attack would come about. We had thought we didn't need a draft, but we started it then. And the blacks in that area were registered at the school where I worked. There weren't any black people on the Selective Service Board, but I didn't get any sense that there was favoritism being shown between blacks and whites, as to who went first to war. Maybe I did not discern the kind of subtleties that I later learned to discern. But I didn't sense anything then. You see, we were so separate that we really didn't know what was going on among the whites.

During the two years she taught in Grenada, Eloise married Brandon Jonathan Hopson, a Baptist minister she had met in Jeff Davis County. He entered the service as an army chaplain, and she traveled with him to bases in Alabama and South Carolina as he ministered to black soldiers in the segregated army.

But a new phase of her life opened in the fall of 1944 when he agreed that she could complete college. It was not at a small poorly funded Mississippi teachers' college, but at Spelman College, the distinguished historically black college for women founded in 1881. It was handsomely supported by the family of John D. Rockefeller. Its alumnae now include Alice Walker and Marian Wright Edelman. Eloise was a full-time student there for two years, receiving her B.A. in English in June 1946. She loved Spelman, a part of the Atlanta consortium of black colleges that includes Morehouse College. It was, she told me, "like a Vassar to the black community."

Her next stop was Japan during the postwar military occupation, where she found it troubling to have servants assigned by the military. She taught at the elementary level while Reverend Hopson continued as a chaplain, but tensions accelerated in their marriage after their return to civilian life at a church in Braddock, Pennsylvania. Reverend Hopson did not want her to teach. "He felt God had called him to preach, but it never occurred to him that I was called to teach just as much as he was called to preach."

After three years in Pennsylvania, Reverend Hopson decided, without consulting his wife, to reenter the service. Separation, followed by divorce, was inevitable. Eloise returned alone to Mississippi, teaching at a small school in Neshoba County, the county that would become infamous for the 1964 murders of James Chaney, Andrew Goodman, and Michael Schwerner.

The principal of her Neshoba school suggested that she start summer graduate work with others from the school at Columbia University. Black teachers had to travel north for the graduate study that was closed to them in Mississippi, and her summers at Columbia in New York City opened up new literature and ideas for Eloise. She was awarded a master of arts degree in English in December 1953.

In Neshoba County, Eloise had been making $1,800 a year, $200 a month for nine months. She didn't know what teachers in the white schools were making. She told a fellow student at Columbia of her financial woes and learned that teacher was making twice as much in Florence, South Carolina.

That system needed an English teacher and Eloise was hired. For nine years, she taught English at Wilson High School in Florence, a city slightly larger than Hattiesburg. She noted that Wilson High School, though also segregated, had much better supplies and equipment than the black schools she knew in Mississippi. In Florence, Eloise paid her poll tax and voted for the first time.

But in the summer of 1959, her mother suffered a second stroke back in Clarke County. Eloise had met Nathaniel Burger, principal of Hattiesburg's black high school, Rowan, while teaching in Florence and, in fact, had applied to teach there at Burger's suggestion. Then Burger had told her that Mr. Blair, the white superintendent, had decided that her salary was too high; he would hire a less expensive "girl" right out of college. Though Eloise was annoyed, she'd been happy in Florence so it hadn't mattered. But it was different after her mother's illness, and this time the move to Hattiesburg worked out.

She was interviewed by Superintendent Blair, who asked her various personal questions including her marital status, and then asked whether she thought all children should be educated equally. Eloise replied: "I'm not sure that all children can be educated equally. What you are able to learn starts way back, and I'm not sure that we can educate them all alike. But I think all of them ought to have the same opportunity. Then each one will take from the system what he is able to take."

Mr. Blair liked that, telling Burger, "She's got all the right answers." Armed with the letter she insisted upon from the superintendent and the chairman of the school board offering her a position, she broke her contract with Florence and came to Hattiesburg.

Eloise taught English at Rowan High School for fourteen years, and also gave private piano lessons. When one of her pupils, Gay Polk-Payton, was seven and beginning piano, Ms. Hopson rapped her fingers with a pencil when she made a mistake. Gay ran out of the house and never returned, but her sister stayed with her lessons and loved Ms. Hopson.[2]

When she came back to Mississippi, Eloise tried to register to vote as she had in Florence. She was denied that right after some of the standard Lynd rigamarole. But Lynd actually gave her the test before pronouncing her unqualified.

I had not thought about the situation really . . . because I was becoming acquainted with a new system, and it was occupying my time. But I remember one day Mr. Burger, who was registered himself, called me over the p.a. system to come up to the library. When I got there, there was Mr. John Doar from the Justice Department, wanting to talk to me about going to Jackson to testify in this voting rights thing. When I agreed, he prepped me for going up there. He said, "Now the lawyers will try to trap you, and don't let them make you change your testimony." I said, "I'd like to see them make me change anything I want to say."

The prevailing attitude of the other black Hattiesburg teachers was let the Rowan teachers do it, and after they get it straight, then we'll all have the vote. I think they were quite satisfied to let us go and break the ice. They were afraid they were going to lose their jobs. And you know, had I been really homesteaded here, I can only speculate what my attitude would have been. Knowing me, I probably would have gone, but then again I might not have.

Miss Hopson was scared by the icy road conditions when she first went to court with David Roberson and others in January. She thought they'd never make it, and then the hearing didn't take place because Lynd and his lawyers didn't come. The second time Eloise went with Vernon Dahmer, whom she termed "a brave person, a determined person. He really believed in the cause and was not one to back down."

Finally the case was moving along. As the second day's afternoon session began, Ms. Hopson's arrival in the courtroom set off that afternoon's procedural skirmish. Her name had not appeared in the amended complaint.

After extended debate, John was permitted to orally amend the complaint to plead the specifics of Ms. Hopson's registration experience—but not without a tirade from Judge Cox: "The government acts like it is so put upon because I haven't set [this case] for trial, and apparently you all are not ready for trial. Now, if you want any more amendments, I am going to give these people a continuance."

Judge Cox had, however, already granted the defendants thirty days to file their answers to the amended paragraphs (the filing of which were not, in any case, necessary under the Federal Rules of Civil Procedure) and was about to give them the same length of time to prepare to cross-examine the "surprise" witnesses.

BY MR. DOAR: . . .

Q. Would you tell the Court what happened when you got in that office?

A. Well, I made known my wishes to the clerk, who gave me a registration form to fill out. This registration form included a section of the Mississippi Constitution and I was told to . . . copy a part of it in the space provided, then write my interpretation of what I had read in the form provided.

Ms. Hopson interpreted Section 233 that the Board of Levee Commissioners was empowered to appropriate land necessary for the construction, maintenance, and repair of the levees in their several districts and to make due compensation to those persons who sustained loss or damage of property in that transaction.

"That's all it said. Now it took a lot of wording to say that, but that was the essence of it, just as simple as anything. And the idea that somebody thought that a certified teacher couldn't interpret that was ridiculous."

> Q. Now, did you have any further discussion with the lady after you completed the form?
> A. Well, during the time I was to copy that section in the registration form, I commented to her that there was not enough space provided to copy that whole section and she told me that she could not discuss the form with me.
> Q. And what conversation did you have with her after you had finished the form?
> A. I asked her when would I know whether or not I had passed the examination. And she said that I should come back in three or four days to find out.

Hopson testified that she did go back in about three days and was told she'd have to see Mr. Lynd who was not in. Another week passed, and this time she told the court that she did see Lynd, that he asked her name, went to a cabinet, picked up her form, and said, "No, you did not pass," that she thanked him and left.

It turned out that Eloise Hopson was not above stretching the truth, at least as to details that were foregone conclusions.

Up there on the witness stand, I lied like a trouper. I was supposed to have gone back and been told that I did not pass. But before I went back to see about my status, Mr. Doar wanted me to go to Jackson. So I just went and got up there and said, "Yes, I went back, and he told me I didn't pass." As far as Mr. Doar knew, I had gone back. I'm not ashamed a bit, I'm shameless.

And see, Theron Lynd didn't remember whether I had gone back or not. If I couldn't read, then there was something wrong with the Bureau of Certification in Mississippi, because I had been certified to teach; it was just ridiculous if they were certifying people to teach who can't read. That big blustery man!

But the inconsistencies in his rejection of teachers certified by the state and hired by his city didn't seem to faze Theron Lynd—or Judge Cox. They showed no surprise that someone with a master's degree from Columbia University might be rejected as unqualified to vote. But the irony wasn't lost on Eloise or the others.

How could it have been that blacks with college degrees were considered not competent to interpret the Constitution, and yet there were whites who had not even graduated from high school who were voting. They didn't have to take any kind of test. To me, that was ridiculous.

In Forrest County, the leaders of the movement to have black people obtain the right to register and vote came from the ordinary people, not the more educated, not the teachers. People like B. F. Bourn and Vernon Dahmer were not teachers.

Yet, as Eloise realized, teachers provided the most damning evidence of Theron Lynd's discrimination. Eloise Hopson was one of those teachers, and that teacher did not forget Theron Lynd. Years later she told me of a time she had been eating in Morrison's Cafeteria in the early eighties: "I felt some eyes on me, and I looked up and directly across in front of me, several tables away, was Theron Lynd, that same Forrest County registrar who wouldn't let me vote. I put on my meanest facial expression, and I stared at him. I don't think I even batted my eyes. I just stared him down."

CHAPTER 12

HERCULES AND ITS INSIDE AGITATOR, HUCK DUNAGIN

Word was passed quickly among some of the black workers at the Hercules Powder Company. "Huck wants to see us—right when the shift ends." Huck Dunagin was not given to calling meetings. He didn't have to. He always seemed to be everywhere as he walked the floor of the plant. Something was up.

Huck Dunagin was big and powerful, a former all-state lineman in high school football. He was the shop steward blacks had elected. And Huck Dunagin was white.

"I'm no integrationist," he told me years later. "If they wanted to keep the races separate in school, that was okay with me. But my men not be able to vote—my men not be able to hold any job they were capable of holding—I couldn't permit that."

Integration of the work force, doing away with the "white man's jobs," had been too hot a topic to be discussed in Mississippi. Huck reserved that for a national union meeting in Portland, Oregon, to which he brought Richard Boyd. There he broke the news to Boyd that he was the black laborer he had chosen to break the color barrier.

Now Huck planned to do something about his black workers voting, and he would do it right at the plant. "If you want to register, you go right ahead," he told a group that included T. F. Williams, Willie Thigpen, Willie Simpson, John Mosley, and the Reverend Sam Hall. "I'll see that you don't lose your jobs."

And they did go ahead—making the trip to Circuit Clerk Theron Lynd's registration office as many times as necessary. They might be denied a loan by a bank—or glowered at in the street—but their jobs would be safe. They had Huck's word.

Rowan High School provided us with five crucial teacher witnesses, and Hattiesburg's black ministers added valuable testimony, but you shouldn't have to have a master's degree—or be a minister—in order to vote in our society. A local industry, the Hercules Powder Company, gave us six solid members of the working class.

In 1912 the company's founding had been celebrated in an unlikely setting in Washington's new Willard Hotel. Row after row of tables filled its ballroom with distinguished-looking diners in black tie, all male, of course. Rarely was such a festive banquet held to commemorate the resolution of a court case, but this was no ordinary case. It was the farewell dinner for the countless lawyers who had worked for four years on the duPont antitrust case and negotiated the creation of the Hercules and Atlas Powder Companies.[1]

DuPont's divestiture was, of course, not voluntary, but rather the result of a successful federal criminal antitrust prosecution commenced in 1907. Price fixing, secret takeovers, and maintaining dummy corporations were among the allegations.[2]

If the period following the Civil War was the glory period of production expansion, with mergers and consolidations leading to single dominant production units in many fields, 1890 and the passage of the Sherman Antitrust Act had signaled its approaching demise. During Theodore Roosevelt's "trustbusting" terms as president (1901–1909), more than fifty antitrust investigations were commenced by the Department of Justice. In its only term, moreover, William Howard Taft's Justice Department then initiated ninety such investigations.[3]

The duPont trial began in September 1908, continuing for more than two years. In June 1912, the trial court approved a negotiated plan of dissolution, and the two new powder companies came into existence, endowed with significant duPont assets.[4] Like duPont, a diversified multinational chemical company, Hercules did not long remain content merely to manufacture explosives. Tree-stump processing plants in Gulfport, Mississippi, and Brunswick, Georgia, were acquired in 1920, and a new plant constructed on a one-hundred-acre tract in Hattiesburg north of Gulfport. Hattiesburg's chamber of commerce had been aggressively seeking new industry, touting the sixteen-thousand-resident community's four railroads, electric streetcars, and new hotel.[5]

Hercules had been in operation for little more than four years when a young Bowdoin College graduate, class of 1917, from Lewiston, Maine, accepted a seventy-five-dollar-a-month position as a chemist in its Joplin plant in Carthage, Missouri. By the end of the year, Leon Babcock, less than a year on the job, was one of eight men in their twenties and thirties described in the company's 1990 history as forming "the nucleus of Hercules' new Engineering and Chemical departments."[6]

High explosives was Babcock's field for Hercules until the end of World War II when he was picked to head its company-wide personnel operation. He visited the Hattiesburg plant four or five times during his fifteen years as Hercules's personnel director, on each visit, walking the floor of the plant with the union steward, Huck Dunagin. Dunagin had first come to Babcock's attention as the Hattiesburg correspondent for the company's employee magazine.

Babcock was almost ninety-five when I talked to him at his condominium in Wilmington, but he had a very clear recollection of Dunagin and his importance to the Hattiesburg plant. "He wrote very well," Babcock told me, recalling in particular one "beautiful poem."

What kind of man was this union leader-poet? Was he a radical, or an understanding businessman in shop steward's clothing? Whatever Huck was, the two men hit it off superbly, walking, talking in Dunagin's little office in the plant, and corresponding between Babcock's visits. "A very fine man . . . very honest, very fair, and very valuable to management" was Babcock's assessment. "He had our point of view. He knew what the problems were in management, and what the company had to do to make a dollar. He was the fairest union man I ever talked to."

In such a situation the company was obliged, both morally and in its own interest, to make certain Dunagin did not become suspect among his own members. The last thing either party would want was Dunagin being thought of as a "yellow dog" in the company satchel.

The employees liked and trusted him well enough to make him their local leader year after year, and they were right . . . He'd make a very strong case for whatever he was talking about with me, but he would always end up on a pleasant note, and he'd very often prove his point.

Babcock would have been interested in a talk Huck gave to an economics class at Mississippi Southern while running the union when it was still C.I.O.-affiliated. Dunagin told the students about an industrial conference he had attended, "The Human Factor in Business and Industry."

"You know, there is more talk and less done about having good labor relations than there is about anything else except the weather."[7] Huck was labor's only representative at the conference, which was held on the roof of a five-story hotel. As he put it: "Only two or three railings separated me from downward space. I certainly did not jump up and say 'I am a member of the C.I.O.'"

Addressing the Mississippi Southern students, Huck called for fair, open, and above-board collective bargaining by management, in return for which its union would kick out all professional agitators, particularly communists. In many respects it was the same straightforward thinking that won the respect of Leon Babcock, but proclaimed in an academic setting.

From 1954 to 1960 Babcock served on the Hercules board of directors. From his earliest days as an employee, he had been acquiring company stock through a payroll deduction plan and had become a very large shareholder. When he retired in 1960, Hercules was considered to be "in the vanguard of chemical profitmakers."[8] True, Leon Babcock had retired, but he had not sold his Hercules stock, and Dunagin believed that the corporate clout Babcock had built up over forty-three years would be around if and when Huck needed it.

Mr. Babcock and I discussed only Huck, but the Hercules unions were not a one-man show. Dunagin had a very able helper of quite a different type. In fact, had he not been the running mate of Dunagin, the great intimidator, A. E. Curry, Jr., eighty-one years old as we sat outside his Hattiesburg home on a pleasant Labor Day, 1994, would have impressed me as physically imposing himself. Curry veered between levity and intensity as we talked.

Five years younger than Huck, who had a bit more seniority, Curry had been graduated from Hattiesburg High School and went to work for Hercules in 1934. A. E. and Huck were eager union recruits and soon took over its leadership, Huck in his natural role of shop steward and A. E. as president.

More important to A. E. was his having been "saved" at a revival meeting at the Broad Street United Methodist Church in 1936. He had "accepted Christ as his personal savior" and given Him his heart to atone for his sins. When I suggested that today he would be called a "born again Christian," he readily embraced that term, but could joke about it. After the revival meeting, the Hercules property manager said so many tools and ladders had been returned that he hoped Broad Street would have another revival meeting again "real soon."

As a man in "the patriotic South," A. E. had felt obliged to enlist after Pearl Harbor Day, despite having a wife and child. His Hercules training caused navy recruiters in Jackson to make him a chief petty officer, and he was able to send home $250 a month. He went on to fly torpedo bomber missions.

Returning to Hattiesburg after more than three years in the navy, he attended what became William Carey College. Curry credits what I considered his remarkable racial attitude for a white Mississippian of his age to his upbringing, despite having a mother who he swore was a member of the KKK, to his being "saved," and maybe also to his union activism. "Give a man his honest due. Don't take things away from them because of race." What Dunagin saw as protecting his own was for Curry Christ's message.

"Everything we stood for, every red-blooded American should stand for." It was nice to hear the rhetoric of the flag being wrapped around equal opportunity in Mississippi in the sixties. A. E. was an industrial pipefitter, and Willie Thigpen, one of our black witnesses, was assigned to him. "I'm going to see you get a chance, but you have to learn to read fractions. Get some Negro plumbers to help you," Curry told him. Some might not have taken that the right way, A. E. knew, but Thigpen understood it was a requirement of the job and made the most of his chance. He and other blacks attained jobs the company said they couldn't do. "Don't let the company say you're not qualified," Curry declared. He wasn't at the Portland meeting when Huck anointed Richard Boyd as the first black in a Hercules white man's job, but, just as Huck had, Curry told the black workers they wouldn't be fired if they went to register to vote.

❖❖❖

Dunagin had not been involved in the trial, so I did not know him at that time, but when I returned to Forrest County to talk with our old witnesses, the Hercules workers kept bringing up his name. Clearly he was part of the story. I wanted to meet him.

T. F. Williams told me that I would never find Dunagin's home by myself. It was way out in the country on Good Luck Road in the Sunrise Community. Although I prided myself on finding my way around the rural back roads of Mississippi, he was right. So T. F. came along for my visit to his old shop steward. While I preferred interviewing people alone, we did get to Dunagin's 125-acre spread, where he once had cattle, and it was good for me to see a southern white man welcoming a former co-worker, an African American, into his home—through the front door—as a friend. In fact, I enjoyed T. F.'s comments and promptings as Huck recalled his career at Hercules for me. And I did not forget that six of the black witnesses for the United States had been Huck Dunagin's men.

Almost eighty-two when we talked, Huck remained a physically powerful man:[9]

I was born June 8, 1908, in Laurel, about 30 miles north of here. Do you read "Dunagin's People"? My son Junior is a syndicated cartoonist in numbers and numbers of papers.

Huck would have been pleased to know that more than a decade later Junior's social cartoons were still appearing on the country's op-ed pages and that I had relevant ones covering the bulletin board outside my office when I taught at Ole Miss Law School in 2000.

My granddaddy, Tapley Dunagin, actually fought in the Civil War, the last two years, went in when he was sixteen. He was born in Alabama, on the Tombigbee River, 90 to 100 miles up from Mobile. He moved to Laurel and went into business when the sawmills started building up there.

When I was about 16, I had an old friend named Matt Giles who told me stories about Civil War veterans. You've read of General Nathan Bedford Forrest, one of the greatest generals ever been. The Germans came over before the war and studied his cavalry tactics and used them. He didn't hardly have any education, but he never surrendered; he never was whupped. How did he win when there were superior numbers against him?

My father, Charles E. Dunagin, was also born in Alabama. He volunteered for the Cuban fracas and was a Spanish-American War veteran. He was supposed to have been shipped out, but just about all of them in the company got typhoid fever . . . and he never went to Cuba.

My mother, Mattie Hudson, was born in Poland, Mississippi—one of the oldest and biggest towns between Hattiesburg and Meridian. Poland was where the Klan lived. Ellisville, just this side of Laurel, was the nest of the Civil War deserters.

In a moving column at the time of Huck's death written for the newspaper for which he was editor-publisher, Charles M. Dunagin, Huck's elder son, described his father's upbringing:

Dad grew up tough, the third of six children of Charles and Mattie Dunagin. Charley, as he was called, was a blacksmith with powerful arms, not given to sparing the rod when it came to my father, who was the most rebellious of the children.[10]

Charley Dunagin did big hammer work as a heavy forger. The family bounced around: Hattiesburg, Wiggins, Laurel, New Orleans, and finally back to Hattiesburg.

According to Huck,

That was when Mama said she wasn't leaving any more. My Pa was raised to believe in the union. He used to work on the railroad, and they were pretty well organized years ago. He wasn't an integrationist.

I was about six when we first got to New Orleans. When we first got there and pulled into the yard, some kids came out, looking through a crack. I threw dirt in their faces. I used to ramble around in the woods on the other side of Hattiesburg and swim and fish in the creek there. And I was ragged, poor. One time I'm walking across the field with a homemade fishing pole on my shoulder and a little string of fish. Some of the baseball players saw me and said, "Who's that, Huckleberry Finn?" I've been Huck ever since.

Huck leaned back and smiled:

I went to Hattiesburg High School off and on. Papa said "Get a job and pay board, or go to school." I got a job in a sawmill, two bits an hour for ten hours—$2.50 a day. I shoveled sand out of a gondola car with no top . . . fooled around, then I decided I'd go back to high school. I was all Big Eight at tackle in 1928, in the biggest high school conference in the state.

For eleven straight years in the 1920s and 1930s there was at least one Dunagin on the Hattiesburg High School football team. Two Dunagins, including Huck, were All-Conference. Huck also played on a strong high school basketball team.[11]

Well, I had enough interest to go to college, but I didn't have a high school diploma. Mississippi Southern wanted me to play football there. So I took the entrance examination and passed. I played football out there in 1929 and '30, and I got to be a pretty good baseball player.

Huck made a decent living while in college. Wash and wear clothes were still in the future, and good clothes had to be dry-cleaned. To acquire him as a football player, the school gave him tuition and the dry cleaning concession. Huck and another student with a car picked up clothes on the campus in the morning and brought them to the dry cleaner in town.

By then he was six feet tall and weighed 185. Huck went in the navy for two years and played tackle on the battleship team.

Back then the rules were different: a large man could do things he can't do now, more than just push. He could grab the back of a man's head, cover his face with his hand, all that. I was pretty bad; I did a lot of things I shouldn't have done.

One of Huck's favorite stories dealt with his whipping a bully on the battleship and the obscene compliment paid him by the defeated. It was a tale he still repeated on his deathbed.[12] "But Dad's veteran's pension got cut off, so I got myself discharged. I liked the navy a lot, but I didn't want to make a career out of it. So I got a job at Hercules."

It was only as a pipe fitter's helper, but Huck started at Hercules on August 31, 1933. His first promotion came in mid-November. In 1934, Huck married Clara Clark. They lived less than a block from the Hercules plant. Charles was born a year later and "Junior" two years after that.[13]

Their sons went to high school in East Forrest, now Petal, and Huck was on the board of trustees that built a new school in order to get certified by the Southern Association. Though it might have surprised some, Huck became a deacon in the Baptist Church.

I got my first job at Hercules because I was a ballplayer. The master mechanic just about run the place then, and he was manager of the semi-pro baseball team that was all Hercules people. I was playing for a different team, and I could catch and play outfield. Hercules had a black team, as well as the white team. The teams didn't play each other, but the blacks probably could have beaten us.

When I went to work for Hercules, roughly three hundred people were employed there. At least fifty per cent of the employees were black. I stayed at Hercules until I retired, except during the war.

The Hattiesburg area had long-leafed yellow pine trees, the best lumber. The sawmills cut them, leaving the stumps that would not rot. They were resin pits and just sat there until the company chemists learned they could extract the resin for different uses in industry, plastics and many other things—including turpentine.

People don't realize what it was like during the Depression. That job at Hercules was supreme back in those days, just having a regular job. I was making $18 a week as an operator's helper. My wife was a registered nurse, getting $12 a week as a public health nurse. They told her they were going to have to let her go and give it to a nurse that didn't have a husband working. There were bread lines out there, and some people would go in a store with sacks and bags and start taking things . . . taking because they were hungry.

The economy had improved by the time the United States entered World War II. In 1943 Huck joined the elite navy unit, the Seabees, as a first class petty officer. The draft had begun, and Huck actually made more money than he was making at Hercules.

Dunagin served mostly in the Admiralty Islands of the South Pacific. The enemy broadcasters in New Guinea told them how they were going to lose and get killed. A younger brother was a marine and was killed in Saipan. Huck was discharged in 1945 as chief petty officer, the highest noncommissioned rank in the navy. By then he was thirty-seven.

In January 1946 I came back to the same job I left, refinery operator. Hercules never had a union until after the war. There was a helper, who had gone in the army and was made a commissioned officer. Some fellows in the plant got some 4-F deal and didn't go. They tried to give one of them promotion over this kid that had gone off and served abroad. They wanted the strike.

Huck still resented Hercules's treatment of that veteran. He relished telling me about the strike:

The whole plant went out, white and black. It pissed me off that they gave this fellow that got the 4-F the promotion over the fellow that went off and came out as a lieutenant, with foreign service medals—so that's when I got into the union, a C.I.O. union, Mine, Mills and Smelters. I made a talk, and they made me chairman of the strike committee. The company didn't think we'd push, but I put on the bulletin board a notice that the plant would be shut down in an orderly manner: carry out all safety precautions, drain all the equipment, everything. They called me in the office and wanted to know about this . . . I wasn't very gentlemanly in there.

Two short blasts of the whistle, and we walked out, shut her down.
That's when we began to get a little attention. The strike didn't last very
long. They gave in pretty quick—a week or so. Some time after that I got
to work just as a steward, trying to get complaints settled.

Huck got to know T. F. Williams in the union. T. F. was first a "sample
boy," who came every hour and took back samples for analysis in the laboratory, to see whether the color of the resin was right or if adjustments
would be necessary.

Huck had a personal grievance against Hercules: he had developed a
procedure that he hoped to patent, but the company beat him to it: "It was
an invention that split the stumps in the ground where they would come
out easier. I was afraid to take them on in court, afraid I'd lose my job."

And there were still professional grievances, too:

People got hurt bad, and the company covered it up. One fellow got his
back burned real bad. I gave them so long to bring him into the hospi-
tal and get him treated, or the union was going to bring him in. They
didn't even want to call his lost time an accident. Mr. Babcock came
down from Wilmington. He told the manager and the superintendent
that he wanted to talk with me.

Beginning in 1947, Huck was formally designated "Union Personnel Representative." He had a whole office at the plant, just handling complaints.
Huck knew his own prerogatives at the plant.

A white preacher named Slim Cameron came in my office. "I want
to ask you something," he said; "You're gonna tell me the truth, aren't
you?" I said, "Slim, I might lie to somebody, but I damn sure wouldn't
see any reason to lie to you."

And he said, "I heard over on the flats that you said you were gonna
whip my ass." I said, "No, Slim, I didn't say that. When I get ready to do
it, I'm not going to tell anybody, I'm just going to find you and stomp
the shit out of you." After a little bit, Slim said, "Well, there's some
doubt whether you can do that or not." And I said, "Well, we'll just get
that settled right now." He got up and took a walk.

T. F. Williams had been listening intently. He leaned forward and urged:
"Tell him about when you integrated the hired labor and what you had

to do to David Travers, that white guy, when Richard Boyd broke the job barrier."

A smile came over Dunagin's face:

That was something. Upstairs, there were barrels and tanks and evaporators. Every hour you'd go to the desk, and you'd make out some reports, and this redneck Travers and some other guys got up there at night with a damned rope, a hangman's noose, made out to hang somebody. It's funny now, it wasn't then.

They wouldn't have pulled it on him like that, hanged him in the building, no, but the noose was coming down in front of him. Richard Boyd tried to quit . . . I had gotten him put on that job in the late fifties, several years before the voting. He was just a helper-at-large, but Richard broke the barrier. It was going to be easier if he wasn't building up any seniority for a first-class job in any one department. I told Richard to hang in there, and he went right on to a first-class job as a crane operator.

Indeed it wasn't funny then. In 1967 in Natchez on the Mississippi River, Wharlest Jackson, a thirty-six-year-old father of five and Korean War veteran, died from the blast of a bomb planted in his truck as he left work at the Armstrong Rubber Company, a plant believed infested with Klansmen and their sympathizers. Jackson was treasurer of the Natchez branch of the NAACP and had just received a seventeen-cent-an-hour raise when promoted to a "white-man's job." It was not the first act of violence against a black employee at Armstrong, which appears to have lacked the kind of leadership Dunagin and Curry provided at Hercules. Jackson's murder remains unsolved.[14]

Hercules's management made a critical decision, siding with Dunagin and Boyd. Travers was laid off. They told him he could come back if he could work with blacks. One wonders if it wasn't Huck Dunagin and his reputation that prevented Richard Boyd winding up as Wharlest Jackson did.

The Ku Klux Klan did burn a cross in front of Huck's driveway. Dunagin offered a reward for the name of the local wizard. Finally, he learned who it was from an informant who didn't want it known that he was the source. It turned out that the Klansman and Huck had known each other since high school.

With an expression of grim satisfaction, Huck told me:

I got the message to him: anything happen around my place, I was going to kill him. He knew darned well if anything happened, the only way he'd stop me from killing him was to kill me. He never gave me any static. The FBI was going against the Klan then and told me some of their tag numbers. I set up a gate so the Klan couldn't drive up here in a hurry and throw a bomb and get away. The gate would swing and lock you in . . . It was going to get them before they got away, and they knew it.

Huck also encountered the Klan in McComb:

My son Charles was editor and general manager of the McComb paper. They have more circulation than they have people living in southwest Mississippi, and he's pretty well known over the country. The Klan threw an unlit pipe bomb in his window with his kids sleeping there. They didn't like what he put in the paper. I went over and sat up a few hours with a shotgun, to see if they came back.

Dunagin continued to be bothered about the difficulties blacks "not having the right to work up":

I started making moves. It wasn't easy. I was chief steward and chairman of the strike committee. We had left the Mines and Smelters. Later on it came out that it was Communist-dominated. But we went with the Gas, Coke and Chemical Workers and later the woodworking union. The company just didn't want to get into any controversy. If they'd have had a choice, most of the salaried would have said "Let the blacks vote." We had the best labor relations of any plant Hercules had. They knew damn well they were going to piss me off good if they tried to fire me. I wasn't worried about that. Home office would have been on them if I'd have told Mr. Babcock. They wanted to treat the employees right, but they wanted the plant run efficiently.

Huck declared that his black workers had as much right to vote as his white workers. Huck pointed out that the white supremacists should have retreated to a common-sense position that voters be able to read and write.

But that wasn't what they wanted. Finally they got it now to where everybody can vote, whether they can read, write, anything else. I gave people the right to work up on the job.

When police cars started dogging behind some colored fellows com-
ing to work—people that were trying to vote, I took a stand that it
would be illegal. My job was to give some protection to members of our
union and our friends who wanted to vote, and, if the police arrested
them on what we considered a trumped-up charge, the union was go-
ing to defend them. They knew that if they went down to try to register
to vote, they wouldn't lose their jobs. It just wouldn't happen. Hercules
nationally wouldn't have wanted that, anyway.

I had a role to play in helping blacks vote generally because if those
at Hercules, a leading company, could get by with it and vote, that was
going to make it easier for the others. That's the stand I took.

T. F. Williams shook his head: "Well, he say he don't want no credit for
it, but my boys never would have got the jobs they have now if he hadn't
moved me so far as to get one of the jobs whites had."

Dunagin smiled at T. F. and said:

T. F. was one of the first ones. They put pressure on him. One day, he
came dragging over to my office, but he wouldn't quit, no backing out.
I told him to get back up there, and he got on back up there.

I tell you the truth, I kind of liked a little stuff.

T. F. Williams laughed, saying, "We had a good time."

Things later changed at the plant. Exhausted by union politics, Huck lost
the election after removing the union from the A.F.L.-C.I.O.

A new bunch at the plant wanted to change things up. I made one
mistake. We had already gone from the Chemical Workers to the
Woodworkers, but I took us out of the C.I.O. altogether, and we went
independent. Keep the money here, I thought, and I shouldn't have.
Anyway, I lost the election. I didn't try. I was going to quit, anyway. I
wanted to stay independent, and they went into the Teamsters. I re-
tired from Hercules in 1971, when I was sixty-three.

Hercules circulated a memorandum to its employees asking if they
wished to contribute to a gift for Huck. Sixty-one employees contributed a
dollar or two. Among them were union leader A. E. Curry, Richard Boyd,
T. F. Williams, and another of our witnesses, Willie Simpson. They owed
Huck much more than a dollar.

Some whites thought I was kind of a traitor, but friends were pretty nice to me. Didn't nobody tell me give up. Two or three white friends did talk to me in a nice way about what I was doing. They didn't think it was right, but they didn't threaten me, just wondering why would I use the union like that. Only reason I did it was because my union members were also my friends. I didn't even talk a whole lot about what was going on to my wife, still sometimes the heat would get on her.

T. F. Williams summed things up: "Well, we had some good times and some rough times, but through all of them—me and him been friends for many, many years. I have to shake with him—more than any of them I know."

Huck responded:

Richard Boyd and then T. F., they're the ones who broke it. Willie Simpson and Willie Thigpen—they were both what I respected as just good, high-class men. Sam Hall was about as good a man as you'd find. I told them, around Hattiesburg and Forrest County, "You're damned fools to think you're going to block it. Do this thing up right. If you don't," I said, "you're going to get it around your throat."

CHAPTER 13

HUCK'S MEN

The Black Workers at Hercules

THE SPARKPLUG FROM PALMER'S CROSSING: T. F. WILLIAMS

The black community of Palmer's Crossing is just down the road from the heart of Hattiesburg. Go over the railroad tracks from the old airport and past the drive-in movie. Turn right just a block beyond the tracks onto Satchel Avenue, and you found at #509 the modest cottage of one of its most prominent residents, T. F. Williams. T. F. and his patient wife, Jessie, raised their family there in a close-knit community of only twelve hundred.

Born in 1918, T. F. was just three years old when his parents moved out from Hattiesburg. Palmers had just a hundred families then. T. F. and Jessie, sister of *Peay* plaintiff R. C. Jones, were married young and had just returned from celebrating their fiftieth wedding anniversary with their five children in Los Angeles, when I first came back to visit them in July 1989. In reminiscing with me, T. F. would often shout "Jessie," and she would join us and straighten him out on a stray detail.

T. F.'s father, Charlie Williams, was the lead man in a sawmill, a job usually reserved for whites. White and black jobs were separate and distinct when T. F. was coming along, just as he would initially encounter them at Hercules. Mr. Williams worked for the Dreyfus family that owned the Dixie Pine Products Company. T. F. was, in fact, named after old T. F. Dreyfus, and T. F. played and swam with some of the younger members of the Dreyfus family as a boy.

After going to work at the Hercules Powder Company in 1942, T. F. stayed there, apart from military service, close to thirty-eight years, until his retirement in 1980. He saw Hercules become aware of the country's changing racial mores:

The Hercules black employees had to go in the back to buy groceries then. I would go to the Hughes commissary instead. Huck Dunagin was a smart white guy who knew we had the votes to get him elected Chief Steward in the union. Hercules went and integrated themselves. They picked several of us black fellows and put us as rolling operators, go all over the plant to work, operate in each building. They showed the whites that we could get along.

Blacks had always been discriminated against, but they did have seniority. Some had been there thirty or forty years. Whites had been given all the good jobs, but T. F. first worked at the boiler room, then operated an overhead electric crane. Finally, he became foreman of the mail room.

T. F. himself had gone to work after spending much of the eleventh grade in a vocational shop where he shoed horses with horseshoes and fixed broken wagon wheels, among other things. His first job was at his father's Dixie Pine plant, where he had run errands even before school was out. It was after the Dixie Pine plant blew up and burned in 1941 that T. F. went to work at Hercules at forty-three cents an hour. On August 23, 1944, he enlisted in the navy. By then, he was up to fifty-four cents an hour.

I wanted to go to the aircraft plant up in Michigan, and they were down here recruiting us. They weren't paying nothing at Hercules. I was ready to go. But I had to get a deferment, and they had to give me a leave, see, because it was a government plant. Well, the foreman tried to show me what I would lose if I were to go up there, already had a home and everything here. And he really was nice, and there was a lot in it. But I wanted to go.

So when the foreman couldn't talk me into staying, he told them in the office. And old man Cook, the super, jumped up and told me, work or fight. See, all they had to do was call the Board and turn you in if you left the plant without a deferment. He said, you work or fight, and I said, hell, I'll fight; I ain't no slave. I went down and volunteered for the navy. My wife like to have a fit. That happened on a Friday, and I got the first bus out that Monday morning. They put me in charge of 21 black men. I went over to Jackson, then to Bainbridge, Maryland, and Great Lakes.

T. F. didn't care which service he entered. He was just mad and wanted to get away from Hattiesburg. "Best thing that ever happened to me in my life. Learned something about the world, and I learned I could be a man.

All you had to do was know a thing, and you could do it. I went to work in the navy, got me a gunner mate, third class, and kept moving up."

T. F. could have reenlisted and probably made ensign, but he felt he could only go so far.

It wasn't like it is now, but I got good experience, and I saw the world. I got on aircraft carriers, the U.S.S. Boxer *and the U.S.S.* Yorktown, *and I didn't get a scratch until 1945 when I got off to catch the ship home from Okinawa. A typhoon blew everything away, and an ammunition dump blowed up.*

T. F. was back at work at Hercules as a laboratory shift laborer December 1, 1945, at sixty-three cents an hour. "I went back to Hercules although I had been very mad when I left. They respected every person—put all the military service time on my seniority. And this guy who said 'work or fight' had died. It was a different plant in a lot of ways."

T. F. joined Forrest County's underground chapter of the NAACP, though he was well aware of some private employers firing blacks who they learned had joined the NAACP. He also knew the eight Palmer's Crossing teachers who were fired after they became members. T. F., however, always wanted to vote.

The first time that I went in and tried to register was when Luther Cox was Clerk. He never could get to you, stand you out there three and four hours, make you come back. I went lots. Later I went up to Jackson to testify about Theron Lynd. John Doar had told me when I got up there, don't let Dugas Shands make you mad.

At 9 A.M. on Wednesday, March 7, 1962, the final day of the injunction trial, T. F. led off our testimony. He and our other remaining witnesses had been up early to get back to Jackson on time from Hattiesburg. Bob Owen examined T. F., who had been paying poll taxes since 1949, and asked what happened when he filled out an application form:

When I just about finished filling out the form, I taken out my pocket dictionary to see some words I didn't understand clearly, and Mr. Lynd's clerk, she saw that and called Mr. Lynd, and he came over and he said, "You are disqualified. Don't you know you are not supposed to use anything?" And I said, "No, sir, I didn't know that. . . . Will you let me fill out another one?" And he said, "No, I can't let you fill out another one." I pleaded with him a while, and he would not let me do it. Then I asked him, "When can I come back?" He said, "Six months." . . . Well, I got up and left.

As I expected, it was M. M. Roberts who cross-examined. It was scarcely two weeks since Roberts, accompanied by the Hattiesburg police chief, had T. F., Reverend Hall and other black Hercules employees who Roberts thought might testify brought to the company offices to be interrogated. Roberts says that T. F. told him that he had advised us he "couldn't go to Jackson because [he] was sick with a bad heart."[1] But T. F. was indeed in Jackson, though that interrogation lingered on both of their minds.

Roberts began by asking a bullying series of questions casting sarcastic aspersions on Williams having carried a pocket dictionary. T. F. conceded that he had brought the dictionary to the office to look up any words he didn't understand. To our side, it was admirable that T. F. cared enough about doing well on his voter application to bring a dictionary. It was a sign of his seriousness, his determination to do his best. To the other side, he was a cheater. That the dictionary was a small pocket version seemed to our side only a practical detail. It was portable. To the other side, it meant he was a sneak, trying to put something over on Theron Lynd and the white citizens of Forrest County.

Roberts attacked T. F.'s credibility: "There's something wrong about this." He implied strongly that T. F. had lied about what he was looking at in the office. A little later he asked, "When you went to see Mr. Lynd and when you were in the office generally, they were always kind to you, were they not?" T. F. replied, "They treated me nice in the office." Roberts should have let it go there, but he asked again, "You have no complaint about the way they treated you, have you?" T. F. Williams replied firmly, "Not the way I was treated, the only complaint I have, I think he should have let me register."

Roberts fell back on the dictionary issue, and T. F. replied: "I got to a word I didn't understand, and I got my little hand dictionary and looked at it, and that was the first thing I taken out, and the clerk walked over there and said, 'You ain't supposed to be looking at anything,' and she went and got Mr. Lynd."

Q. Theodore? You say a girl came and told you—a lady in the office told you that you were not to look at these papers?

A. She told me I wasn't supposed to. And then she went and called Mr. Lynd over . . . I was getting information about a word in the dictionary. I didn't use anything until I got ready to fill out the Constitution. Then I checked over some words to see whether I was right.

Roberts moved on to a piece of paper T. F. had with him with notes about citizenship and constitutional rights and demanded to know where that came from. T. F. replied: "That was from the encyclopedia . . . I had been studying that because it said you had to have that to vote and I had been studying the Constitution. . . ."

Q. Did you talk to anybody about what you might need?
A. No, sir, I hadn't talked with a soul, but I knowed some of the things that it taken to be a citizen and I took it to refresh my memory on it.

Isn't it true, Roberts demanded, that Preacher Jones was responsible for T. F. and the other Hercules workers going to register?

A. No, sir, I didn't get no preacher to take me. The record shows I have been going up there. I wanted to register. . . .
Q. So he didn't have anything to do with your going, but you went up there with a group?
A. Yes, sir.
Q. And there were eight or nine or ten of you and you all went from Hercules, didn't you?
A. Yes, sir. . . .
Q. The truth about it is that Mr. Lynd tried to get you to give him that paper you had, didn't he, and you would not do it?
A. No, sir, he never did try that. He taken that Constitution card he gave me, but he didn't ask me for my paper.
Q. Do you deny that he asked you for the paper?
A. Yes, sir, I deny he asked me for the paper. . . .

Roberts droned on in the same vein, but T. F. never broke.

THE QUIET CUSTODIAN: SHERMAN JACKSON

Sherman Jackson died before I began this book, but his memory remained vivid in his family and in his community. A janitor at Hercules, he was so much more than that. "Sherman Jackson was kind of a quiet fellow," his Hercules co-worker Willie Thigpen told me. "If he knew you real good, he were real friendly. He got to know me good." Together they were regulars at football games, either at Jackson State or the local high school.

Sherman Jackson was born in Alexandria, Louisiana, in 1910. His family moved first to New Orleans and then to Hattiesburg, where Sherman was graduated from Eureka High School. He felt that he was academically a year ahead of his grade when he arrived.

Sherman Jackson, Jr., the oldest of his four sons, became a Jackson middle school teacher and coach.[2] His brothers went off to Los Angeles, Houston, and Syracuse, New York, but Sherman Jr. stayed. He had studied or traveled throughout the United States and Western Europe, but Jackson, Mississippi, remained his home. "I know there's a lot of prejudice here," he said, "but I find that any place you go. People go to these other places, and sometimes they want to talk down about the South, but I find they are in worse shape than we are here."

His father hadn't gone to college, but his Sherman Jr. felt he was "educated far above his high school. He knew current events. He wasn't afraid of nobody, and he didn't like the idea of somebody saying that he couldn't vote. That was one of his rights, being able to vote. He didn't talk down to nobody, but he didn't let anybody talk down to him."

The *New Orleans Times-Picayune* was delivered to the home of Sherman and Josephine Jackson in Hattiesburg, and they also read the *Reader's Digest*, the *Pittsburgh Courier*, and the *Chicago Defender*.

> *He kept a scrapbook about Joe Louis, and about the war, about Pearl Harbor. He always mentioned the problem of blacks not being able to vote. Said that that was one thing he was going to be able to do. He used to talk about how you had to pay to vote, how they had a poll tax and how you had to take a test. And he said there wasn't anything they could ask him on that test that he couldn't tell them about because he was well versed in the Constitution. He said if they didn't let him vote, it wasn't because he couldn't pass the test or he didn't pay the poll tax. He was going to keep trying.*

Sherman Jackson had made a name for himself in Hattiesburg. He booked dances and even brought Louis Armstrong to old Love's Hall.

> *Lots of times he'd be singing around the house, so we learned a lot of songs, Cab Calloway songs like "Minnie the Moocher,"—you*

know—"Hidey, Hidey, Hi—Hodey, Hodey Ho." He didn't play an instrument, but I got my scholarship in trumpet. We didn't have a recording machine, but we talked about music all the time.

Sherman Jackson also always knew what was going on in his community.

We four boys never did think anything could happen that he wouldn't know—because that was during the time where everybody raised you. If something happened on Mobile Street where black people hung out, if anybody said anything to you, if you didn't act right, he'd know about it because he knew everybody along the street.

The Jacksons were a close-knit family. Sherman, Sr., was firm, but loving, and he had a sense of humor.

He always took care of our needs, even during the depression. I remember our first house, a shotgun house. He didn't go to church that much, but he always sent his dues in to Mount Carmel Baptist Church. My mother was more of a church-goer. We went with her to the Church of God, Pentecostal, though I became an Episcopalian when I was in college.

Hercules had been a good employer for Sherman, Sr., but he didn't want his sons working around the chemicals there or cleaning out those railroad tank cars. His sons would go to college. "He kind of leaned toward Tennessee State, but he let us make our own choice. He had us talk to people that had gone to different colleges. So we got a little insight into college life before we even started. I went to Jackson State and my youngest brother to Texas Southern."

Sherman Jr. wanted to watch his father testify for the United States. "I drove down there, but there were police around the courthouse in downtown Jackson, and one of the officers told me, 'Just get off, you can't go down there.' I never did get a chance to see him."

While Sherman Jr. was frustrated outside the courthouse, his father was being bullied inside by Dugas Shands. Jackson's first attempt to register had been at the end of January 1961. He had gone to the courthouse with eight or nine other black workers at Hercules, and had actually seen Theron Lynd, who asked him how long he had lived in Hattiesburg and where he worked. Lynd then told all of them except the Reverend Miles Jones to wait outside. When Reverend Jones emerged and told them he had not been registered, Jackson went home.

He returned about a week later and was permitted to fill out a form. He did a short but adequate interpretation of a constitutional provision dealing with uniform taxation throughout the state. For "duties and obligations of citizenship," he wrote: "Uphold and defend all laws of city, county and state government." Yet the big NR, not registered, was inscribed on the top of his form.

After Jackson testified that he paid his poll tax every year, it was time for Dugas Shands, who appeared to be salivating at the prospect of cross-examining a janitor instead of a teacher: Sherman, did you complain to the Department of Justice? Did you send for the FBI? No, well how in the world did they get to you? You don't know, well, what are you doing in this lawsuit? Who was with the Department of Justice men when they came to see you? Come on, Sherman, let's be serious about this thing. How many times did they come?

Jackson had not been back to learn of his rejection directly from Lynd. He blamed the flood, and Attorney Zachary explained to the court that Hattiesburg had indeed had a bad flood the preceding February. Jackson had written "34" for his election district and "Library" instead of "Forrest" for his county, though he obviously knew the name of the county he lived in.

JUDGE COX: Who wrote that in there, Sherman?
A. I did.
JUDGE COX: You didn't know what you were writing that in there for?
A. I was confused on the district.
SHANDS: Now you know why you didn't pass, don't you?
A. Yes, sir.
JUDGE COX: Is that why he didn't pass?
SHANDS: I don't know why he didn't pass. I merely asked the question.

Lawyers do merely ask questions, but everyone in the courtroom knew that Jackson's race was why he had not passed. There would, however, be no stipulation as to that. Willie Thigpen had, in fact, told Jackson that he was told that none of them had passed. John Doar brought that out in an offer of proof on redirect examination, though Judge Cox did not permit it to remain in the record.

Jackson's testimony was not as strong as he had told Sherman Jr. it would be, but his application more than met the standard by which whites were registered.

WILLIE THIGPEN, BACK TO HERCULES FROM THE LEDO ROAD

Sherman Jackson's buddy at Hercules, Willie Thigpen, was born in 1916, the eldest son of a farmer who moved from Jones County down to Hattiesburg. Roy Thigpen, only nineteen when Willie was born, died during an appendix operation at the age of thirty-one. Willie's mother died in childbirth in 1921 when he was five.

> *My mother's mother, my grandmother, Alice Kelly, took care of me and my two younger brothers for six years after my mother passed, until my father re-married, and I come to Hattiesburg with him. She was one of the Kellys in Kelly Settlement in the south end of Jones County. She was mighty strict: show up on time, eat the last bite, and do the chores. But growing up in the Kelly Settlement was fine: no electricity, but we had an eight-grade school, White Oak. I went through the fourth or fifth grade out there.*
>
> *O. B. Kelly was a white slave owner. He owned my great-great-grandmother. My grandmother could remember when she was small, the Civil War ended, the soldiers came through and told her, "You all are free now; you all know you are free now?" Religion was very significant to my grandmother. She went to Shady Grove Baptist Church, and I went there too, dressed up, every Sunday. The Sunday School classes we were in, you know how kids are; sometimes we'd play. But better not let them see you; they'd come get you right out of church. I stayed in Kelly Settlement until I was 12.*
>
> *I used to read a lot. We didn't get a newspaper in Kelly Settlement. We did in Hattiesburg. I used to read the black magazines, Ebony mostly, and Jet. I went up to the eleventh in Eureka High School, but I didn't get my high school diploma until I come out of the Army.*

Vernon Dahmer was Willie's uncle. His first wife was Roy Thigpen's baby sister. Willie never forgot Vernon's belief: "If you don't vote, you ain't nothing" and desire that everybody be upgraded, but he thought his uncle Vernon was "too friendly."

What I mean by that, just before he was killed, he built a new house, and I think he thought some of the whites was his friends, but they wasn't. A bunch of them used to stop and talk with him and buy lumber from him. And he showed them all around his house and in his house, everything. I believe that's how they knew so much about how to get to him.

Willie Thigpen's first job was clearing land for Vickers Platform from 1935 to 1939. Then he was an express handler for Railway Express in Hattiesburg until he was drafted into the army in 1942. He and Iola Lee Williams had married in 1935 when he was nineteen and she was seventeen. They didn't have a place of their own so Mrs. Thigpen stayed with his aunt in Hattiesburg while he was in the army.

I spent my army service in the CBI. I know you heard of the Ledo Road; I was on it. That was something—hot and rainy—in Northern India. We were at the foot of the mountain. It went from Ledo on up through the jungle and finally over the mountain. I must have been there 24 of my 28 months overseas.

After the Burma Road for supplying the Chinese was cut by Japanese forces in 1942, the western allies built the Ledo Road from Ledo, India, to Kunming, China. The only alternative means for supplying the Chinese had been hazardous airlifts over the eastern edge of the Himalaya Mountains.

I went into the Army in November, and on February 22d I was on my way overseas: from Newport News to Oran, Africa; from there to Calcutta, India; then up through India by train, and stopped at the Chabua Air Force Base. That's where we were headquartered the whole time I was there. Signal Corps. We went over in China once, through Burma. We built telephone lines just like a telephone company here. When I was discharged, I was T-4. I tell people now, I couldn't hold a full field pack if they was going to shoot me. We were just a telephone outfit, never went on a hike and never owned a pack. My telephone office did real good, and I got along fine with white soldiers while I was on the base.

Thigpen was honorably discharged from the service in the middle of 1945 and returned to Hattiesburg and to the job he left at Railway Express.

I always had thought about registering to vote, but you had to pay poll tax then to vote. I said: well, if it ever gets to where I can register, my poll tax will be paid. I paid that to the Sheriff, the tax collector, but I didn't try to register at that time, no.

They'd have NAACP meetings, all that, but the head teacher was afraid to go try to register on account of his job. And I didn't know but three colored people in Hattiesburg that were registered: Richard Boyd at Hercules, the druggist, Hammond Smith, and Reverend Willard.

After being laid off by Railway Express in 1949, Thigpen went to veterans school at Rowan and earned his high school diploma. On July 13, 1950, he went to work for Hercules, making fifty-five cents an hour. The first time there was voting activity among Hercules workers was 1960–1961. Thigpen gives the credit to Huck Dunagin.

You know, at that time what kept most colored folks from trying to register, your job was threatened. We had a meeting, and he said: "You go and try to register. Don't worry about your job because that won't cause you to lose it." He was a white man, as old as I was. He had been in the service too. I don't know what got him interested in this. He had a lot of support from the colored to get elected as business agent because they run folks against him several times, trying to get him out. Back at that time, folk would maybe bring up something on you that wasn't true; get you fired. Maybe they'd just want the black to get fired.

I imagine nearly 50% of the Hercules workers were black about 1960, but there were still so-called "white jobs" as opposed to "black jobs." I had started as a day laborer ten years before. By 1960, I was switchman on the railroad. Huck Dunagin talked to, let's see, T. F., Dewey Johnson, Sam Hall, me. Sam Hall was the most quietest fellow I ever seen, and he winds up preaching.

Thigpen had told Civil Rights Division attorney John Rosenberg, and later testified, about his first visit to Theron Lynd's office, February 1, 1961. By then he was a pipe fitter's helper at Hercules. Deputy Clerk Dorothy Massengale gave Thigpen an application form and a card with Section 121 of the Mississippi Constitution on it, concerning special sessions of the legislature called by the governor.

The only help he got from her was receiving an extra sheet of paper since there wasn't room enough on the form for him to write the section.

His interpretation was that the governor was "to govern the affairs of the State and is the head of our state government." As to the duties and obligations of citizenship, Thigpen stated: "It is our duty to obey all laws of our State and to pay taxes to support all the law." It hadn't satisfied Theron Lynd. When Thigpen returned the following Monday, Lynd went to his file cabinet and told him he didn't qualify. Shands cross-examined Thigpen on his failure to have signed the application or to name his election district, and Thigpen conceded that he had "missed some of it."

On October 16, 1961, Thigpen filled out a second application. This time he was given section 72 of the constitution on how to override a gubernatorial veto. And this time the purported reason for rejection appeared on the form. He had not completely copied the lengthy section.

I know the lawyers from the Civil Rights Division were in my house two or three times. I remember getting a subpoena to come to Jackson, and I remember testifying, oh yes. I remember John Doar asking me questions. I had never been a witness in court before. I remember Medgar Evers was at the trial in Jackson when we were there. I had never met him before that.

Medgar Evers would live for another fifteen months before being assassinated by Byron De La Beckwith. It was appropriate for him to have been in Judge Cox's courtroom to see the beginning of the end for Theron Lynd.

PREACHER SAM HALL: IN FOR 100 PERCENT

The Reverend Sam Hall lived with his wife, Corinne, right up the street from Addie Burger at 405 Francis Street, behind the Mary McLeod Bethune Elementary School. He testified between two of our white witnesses, Helen Coughlin and Steve Barter.

Delivered by a midwife in Franklin County, Mississippi, in February 1916, Reverend Hall's education ended with the eighth grade, as with most black Mississippians of his day. Like others at Hercules, he had previously worked at the Dixie Pine Mill. In 1939 he moved to Hercules as a laborer.

At first, he filled sacks and sewed them up. From that lowly start, Hall became a sample collector, taking samples of finished products to the laboratory for analysis and cleaning the laboratory equipment and floors. When Hall became one of the lead men in the section, fellow witness John Mosley worked for him. Mosley told me later, "Sam Hall? Oh, he's in for 100%. He'd see that things stayed in order inside, carry out whatever assignments. All around guy."[3]

"The most quietest fellow" Willie Thigpen had ever seen traveled the nineteen miles each way to the Mount Hebron Baptist Church in Sumrall each Sunday to preach.

Richard Boyd remembered Sam Hall going across the street from work: "He would sit down, just start crying, praying. I'd go ask him what was going on. He said, 'I think I've been called.' I said, 'If you've been called to preach, you should go ahead and preach.'"[4]

Boyd and Hall worked days, Monday through Saturday, when they were the Hercules laboratory's sample collectors. Monday through Wednesday, Hall was in charge; Thursday through Saturday it was Boyd. Boyd had more laboratory seniority, and Hall had more plant seniority. Huck Dunagin had posted the job on the bulletin board, and they both put in for it. Huck made them co-leaders.

In 1941 the Hercules workers had started organizing a union, and it was certified the following year. Becoming unionized got them talking about their rights. One of the rights the black workers lacked was, of course, the right to vote. Boyd recalls: "Sam and I got a chance to go in all the buildings where they were making stuff, taking samples, and talking to the people that worked down there. And we decided that whenever we had a day off, we would go down and try to register to vote."[5]

While Boyd was one of a dozen blacks eventually registered by Luther Cox, Hall was rebuffed. There was progress at work, however. By March 1957, he made $1.55 an hour at his job as a lab utility helper. But he was still unregistered when Theron Lynd succeeded Cox as circuit clerk two years later. Reverend Hall testified about his first attempt with Lynd:

In '61, the last part of January, we went up there to try to register, a group of us Negroes. We went in there about 4:15, and Mr. Lynd asked Miles Jones how long had he been in Hattiesburg. He asked Sherman Jackson how long had he been. He asked Cornell McCree and myself how long. We all told him. Then he said, "You, Miles Jones,"—pointing to him—"you come on in, and the rest of you go back in the hall and wait till I send for you." We stood there in the hall and waited till Miles Jones come out another door and told us that was going to be all for this day.[6]

Reverend Hall returned to the office about a week later, February 4, 1961:

*When I walked into the office, Sherman Jackson was there, filling out
a paper. A lady there told me to go back in the hall . . . In a little bit,
Sherman Jackson came out . . . I went back, and she told me to go back
in the hall till she get ready for me. A few minutes later, she called me
back in, and I filled out the blank, all except them oaths. Well, I turned
to the lady to ask her concerning these oaths, and she told me that she
couldn't tell me. So then I laid the paper up on the counter and I left.[7]*

Sam Hall was forty-five when he filled out the application form. He had
paid his poll tax for eight years. He was asked to interpret section 165 of the
constitution on judicial conflicts of interest. His simple phrase indicated he
understood the heart of the issue: "when the parties know about the case or
of kin." For duties of citizenship, Hall said: "A good citizson one who obey
the laws and do all he can for his State and country." Not a bad answer for
a segregated eighth-grade Mississippi education of the 1920s, but not good
enough to be registered by Theron Lynd.

Hall was cross-examined by M. M. Roberts, who had interrogated him
at Hercules February 20:

Q. You filled out this form one time, didn't you?
A. Yes, sir, that's the onliest time I filled it out.
Q. And you never did go back to determine what became of it did
   you?
A. No, sir.[8]

M. M. Roberts contended the case was being stirred up by the Justice
Department in Washington, D.C., not by the rejected black citizens in Mississippi, with questions such as "They brought you to Jackson, didn't they?"
But Reverend Hall replied, "I came to Jackson today myself."[9] Roberts brow-
beat him, but he told the truth and survived.

There would be change in Forrest County. In little more than three
years, by then registered, he would be called by Theron Lynd to serve on
the grand jury, voting on proposed indictments for felony offences. And he
performed regular trial jury service in both 1970 and 1976.

In 1973 Reverend Hall was diagnosed with coronary artery disease, but
he continued to work at the plant. A 1977 company performance review
cited his "quality of work" and "cooperation."[10] When he retired on March
1, 1979, he was a laboratory senior crew leader. Some sixty-five fellow workers contributed between one and ten dollars each toward a richly deserved
farewell gift for Sam Hall.

Reverend Hall died of cancer of the pancreas just two years later, in August 1981. He had helped make Forrest County a better and fairer place.

JOHN STEVEN MOSLEY, NOT "WILLIE"

The most complex of the Hercules workers, John Steven Mosley, was born in Jackson in 1918. His father farmed the flat land of the Mississippi Delta. After his parents divorced, Mosley shuttled back and forth, living mostly with his father in the Delta, but also with his mother in Jackson.

Moving from home to home made schooling difficult. At one point when Mosley was with his sharecropper father, he enrolled in Doddsville Institute in Senator Eastland's hometown in Sunflower County.

> *In Belzoni, my father and we four children worked for a lawyer, James Stanbury. We'd take care of maybe 15 acres: King Cotton. However, on our own we raised sugar cane syrup, milked cows, had chickens, our own vegetables. The rest of it would be for the farmer.[11]*
>
> *In Inverness, we worked for A. B. Jones. Most I could do was get out and try to chop cotton. I was too small to do most anything else except take care of the livestock. My father and Mr. Jones got along fine, but my father was a person who didn't stay in one place too long. If business did not come out like he thought it ought to, he would leave and go where he could do better in the financial part.*

So after two years, Mr. Mosley moved to Cottondale, still in the Delta, and began working for George B. Wilson, Jr.

> *I was a young teenager then, and Wilson just didn't like me. I told him off. So I left there; some things you can brush off, and some things you don't take. Another white man there struck me, and we had a tussle. He reported to Mr. Wilson that I was trying to kill him. Mr. Wilson came down with his shotgun as if he was afraid of me. I had worked in his house, painted the floor, mowed his lawn, yet he had a big shotgun. He said I was trying to take a white man's life. I hadn't tried to take that man's life. He had hit me with a two-by-four, so I grabbed it, and took it away from him. I could have hit him, but I didn't. Anyway, Mr. Wilson didn't like that. It was kind of a crucial time. You didn't raise your voice too much then to a white person.*

So Mosley left. He was in the seventh grade and returned to his mother in Jackson. He worked part-time and went to school part-time until he dropped out in the ninth grade. His mother had remarried, had two children with her new husband, and John had to take care of himself. He and his sister went back to Cottondale. Their father had become ill, and the white man that John had tussled with had been fired. Mrs. Wilson hadn't been in favor of his leaving in the first place.

It wasn't too far from where Emmett Till, just 14, was murdered, Tallahatchie Road. They snatched him up, take him, interrogated him, strip him of all his clothes, shot him through the head, and tied a wire around his waist, and placed weights that they thought would hold him to the bottom of the river. But a young man out fishing discovered him. That was a place I didn't hang around too much.[12]

The reaction in the black community was muted, by necessity. Mosley told me, "If the black man would say something to the white man, a white lynching group'd come by night and take him out and hang him. Some of their white friends didn't approve, but they was afraid they'd be called 'nigger lover.'"

Mosley went to school after Christmas until the planting of cotton began in April:

You try to get all of the cotton seeds planted by Good Friday. I'd have to leave school then. Everybody be rushing around to get the seeds in by Good Friday—an old tradition they had—means we have a good crop. I didn't see why it made any difference because some seeds planted after Good Friday done just as well.

Mosley's father was superintendent of Sunday School at Cottondale. He had taught Sunday School at Inverness and at Gum Grove Baptist Church near Belzoni. So the children had to go to church. There was no question about that.

Those were horse and buggy days. Dad had to load us up and ride 10 miles out to the Gum Grove Church. Reverend R. J. Hawkins was pastor of the church. His sermons had so much influence on us that we kids would try to imitate him. I accepted Christ as my savior under Reverend Price in Cottondale. I made public my feelings toward being born again as a Christian. I was baptized, and I studied the Bible.

Mosley's father was a good Bible scholar and taught him things that Mosley still recalled as I talked to him. One lesson when he was eight or nine dealt with putting God's Kingdom first. That never left him, and he taught the same lesson when he was a Sunday School superintendent himself before having heart surgery. He told me how he got to Hattiesburg:

I was working with a construction company on an air base in Jackson, and the man wanted to bring most of his employees with him to Hattiesburg so they'd have somebody there who would know what to do. About 100 of us came down, and I've been in Hattiesburg ever since. We built barracks in Camp Shelby. That's when I moved from construction work to the warehouse and shipping department. We finished that job, and they left to go to Alabama. I refused to go with them. So the Colonel at Camp Shelby asked me what was my classification. I told him I was 1-A. He said, "You're working on the home front here with me; you're a good man, and you know what to do." So I delivered merchandise to 52 stores.

The colonel had Mosley reclassified but made it clear the new classification would hold only as long as Mosley remained with him. So Mosley worked there until the camp began to close.

I knew I had to find me a job, and I got one with the Merchants Company in the shipping department. That's where I met my wife, Lorraine Jeanette Wortham. She put the government stamps on cigarettes for the cigarette and tobacco department. I built this house in 1946. She went back to school at Jackson State and Alcorn A. & M. and taught school for 30 years in Lamar County. We didn't have any children.

Mosley's interest in voting had begun when he was a teenager, and his father used to read to him from the *Memphis Commercial-Appeal* about Franklin Delano Roosevelt.

When I came to Hattiesburg, Luther Cox was Circuit Clerk. I go up there to try to register, and I was turned down. Things were getting heated up. He said, "We're not allowing you to register now, but I think they're going to change that." But he died.

I only went to Cox that one time. He said he wasn't registering black people, so I didn't go back up there. Some guys from my Masonic lodge went several times, and he gave them a few words: "I told you the other day; I told you a second time; why are you back here?" I didn't go back because naturally I didn't want to disturb him. He might have thrown me in jail.

Cox was a slender, small guy, wore glasses, slightly tan complexion. I did have a picture of him. Y'all came here one day, and I showed it to John Doar. In the paper it said, "If I'm re-elected as the circuit clerk, I will continue my job as allowing certain people to register and vote." So Doar asked me what was I going to do with it? I said, "I'm going to keep it for evidence in case it's needed."

Theron Lynd came in, just as tough as Cox. I thought I knew him from talking when I took work to his old company on Pine Street. He was a friendly guy then, but he wasn't going to allow you to register.

By 1959 when Lynd became circuit clerk, Mosley had been working at Hercules for eight years. Mosley didn't feel the black workers had any problems out at Hercules.

Huck Dunagin was the head of our house union. We used to have a union meeting once a month. People began to ask questions, "How many of us are registered?" Irving Rube said, "They won't let us." And Huck told us, "Go in and try, anyhow. Go back. They may change their mind."

One day after work, about 4:30 P.M., Mosley went to Lynd's office with his friend, Robert House. Mosley had gone too late. He was given an application by a woman behind the counter and a card calling for him to interpret section 211 of the constitution concerning the leasing of sixteenth section lands in the Choctaw Purchase. He had no hope of completing that by 5 o'clock. When his half-hour passed, Mosley was told he could try again in six months. "I met John Doar with you. I was subpoenaed to go to Jackson. I said, 'Now my wife is ill,' and you said, 'No, you've got to go or else you're going to go to jail.' Naturally, you had your program made up."

I doubt if I mentioned jail, but I'm sure I told Mosley that he'd get in trouble if he didn't obey a subpoena. He remembered his two trips up to Jackson, skidding the first time with Reverend Chandler, but then testifying when he went the second time with Willie Simpson.

Mosley told me he wasn't scared when he went to Jackson, that he never feared anyone up there because he used to deliver groceries to some of Judge Cox's relatives. But he sounded scared as John examined him about his one attempt. Shands's cross-examination concentrated on Mosley's not having gone back, and Shands repeatedly called him "Willie." No matter what he was called, however, John Mosley was another African American who should have been registered to vote in Forrest County.

WILLIE SIMPSON: HE PLAYED BALL, TOO

Baseball has an important place in the Hattiesburg history of the Hercules Powder Company. Huck Dunagin may have been better known locally as a football player, but Hercules was more interested in his ability to catch and play the outfield for the company's white baseball team. Baseball skill also enabled young black men with athletic talent to obtain secure jobs with Hercules, where ultimately they were led by Dunagin as their shop steward.

Richard Boyd recalled his own coming to Hercules and the man responsible, John Alva Stiglets:

> *Mr. Stiglets, the master mechanic, was kind of the overseer of both the white and black Hercules teams. He was the one responsible for getting those teams organized, getting money out of the company to finance the teams.*
>
> *So one Sunday we had a game down there and I was playing first base for the other team. That particular day I hit a home run, and he asked one of the fellows that was working at the plant at that time, "Where does he work?" "He's working at the Compress." And Mr. Stiglets said, "Why isn't he working at Hercules?" "They won't hire him." I just say it like he said it, "The hell they won't. Just tell him to be out to the plant tomorrow morning." And that's the way I got hired.*

Boyd played for Hercules's black baseball team for three years until the company stopped sponsoring baseball teams.

Willie Custer Simpson, another Hercules ballplayer, was born in 1914, about twenty miles up the road in Ellisville in Jones County. Willie was the son of Henry Simpson, a drayman who made deliveries and hauled furniture and anything else in need of hauling. They lived right among whites.

> *Our father always told us how to come up, treat white people with respect. We never knowed no problems. I never wanted to do what the white man did, anyway. We were brought up to be independent. When I'd go to Hattiesburg to pick up something, we would wait until after*

the white folks got waited on. I remember, in Hattiesburg Hardware, the first time that I didn't have to wait. I was in a hurry, hoping I'd get waited on and come on out. Well, a white man come in, and the clerk, he went around to the white man. But that white man said, "No, he was here first." So the clerk waited on me. I'll always remember that. All white folk are not alike. They're different in the daylight like dogs.

His mother had been Olivia Anderson. She was married three times.

My daddy was the last man she married, and she was his only wife. I was the oldest son of his five children. When I was growing up, my daddy and mamma were big readers: papers, Laurel Leader, *books. I read all them old Wild West shoot-em-ups. I read everything. After we got to Hattiesburg, we bought the Pittsburgh* Courier *and the Chicago* Defender. Life *Magazine back in them days was real popular.*

Ellisville just went to the eighth grade. I finished seven grades there, and my mama wanted me to go to Oak Park in Laurel that was just opening up. I did the eighth, ninth and tenth grades there. When I moved into the eleventh, they called for me to pay tuition. And the old man say he didn't have it, $12. The whole year was $24. All the rest was paid for. $12—and the old man didn't have it. All he could do was feed us, and pay light bill, telephone bill.

So I did the eleventh grade at Hattiesburg where they didn't charge me the $24. See, I stayed with my sister. I could have done the same thing in Laurel, stayed with my aunt, but we didn't know that until afterwards. Stay with your kin and let them be your guardian. Then you don't have to pay.

After Willie finished the eleventh grade, he set off for St. Louis.

Some friend that came by said my half-sister was hollering for me to come. We hoboed up there, and I used to hobo down here to visit. Can easily catch some freights; wasn't no problem. They had me repeat the eleventh, and then I had hard subjects in the twelfth, and I didn't finish. I got a high school diploma because I took a correspondence course out of Chicago. It was my own idea to come home again. That's when I got the job at Hercules.

And that's when Willie became a force on the Hercules colored baseball team.

They hired me in April 1935 when I was going on 21. I played left field, pitched, second base, third base. I could hit a baseball 500 feet. See, my daddy was a ball player, and all us men played baseball. I was one of those big, long ball hitters. We'd play ball like Monday and Tuesday. They let us off.

We played against big teams from Bogalusa and Laurel; New Orleans; Canton, Mississippi. A team from Eastern Bogalusa had a big factory. Man, you get in that town, it smelled like cabbage. After you stay there a while, it was all right. And they had big saw mills. We played so many teams. They didn't allow blacks in professional baseball then, and in the colored leagues you played day and night. I ain't wanted nothing of that.

When Willie first went to Hercules, he did common yard labor for thirty cents an hour.

I was pretty big, so the foreman for where they pull those big tanks, said, 'I want him,' big young buck, you know. I went to 32 cents an hour, two cent raise. That was money back in those days. All you do is eat well and pay rent. I worked at Hercules forty-one years and eight months and got a pension.

By the time Willie retired in 1977, he was making $6.25 an hour.

We had to pay poll tax—without voting. I didn't like it, but I didn't buck it. I paid the poll tax . . . I could live without voting—maybe. When everybody talked of voting, first place, you had to check with the company you worked for—or they would fire you. They fired some people around here. We wanted them to let us Hercules workers vote and let our teachers vote. Most of us owned our own homes, paying taxes.

Big Huck Dunagin, the head of our union, said, "You go up there and stay in line and try to get registered. Stay there until 5 o'clock when they close up on you." We stopped by Huck's office, coming in as we got off the shift, see. And he was telling us what to do. Man, I was ready to go then, when I knew I wouldn't lose my job.

On February 1, 1961, Willie was given an application. He needed an extra page to write out the constitutional section on uniform taxation that he was assigned. His interpretation was to the point: "All property in each county shall be tax equal, according to its value." He included being a church-goer as one of the duties and obligations of citizenship, something with which most Mississippians of that day agreed, regardless of race. Deputy Clerk Dorothy Massengale witnessed his affidavit.

> *When I went into the circuit clerk's office to fill out these forms, oh, they were just as nice as they could be. "All right, Willie," said old big Lynd. He was a great big . . . I knew him when he was a youngster, too. I guess he'd be coming from school. I go to work by his house. And I see him a lot of times. So when he got to be clerk, he knew me, and I knew him. He'd tell me, "Well, Willie, you didn't pass." It was a mess back in them days. But I knew how to act. I had to stay in my place. No problem. They wrote "N. R." I was rejected; sure was.*
>
> *Oh, I felt so bad. I turned around and come out of there. I could have cut that cat's throat, but I knew that wasn't right. I go back and try again. And he tell me, "Willie, you didn't pass." We had five children, and I wasn't going to jeopardize . . . No, not until you lawyers fighting the case got down here and changed things.*
>
> *Sherman Jackson worked with us cleaning cars. I knew he wasn't scared to go, and I wasn't scared to go—not when Huck said we're not going to get fired. So I went in again and filled out another form in September 1961, and three or four in all.*

In September, Simpson's section dealt with the legislature's powers to create and alter corporations. His interpretation basically recited the constitutional provision. This time he left church-goer out of the duties and obligations of citizenship and substituted "a builder of his city and community." That didn't work either. Now it was "N. Q." written on the rejected form, rather than N. R.

Bob Owen brought out those facts on direct examination. Dugas Shands then harshly cross-examined:

Q. Willie, how many times did the F.B.I. men come to see you?
A. At least once.
Q. Come on, Willie, how many times did they come? You remember that. You remembered this other stuff.
A. At least once.
Q. I didn't ask you that, I asked you how many times they came. . . . Did you send for them?
A. I didn't. . . .

Q. How do you think they found you?

A. Through our chief steward . . . I went to him and asked him would my job be jeopardized if I attempted to register, and he said no. I wanted to vote and I went to him first to see would it jeopardize my job.

Q. Your job has not been jeopardized by your efforts at registration, has it?

A. It has not. . . .

Q. Did you ask anybody to help you on this?

A. I did not . . .

Someone wandering into the courtroom might have thought Simpson was a criminal defendant who had made the mistake of taking the witness stand in his own defense. Rather he was a black Mississippian who just wanted to vote. Shands's long, hectoring cross-examination tried to establish that Simpson's applications had been rejected on factual matters. Shands also declared that Simpson had signed the application in the wrong place:

Q. Now, on your application of September 27th . . . you didn't sign on that bottom line that you couldn't read a while ago.

A. Well, I read it.

Q. You didn't read it right, did you? Huh?

A. My eyes are not quite as good as they were a few years ago.

THE COURT: Can you see without glasses? You don't have glasses on.

THE WITNESS: I can see—but not as good as I should. I don't have glasses, but I am going to Dr. Busby and get me some. But when I filled out the application I could see better, the lighting was better.

THE COURT: You could read and write better?

THE WITNESS: I can see real good with 75 to 100 watt bulbs. I can read clear.

THE COURT: You can read and write, right?

THE WITNESS: That's right.

THE COURT: How much education do you have?

THE WITNESS: High school.

THE COURT: What does that mean?

THE WITNESS: That means all except chemistry.

Recalling the trial, Simpson told me:

The trial in Jackson was the only time I testified. I was supposed to have been wearing glasses. I sometimes wore my wife's glasses. And the day I testified, I didn't take my glasses. So I couldn't read up there. But I knew it was right to vote. If you pay taxes, like this guy told them, give me liberty or give me death. But I couldn't afford to lose the job with five children. No, Lord, that wasn't that important to me, to tell you the truth. But now it is. I believe in it.

And I had joined the NAACP. At that time Hercules didn't want you to join the NAACP, and you couldn't say nothing about what you belonged to, or Hercules would run you away from there. So I said, well, I just go and pay my dues; I know they were doing a good job trying to help the blacks and nothing jeopardized my job.

Helen Jones was eighteen when she and Willie married in 1936. She finished high school the next year, but college was postponed until after their five children were raised. In 1958, she earned her degree from Jackson State and taught first grade in Palmer's Crossing. Mrs. Simpson once taught Vernon Dahmer's daughter Bettie.

She did not try to register as early as her husband. There was no "Huck Dunagin" in the county school system, and she was afraid of losing her job. On her application to become a teacher, she had been asked if she was a member of the NAACP. That fear made her very leery of the arrival at their door on one occasion of storekeeper B. F. Bourn.

It wasn't that Mrs. Simpson didn't know Bourn. She had shopped at his store on Mobile Street. But she knew also of his involvement with the NAACP and civil rights generally, and she wanted to know if he was there to collect two dollars to put toward their poll tax and how that might endanger them. "I told my husband that B. F. Bourn should go away because I don't have a job then, see. I had children and everything." Those children were very important to both of the Simpsons. They all obtained master's degrees and, in two instances, doctorates. They could be proud of their parents,[13] and also recognize what B. F. Bourn did for their community.

CHAPTER 14

B. F. BOURN, STOREKEEPER AND FREEDOM FIGHTER

As a sixteen-year-old with a ninth-grade education, Benjamin Franklin "B. F." Bourn was a laborer at Meridian Fertilizer, but as an adult, in the era before shopping centers, he ran the grocery and meat market at 523 Mobile Street in the heart of black Hattiesburg. It was profitable, and B. F. acquired eighty acres of farmland in Kelly Settlement, raised cotton, and sometimes had as many as thirty-seven head of cattle and fifty head of hogs, as well as five houses. In 1946 he was a leader in establishing Forrest County's NAACP chapter.

B. F. and his wife, Arlena Oatis Bourn, a teacher, raised seven children in their big orange house on Old Airport Road in Palmer's Crossing. All but the eldest attended college. B. F. was determined to try to bring about change. Years after B. F.'s death in 1973, Booker T. Bourn described his father as "always in the civil rights movement, going all over for meetings." Booker showed me an NAACP certificate documenting his father's first fifty-dollar payment toward life membership in that organization, a payment made in 1969, when fifty dollars was still a lot of money.

Booker told me about the five-foot cross that the Klan burned in front of their home. It made B. F. Bourn feel that he had to carry a pistol. Booker explained his father's economic success: "My daddy was independent of the white man. He didn't depend on the white man for nothing. We were making a living." Booker, however, felt he personally had lost jobs at white-controlled companies because he was B. F.'s son.

B. F. was our final Tuesday afternoon witness. Since it had occurred prior to Theron Lynd's taking office, Judge Cox did not permit Bourn to testify that he had been a registered voter prior to Forrest County's 1949 reregistration or of the subsequent rejections that led to his being one of the plaintiffs in *Peay v. Cox*. John Doar took Bourn through the four occasions between March 1959 and January 1961 that he went to the circuit clerk's office seeking to register but was turned away by one of the female deputy clerks. He "would have to see Mr. Lynd."

Then it was Dugas Shands's turn:

Q. Did you send for the Department of Justice in this lawsuit?
A. No, sir.
Q. How did they get your name?
A. Well, I don't know how they got it, but I made some complaints after I was denied. . . . I have made complaints to the Justice Department, and I have also made complaints to the Civil Rights Department. . . .

Shands repeatedly nagged at Bourn, suggesting that he had "sent for" the FBI, reminding him that he was under oath, and finally getting him to admit, under pressure, that he had never actually asked Lynd to register him when he posted bail for Clyde Kennard. Shands demanded, "If you really wanted to register, why didn't you mention it to Mr. Lynd when you were in there? . . . You don't know?

A. Yes, sir, I do know. Because I actually didn't go in for that at that time.
Q. Why didn't you mention it to him when you saw him at the Kennard trial?
A. I don't know that I even saw him at the Kennard trial.

Shands tried another tack:

Q. Have you ever been convicted of any crime?
A. No, sir, nothing more than a stop sign, a traffic light and a stop sign. Nothing more than that.

The NAACP had been highly supportive of Clyde Kennard, as Kennard tried to defend himself against sham prosecutions. Bourn was a logical person to put up the bond for Kennard to at least keep him out of custody during his trials. It would have helped his testimony if he had spoken to Lynd about registering in those encounters. However, one should not second-guess the decisions of a highly visible black leader pressured as Brown was.

In its 1978 history, the Forrest County NAACP branch described Kennard's ordeal and subsequent death trying to enter the University of

Southern Mississippi, and asserted its own role in the desegregation of the university. The program for the branch's Annual Freedom Fund and Award Banquet that year was dedicated to five NAACP freedom fighters: Vernon Dahmer, the Reverend Wayne Pittman, the Reverend W. B. Ridgeway, the Reverend M. L. Barnes, Jr., and B. F. Bourn.

CHAPTER 15

THE REVERENDS JAMES C. CHANDLER AND WAYNE KELLY PITTMAN

Annette Wilson lives just a few houses down Spencer Street from Mount Zion Baptist Church, which her husband, Harper, attends. But her allegiance has always been to Hattiesburg's oldest African American church, Mount Carmel Missionary Baptist Church, established in a log cabin in 1888. She was just a girl when the Reverend Dr. James C. Chandler became pastor of her church in December 1954, and she came to love him for his support of the church's youth and their activities. Mount Carmel's hundred-year history describes his arrival as pastor as ushering in a "new era of progress" as he stressed active participation by all.

Lillie McLaurin, the Mobile Street news dealer, was twenty-seven when Reverend Chandler was called to the Mount Carmel pulpit. She was already a keen observer of the black community scene, and she knew her church. "For the first five months, he was teaching, not preaching." She detected a certain restlessness in the congregation. "He hadn't preached like they were used to." So she was blunt with her new minister. "The membership wants some gravy, holler a little."[1]

Chandler did, and the "Amens" started to flow. Small, dynamic, and outgoing, he became the best preacher in town. Minnie Daniels Halyard, sixteen at the time, remembers how good he was with teenagers, how he knew all their names, what a strong Sunday School he ran.

The third Sunday of each month was Youth Day, with children coming to Mount Carmel from all of the nearby Baptist churches. Both junior and senior choirs were considered without peer in the community, and Chandler started a Men's Day and a Women's Day, to spur a little gender competition in generosity. The church was $8,000 in debt when Reverend Chandler

B. F. Bourn, storekeeper and freedom fighter, 1957. Courtesy of the Bourn family.

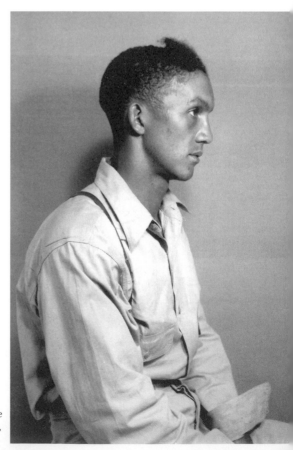

The Reverend Sam Hall's employment picture at Hercules Powder Company in Hattiesburg, 1939. Courtesy of Maynard Tuck.

Jesse Stegall when he testified in 1962.
Courtesy of Jesse Stegall.

Jesse Stegall reviewing his application
form in 1989. Courtesy of the author.

Eloise Hopson at her piano, 1989. Courtesy of the author.

Addie Burger in front of her husband's diplomas, 1989. Courtesy of the author.

everend and Mrs. Wendell Phillips Taylor, 1990. Courtesy of the author.

avid Roberson with two of his students at Roberto Clemente Community Academy in Chicago, 1989.
ourtesy of the author.

T. F. Williams, the sparkplug from Palmer's Crossing, 1989. Courtesy of the author.

Willie and Iola Thigpen, 1989. Courtesy of the author.

—AP WIREPHOTO.

CHECKING RECORDS in his office at Hattiesburg, Miss., Monday afternoon shortly after learning he had been convicted of civil contempt by a federal court of appeals in New Orleans was Forrest County registrar Theron Lynd. Lynd was accused of discriminating against Negro voter applicants in violation of court injunction.

Registrar in Mississippi Found Guilty of Contempt

ST. BERNARD HIT BY FREAK WIND

Damages S c h o o l, Pool

Vote Official Convicted by Appeals Court

Theron C. Lynd, Forrest County, Miss., registrar of voters, was found guilty of civil con-

ron Lynd still at work after g found guilty of civil tempt by the Fifth Circuit, 3. Credit: Associated Press.

Lynd's successor as circuit clerk, Marian Brown, changed the registrar's office, 1989. Courtesy of the author.

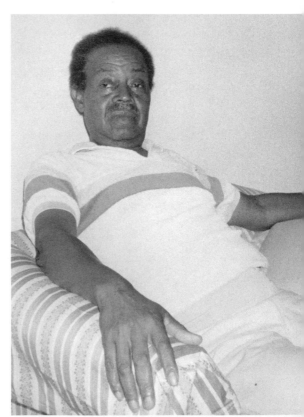

R. C. Jones, a Peay plaintiff and mentor to David Roberson, 1989. Courtesy of the author.

Sam Hall, affectionately called Reverend by his many friends, took early retirement recently after 41 years of service. Although he retired from Hercules, we're sure he is still serving as pastor of the New Hebron Baptist Church in Sumrall. He also has many years of service at this church.

The Baptist preacher Sam Hall as he retired from Hercules after forty-one years, 1979. Courtesy of the Hall family.

The first black in a "white man's job" at Hercules, Richard Boyd, still smiling despite its having taken fifty attempts before Registrar Luther Cox registered him, 1991. Courtesy of the author.

The priest who helped, Father John Izral, with the author in New Orleans, 1993. Courtesy of the author.

T. F. Williams and the author renew acquaintances in Palmer's Crossing, 1989. Courtesy of the author.

Judge Thelton Henderson, 2009: as a young lawyer, Henderson was the first African American on the Civil Rights Division trial staff. Courtesy of Judge Thelton Henderson.

Fifth Circuit Judge Richard Rives saved John Hardy from criminal prosecution, c. 1962. Courtesy of Fifth Circuit Clerk's Office.

n Doar receiving, on behalf of Civil Rights vision lawyers (1960–67), the Humanitarian ard of the Choral Arts Society of Washington, ⌐., at its annual concert in memory of Dr. King. uary 11, 2009. Courtesy of Margot Shulman.

Two of "The Four" who saved the Deep South: Judges Elbert Tuttle (*left*) and John Brown, 1956. Courtesy of Fifth Circuit Clerk's Office.

Vernon Dahmer, Jr., thinks of his father's sacrifice as he watches President Obama's inauguration with his brother Dennis (*left*) and thirteen-year-old Deryk Dahmer at the family home in Kelly Settlement, 2009. Courtesy of Rick Guy, *Clarion-Ledger*.

Judge John Minor Wisdom of New Orleans, one of President Dwight Eisenhower's gifts to civil rights, 1960. Courtesy of Fifth Circuit Clerk's Office.

The leader, Vernon Dahmer, c. 1964. Courtesy of crmvet.org.

...nonstration on the morning of Vernon Dahmer's funeral, January 15, 1966. ...rtesy of Mississippi Department of Archives and History.

Burke Marshall, with Attorney General Robert Kennedy, 1962.

A 1961 Herblock cartoon, © The Herb Block Foundation.

The Reverend Wayne Kelly Pittman told CBS News, "A voteless person is a hopeless person."
Reports on September 26, 1962, over the CBS Television Network.

wonder Huck Dunagin is smiling—
nen had become voters, c. 1970.
rtesy of Charles Dunagin.

became pastor. In two years that amount was paid off, and Christmas Day 1956 was celebrated with a mortgage-burning ceremony.

Addie Burger was one Methodist who used to visit Mount Carmel. She always enjoyed the church while Reverend Chandler was there. Andrew Wilson, a leader in the Hercules labor movement, was a member of Mount Carmel at the beginning of the sixties. He felt close to Chandler, admiring his recitation of the Baptist Covenant in conjunction with communion, and his call for people to be judged by their example, not by words. He recalled Chandler's participation on a "Bi-Racial Committee," which wasn't biracial, but which did lead to a more vigorous NAACP chapter, and also Chandler's declaring that they were citizens of two worlds and should obey the law of the land as long as it didn't supersede the law of God.

Reverend Chandler's popularity with the youth of his church did not carry over to all of the older members. On December 10, 1958, three of them complained to a Sovereignty Commission investigator that Chandler "had them thrown out of the church because they had objected to his dictatorial practices." They alleged that Chandler was requesting that each member donate ten dollars a year to the NAACP.[2] However, the Reverend R. W. Woullard, a funeral home owner who identified himself as an opponent of the NAACP, told the investigator that the three were "malcontents" and that their statements about Chandler and the NAACP were untrue.[3]

Reverend Chandler was born in State Line, Mississippi, in 1905. He attended the Meridian public schools, then moved to New Orleans where he attended Booker T. Washington High School and earned degrees from Dillard University and Union Baptist Theological Seminary. He testified on the second day of the trial.

Chandler had been, as he wrote on his application form, at Mount Carmel for six years, nine months, and sixteen days when he and the Reverend Wayne Pittman went to the circuit clerk's office about 11 A.M., September 28, 1961. It took about fifty minutes for him to fill out the form, squeezing lengthy section 273 on amending the state constitution into the minimal space provided. His interpretation "A democratic form of government" might not win a prize, but "Paying of taxes, obeying the law, participating in the affairs of government" was certainly a solid answer to the duties and obligations of citizenship.

Lynd told them to check back in two or three days. On October 2 and again the following day when they came by, Lynd was in court. On the fifth, Lynd was there and told them, as a deputy sheriff stood by him, that they had "failed to qualify." Reverend Pittman asked what had been wrong, and

Lynd replied that he wasn't supposed to tell, but they could try again in six months.

Despite resistance from Shands and Zachary, Judge Cox ordered that we be given a copy of Chandler's September 28 application. It was the first time we had seen it, and John Doar placed it in evidence, telling Shands he had no statements by Reverend Chandler, FBI or otherwise, to give him.

Shands then cross-examined: "James, I believe you testified that you didn't quite understand the request of the application to write your interpretation of the Constitution, is that right?"[4]

A. Well, I haven't said that.
Q. You didn't say that?
A. No, sir.
Q. What did you say about your understanding of the interpretation that they asked you?
A. I said that I was asked to write in a section of the Constitution.

Shands inquired whether Chandler had talked to any of us seated at the government's counsel table at the time of his application, but the only division attorney he had talked to by then was Jay Goldin, who was not present at the trial.

Q. You understand that you are here to tell the truth, sworn to tell the truth, the whole truth and nothing but the truth?
A. That's right.

After more skirmishing, and repeated attempts to confuse Reverend Chandler's memories of his contacts with us, as well as to have him admit that he had made statements to the FBI, Shands continued:

Q. Have you made any appeal to the election commissioners of Forrest County, Mississippi?
A. I have not, sir.
Q. Have you made any complaints to the Department of Justice?
A. I have not made directly any complaints to the Department of Justice.
Q. Well, who did you make it through? That's what I thought. I wanted to get that information from you. What were the indirect complaints you made?

A. I have not filed a complaint with the Department of Justice relative to this voting.

Q. Did they come to see you or did you go to see them, the Department of Justice men?

A. The gentlemen from the Department of Justice visited with me.

Q. You didn't ask them to come to see you?

A. I did not.

Q. How did they get your name? You know that, preacher, don't you?

A. They could have gotten it from most any source because I am a citizen of Hattiesburg, and they certainly could have gotten it from the registrar's office.

Shands then ridiculed Chandler because he had signed both the General Oath and the Minister's Oath on the form:

Q. You didn't know you were supposed to take a preacher's affidavit? You took a general affidavit, didn't you?

A. Well, let me check, sir.

Q. It's right there in front of you, can't you see it?

THE COURT: Go along, let's don't take so much time studying it.

A. I—I—I was misled with the application blank and I wrote in both of them, the Minister's Oath and the General Oath.

Then Shands berated Chandler for not knowing what precinct he lived in. The number of American voters who know what precinct they live in is so small that campaign workers collecting petition signatures routinely instruct the voter to leave the precinct blank. Campaign workers fill it in themselves after checking the voting lists. Chandler's confusion over the precinct he lived in was even more understandable, when he had never been permitted to vote there. Dugas Shands portrayed it as a damning mistake, but Reverend Chandler would later be the first of our witnesses to be registered by Theron Lynd after the Fifth Circuit entered the injunction we had sought from Judge Cox.

He stayed at Mount Carmel, the largest of Hattiesburg's Baptist churches during his pastorate there, repaired it following a fire, then moved on to a church in Laurel before returning to New Orleans where he died.

"A VOTELESS PERSON IS A HOPELESS PERSON"

Lawyers with a choice of witnesses never put the same person on the witness stand to testify in three successive trials involving the same parties unless that witness is a strong one.

The Reverend Wayne Kelly Pittman was such a witness. An African Methodist Episcopal minister of the gospel and also an interior decorator, Pittman was the only one of our witnesses called in all three proceedings of the trial stage of *United States v. Theron Lynd.* He testified, not just at the March 1962 preliminary injunction hearing, but at the September 1962 contempt trial conducted by the Fifth Circuit in Hattiesburg, and then the anticlimactic April 1964 trial on the merits.

That was appropriate. Reverend Pittman had known Lynd since the registrar was a teenager working on the oil truck his father drove through Hattiesburg. It was also remarkable because, unlike our other black witnesses, whose backgrounds were exemplary, Reverend Pittman, who was born in 1907, had pled guilty to burglary when he was twenty-seven and had been sentenced to four years hard labor in the state penitentiary.

Back in the community, he had been sufficiently determined to vote that he had a bill introduced in the Mississippi legislature by Senator Curran Sullivan of Forrest County. He had been forthright enough to put down his conviction on his voter application form, even though the application inquired only as to other offenses. Bill 256, enacted by the Senate and House and signed by the governor in March 1942, declared that Pittman's "right of suffrage and citizenship" had been restored, though why the state's white bureaucracy acquiesced in Pittman's desire remains unclear.

When Reverend Pittman was interviewed by CBS News in 1962, he explained his strong desire to vote: "A voteless person is a hopeless person."[5] He went on:

> *I believe that voting is a prerequisite to first-class citizenship . . . I believe if I become a qualified voter, along with other Negroes in Mississippi, that we'll be able to speak and get certain things that we think we are entitled to . . . They feel and know that they are not obligated to us . . . Voting would make you feel that what the civil government represents for all of its people will include you too.*

I sat in the comfortable Hattiesburg home of Earline and Richard Boyd, talking about Reverend Pittman. Richard told me Reverend Pittman and his younger brother were very talented and ran the projector at the black movie house on Mobile Street. He had known him before he met Mrs. Boyd: "His brother was a classmate of mine. Reverend Pittman went to Tougaloo College, and his field was mostly interior decorating. He had gotten very interested in the church while he was there, and I guess he got the call to preach."

Earline had sung with Pittman in the choir at Zion Chapel. She remembered him as president of the choir:

And he didn't want you to talk; he let you know. He was very stern about whatever he was into. He was also a very good carpenter and interior decorator. That was his profession, yes. He did this house, the kitchen—and the addition of the den. He believed in equal rights and was very active in the NAACP—at one time he was local president. After he was president, he continued the same tradition and was determined to try and get black people registered.

Our conversation turned to Reverend Pittman's family life.

He was a married man but had no children. He was sent by the Annual Conference from one place to another: Picayune, Natchez, a long ways, then from there to Gulfport and St. Paul AME Church. And that's where he died, at the parsonage at that church. But he was still just visiting. He had kept his residence here and was just down there to preach. Worked whatever, whenever. People really loved his work.[6]

Reverend Pittman had gone to high school in Hattiesburg with Nathaniel Burger, the black high school's principal, who was permitted to vote. Pittman had tried to register to vote, not just with Theron Lynd in the 1960s, but in the early 1950s when Luther Cox still held the office. He was greeted by the old refrain from both registrars: "It's a little late, it's closing time . . . you have to come back some other time."

Each January, Pittman would pay his property tax, pay his poll tax, and try to register. The second time he saw Luther Cox, Cox said he could not register him because of the lawsuit brought against him by local blacks, though Pittman was not one of those plaintiffs.

Around 1955, he made his last try with Cox as part of a group of twelve or fourteen. They entered the office from two directions. "Mr. Cox was disturbed," Pittman testified at a later hearing, "and he said, 'I can't register any of you, there's too many of you; don't come in here like this.'"

Now he was to testify about his attempts to register with Cox's successor, Theron Lynd, particularly on the morning of September 28, 1961, when he went to Lynd's office with Reverend Chandler. They found Lynd seated on a stool in a corner of his office, and Lynd gave them registration forms to fill out at opposite ends of the counter.

JOHN DOAR: Now, is Mr. Lynd in the courtroom this afternoon?

A. Yes. The gentleman there with the glasses on, the stout man.

Q. Now, did you receive any instructions as to how to fill out the form?

A. No, sir.

Q. And did Mr. Lynd give you any section of the Mississippi Constitution to interpret?

A. Yes . . . Section 165. Seemingly, it had to do with a person being carried to court or to be tried, and that if the judge who was presiding was related by consanguinity or affinity, that this judge would not be permitted to preside, and that another judge would be appointed by the governor or some other power to preside over that particular case.

Q. Do you know what "consanguinity" meant?

A. Related or kin by blood.

Q. And "affinity," do you know what that means?

A. . . . It is the relationship involving the marital ties that we sometimes refer to as marriage.

Q. And when you finished the form, what did you do then?

A. I—well, before I completed it . . . I discovered that I was not going to have enough . . .

MR. ZACHARY: Now, we object to that, if the Court please, that is not responsive to the question at all.

THE COURT: I sustain the objection. Let's just answer his questions. Have you got his question clearly in mind, Preacher?

Reverend Pittman certainly had the question in mind. He had handed in his application and thanked Lynd, who told him he could come back in a few days to find out if he passed. Lynd was not in the office the first time they returned, but on October 6 he was. Lynd looked at the forms and said:

"You failed to qualify." . . . well, I said, "Mr. Lynd, can you point out the question or questions where we failed, and is it a possibility of an

amendment or correction of those questions?" and he again said, "You failed to qualify," and I thanked him and turned to walk out of his office . . . as we approached the door leading to the corridor, Reverend Chandler stopped and turned and said: "Mr. Lynd, can we try again?" Mr. Lynd's reply was: "Yes, the law says six months from the day on which you tried."

Dugas Shands took over: How many statements did you make to the Department of Justice men? To the FBI? However, only division lawyers had interviewed Reverend Pittman. Our notes were our work product, not to be handed over.

> Q. I show you the last page of (your application). You signed and filled out both oaths, didn't you, Wayne? You didn't fill out that application correctly, did you?
> A. If I did that, I did not.
> Q. That's right; that's the way you filled it out, isn't it?
> A. It is.
> Q. You know now why you didn't pass, don't you?
> A. No, sir, I do not.

Reverend Pittman was not backing down to Shands, who then suggested that Pittman had failed because he wrote in the wrong precinct. Pittman replied: "When I was a kid we used to have fires in our section of town and when they would blow the whistle for fire they would blow it four times for our part of the town, and we lived in the fourth ward, so I assumed I was still living in the fourth ward."

> SHANDS: Do you know that there are no precincts in Forrest County that have numbers?
> A. No, sir, I didn't know it. . . .
> Q. When you came back and were told that Mr. Lynd was out and was up in court, you didn't go up in court and look for him?
> A. I wasn't told where he was. I was told he was out. . . .
> Q. You were not told that he was up in court?
> A. Not me.

Shands concluded with a series of questions designed to humble Pittman for operating his decorating business without a license and without paying taxes on it.

Addie Burger recalled her fellow witness as "just a smart, civic-minded person." Jesse Stegall agreed, considering Pittman "a smart person and a very solid individual . . . what he believed in, he believed in."[7]

Without our successful appeal from Judge Cox's inaction that I describe later, there would have been no realistic opportunity for that smart, civic-minded African American person to vote in Forrest County. On April 25, 1962, shortly after the Fifth Circuit preliminarily enjoined the circuit clerk from discriminating against African American applicants, Reverend Pittman took a certified copy of his restoration of rights to Theron Lynd.

Still he was told by Lynd that it would take him two or three days to think about it. It was another stage of the runaround in which Pittman kept returning to the registrar's office, never to find the circuit clerk in. Finally, after another month of being denied the ballot that the Mississippi legislature, twenty years before, had declared he had a right to, Pittman found Lynd in his office. Pittman testified in the second trial, the contempt trial, that Lynd "said he wanted to be frank, that he had forgotten it." Lynd told him, however, that he could come and fill out a form any time he wished. Not surprisingly, Lynd was "pressed for time" that particular day, and it was, as was so often the case, "almost closing time."

On the afternoon of June 2, 1962, Reverend Pittman got to fill out another application. By then a different Mississippi legislature had been active. New laws had been enacted: the names of applicants would be published in the local press, and they could be challenged by any voter who contended that they lacked "good moral character."

"I cannot pass on this now," Lynd told him. "You will have to give me a little while. It will take about ten days after you have filled out this form for publication in our local papers and following that . . . there will probably be fourteen days that we will have to wait to see what the outcome is."

Reverend Pittman returned June 26, but he was, Lynd informed him, eight or nine days too early.

Well, I didn't go back any more until July 26th . . . I asked Mr. Lynd if he had heard anything about this publication of the names of those seeking to register and vote, and he said: "Yes, you come on back here." And he went to the file and looked at the form, and he asked me where did I live.

I told him, and he asked me what part of town was that street located in. I described some of the buildings there that he would probably be familiar with, and he said, "Yes, I know about where that is. You will be in the Library district." Then he got a large book down from the shelf and wrote several words in it and said for me to sign there. He closed the book, and I thanked him for it.

Was it too good to be true? The years of frustration had made Reverend Pittman a little cautious: "Aren't there other credentials . . . that would authenticate my becoming a registered voter other than the two consecutive poll tax receipts? And he said, 'No, you need no further credentials. Those two poll tax receipts alone will suffice.' I thanked him and left the office."

The next day Reverend Pittman went over to city hall to register for municipal elections only to be told that the Forrest County clerk's office should have given him a registration card. It was another trip to the courthouse and then back to city hall with the card.[8]

It was just another day in one African American man's fight for basic rights of citizenship in Forrest County, Mississippi, in 1962. The publication requirement just adopted by the Mississippi legislature was a blatant attempt at intimidation, as was Shands's harassment concerning licensing.

The quiet, stately determination that carried Reverend Pittman through a stay in a Mississippi prison to a legal restoration of his civil rights and a calling to the ministry was not, however, about to succumb to harassment or intimidation. He voted during the last twenty years of his life.

Asked by a CBS interviewer about the white concern that blacks wanted to take over the government, Wayne Kelly Pittman replied: "I don't believe the Negro is that strong, and I definitely know that our government is not that weak."[9]

CHAPTER 16

THE REVEREND
WENDELL PHILLIPS TAYLOR

Get out of this land of hate, you sincerely implore,
Leave the demagogues, and march to a friendly shore!
Why do I live in this horrible land of the South, you ask,
And struggle and strive at a futile and hopeless task?
To your question I have only a simple answer, my friend:
Here is the battlefield, here the battle we must fight and win.

(FROM *I DO NOT VOTE* BY REVEREND TAYLOR)

All of our black witnesses were distinctive and impressive in their own ways, but Reverend Taylor had a unique aura of sophistication. (On a personal note, on my first visit to the Taylors, it was Mrs. Taylor who introduced me to the pleasures of grilled catfish.[1]) But it wasn't just Reverend Taylor's sophistication, his two degrees from Columbia University, or his column, "Perspective In Black," for the *Mississippi United Methodist Advocate* that made him different from our other witnesses. He had been registered to vote in New York City and in two other Mississippi counties before being rejected in Forrest. He had also led the NAACP chapter in Meridian, Mississippi.

Reverend Taylor, named for the Boston abolitionist Wendell Phillips, was a Methodist minister with keen insight for his church. He told me:

Methodists are losing membership, and you have Pentecostals gaining by leaps and bounds, Southern Baptists, also. That bothers me because I think one of the reasons why they're gaining is that they are offering some very hasty solutions to very severe social problems. It is all a matter of this kind of individual salvation, no social responsibility.

The tenth of fourteen children, Reverend Taylor was born in 1915 in a rural part of Rankin County, about twenty miles from Jackson. His mother was staying with her in-laws while his father, also a Methodist preacher, was at the annual conference. His paternal grandparents, who had been slaves in Virginia, had a two-hundred-acre farm. Cotton was their money crop, but his grandfather raised what they needed to live on, and had cattle, hogs, and bees for honey. His grandmother Annie and a great-uncle were among the first black teachers in the state.

Reverend Taylor told me about John Preston, a mulatto, who was his grandmother's uncle. There was also mixed blood on his paternal grandfather's side. His maternal grandfather, John Wesley Little, another minister, was fourteen years old when slaves were freed. He told young Wendell he hated slavery so badly he wanted to break his arm to keep from working. He was within four months of turning one hundred when he died.

Wendell's father did not stay long in any one church, but three of his five sons became ministers. Wendell's older brother Prince Albert Taylor, Jr., was the first African American bishop in the United Methodist Church to serve an episcopal area made up of predominantly white congregations. He served all of New Jersey between 1964 and 1976, while residing in Princeton.

"How did my parents support all those children?" Reverend Taylor laughed.

They were hard workers, and my oldest sisters Annie and Helen finished high school and helped out by teaching. You were a top-rated teacher then if you finished high school. Rural schools ran four or five months—about six months in the city. The whites would go a month or two longer than blacks.

Wendell's first school had one room, two teachers, and eight grades in Vaughan, Mississippi, a progressive community that sent many of its children on to high school in Meridian or Jackson. In 1921, the family moved back to stay with his paternal grandmother after her husband died. There was plenty to eat, and meadows and streams to roam in, but Wendell felt his grandmother didn't like him: "She was a little more partial toward those that had the lighter brown skin color."[2]

I learned nothing during the year back in Rankin County. My oldest sister knew more than the teacher did. Teachers were hired by the white superintendents. In 1950, some teachers were in the service of the superintendent on his farm in the summer time. The trustees of black schools were just figureheads; they reported to the superintendent what was going on. When February came, school was just about over.

In addition to preaching, Wendell's father taught wherever they went, to help make ends meet. In Mississippi in the 1920s, most African American teachers earned only twenty dollars a month. When Wendell started teaching in 1937, he was paid thirty dollars a month.

As his father moved on, Wendell attended different schools in the eighth, ninth, and tenth grades. As a teenager, he was small but tough, and took care of his brother Walter. Wendell was out of school for half a year after the tenth grade at Lanier High School in Jackson. It was the middle of the Depression, and his father was the pastor out in Jasper County. They would have had to rent a house in Jackson, or stay with someone and pay board, and their father didn't have the money for either. Only four cities had public high schools for blacks: Jackson, Hattiesburg, Laurel, and Vicksburg. Public education for blacks elsewhere in the state mostly ended at the eighth grade.

Wendell's three youngest siblings were sent to stay with older ones. Wendell stayed with his parents, but the only job he could get was teaching school for two weeks filling in for his father. He and a brother loaded coal cars in the summertime, and Wendell worked on the farm for ten cents an hour.

In the small rural towns the Taylors generally were in, there was little to read. Newspapers were hard to find and provided no positive coverage of African Americans. There were church magazines and books his father had accumulated over the years. Occasionally, they got copies of the great black paper, the *Chicago Defender*, but Wendell did not get acquainted with the *Pittsburgh Courier* until years later in college. Sometimes, since his father was a minister, they would receive mission boxes to be distributed, and an occasional box of books. But that was about it. There were no available public libraries.

After they moved to Hinds County, Wendell went to Mount Beulah College (Southern Christian Institute), a fine high school operated by the Disciples of Christ, where he met his wife, Geneva Chambers. Wendell was valedictorian of his class and continued through junior college there.

Wendell and his siblings were taught by their parents that they were as good as anybody else. He did not lack confidence, telling me that he had enough talent to have played professional basketball. He deeply resented it when dark-skinned people were treated by whites as virtual animals, and Reverend Taylor's description of blacks being arrested in the unrest that followed the murder of Medgar Evers underscored that: "Young blacks were being arrested by the hundreds and herded off to stockades in the fairgrounds."

Their father had participated in a small underground railroad to save African Americans from sharecropping in the Delta. During the worst of the Depression years 1930–1933, they rented land and bought only what they actually needed. Their parents talked about voting, but feared they'd get in trouble, and believed that, if they did vote, they would have to pay a cumulative poll tax for every year that they'd been old enough to vote.

When Reverend Taylor finished junior college, he substitute-taught in the elementary school at SCI for a month, then enrolled at Clark College and Gammon Theological Seminary in Atlanta, graduating in 1937 with a year's break caused by a false positive on a TB test.

A friend at Clark was working at the Civilian Conservation Corps (CCC). Reverend Taylor went to Shreveport and enrolled in the New Deal's CCC soil conservation program. While there, he and Mrs. Taylor "snuck off and got married by a Baptist minister." He was twenty-two.

Reverend Taylor decided to become a minister while he was in the CCC. One rainy Sunday, he didn't go to church.

Protestants were a little lackadaisical about that. I would have to go with the Catholics to the early morning Mass and wait in the city until they came back in the evening. That Sunday was so bad I just decided not to go along with them. I was reading the 11th chapter, 24th and 25th verses, from Hebrews*: "By faith, when he was grown up, Moses refused to be called the son of Pharaoh's daughter, choosing rather to share ill-treatment with the people of God than to enjoy the fleeting pleasure of sin."*

Feeling that God was speaking to him directly, he went home to study for full-time ministry and was accepted on trial.

His first church was in Union, Mississippi, where the parsonage was a new house but unfinished. Sometimes they couldn't keep the rain out. His salary was three hundred dollars a year, but he didn't always get that much.

Reverend Taylor was exempted from the draft later because he was a minister.

*My wife wanted me to go in as a chaplain. She could just see herself go-
ing around, traveling. I saw enough in the C.C.C. camp, what a chaplain did, really turned me off. The chaplain answers not to God but to
the government. The flag came first, and God second. I was supposed
to be his assistant, but I couldn't assist that.*

In 1940, he became an elder, and they moved to Meridian. When war
broke out in 1941, blacks were still not voting there. The Taylors both liked
Meridian. Wendell was the first man hired to teach in the junior high
school, and he also helped handle registration both for the draft and for
rationing.

Reverend Taylor was thinking about continuing his education. His
brother-in-law, William James, was preparing to leave his pastorate at the
East Calvary Church in New York City, and he asked Taylor to take over
there. In June 1944, Reverend Taylor arrived at the little brownstone store-
front at 2085 Fifth Avenue. It had a day care center on the first two floors,
sponsored by the Mayor's Committee for the Wartime Care of Children,
with the parsonage five floors above.

Taylor studied for one semester at City College, then enrolled at Columbia University's College of General Studies. He took a full load every
semester, mostly in the evening. He liked Columbia and the church.

*I majored in Sociology at Columbia. The caliber of instruction and
the teachers . . . they were very competent, very professional. I got my
bachelor of science degree in 1948, and my master of arts in education
in 1949. I was on probation for one semester. I thought they figured I
couldn't make it because I came from the South, but I did, and when
I finished my college work, I got a tuition grant as a "Dean's Scholar"
for my master's work.*

Reverend and Mrs. Taylor both voted in New York. At that time, registration rates in Harlem were the lowest they'd been since the Civil War. All
the Taylors had to do to register in New York was to sign their names. Wendell wrote two poems, the first castigating the New Yorker for his lackadaisical attitude toward voting, the second the sad lament for the Mississippi
black who was not permitted to vote that begins this chapter.

After getting his master's degree, Taylor first taught history and sociology at a state junior college in Mobile, Alabama, then moved to Rust College in Holly Springs, Mississippi. He had intended to return to Columbia

to complete work for a doctorate, but came to realize that his first love was not teaching but the pastorate, for which he needed no doctorate.

In 1951, Reverend Taylor was appointed to St. Paul's Church in Meridian, Mississippi, one of the major churches within the conference. There he met Medgar Evers and became president of Meridian's NAACP chapter. He had never belonged before.

The first time I met Medgar, he was a friend. He was that kind of person. Medgar traveled throughout the state as field secretary, trying to get chapters organized and actively involved in the social and political scene.[3]

My church was one of the few churches in Meridian that the NAACP could meet in. Charles Darden, a member of my church, was chapter president before me. He sold rings and pennants for high school graduation. So he had an independent business, and he was a kind of an agitator about the administration of the school system. Gloster Current, the field secretary for the National NAACP, spent time at our house. We were in the process of getting folks registered. When I went to register to vote there, I had no difficulty. I just signed my name. That's all.

Reverend Taylor laughed:

I don't know if my predecessor at St. Paul's, Reverend L. E. Johnson, let the NAACP meet in the church. I doubt it. We had about fifteen or twenty at our NAACP meetings in Meridian. I remember one of my trustees saying that having the NAACP in our church would jeopardize the job of some of the teachers who worked at the public schools. I told him that if they felt that way about it, they could join another church, because our church was open for any type of activity that was for the advancement of mankind, and the NAACP was that type of organization. But some were afraid that it would endanger the jobs of teachers who didn't even come to the meetings, just because they belonged to the church.

Reverend Taylor was president of both the state chapter of the Southern Christian Leadership Conference and the Meridian chapter of the NAACP. Neither Dr. King nor Dr. Abernathy visited him in Meridian, though he did meet with them in Memphis. But the SCLC never did get very strong in the state.

Reverend Taylor was not afraid to state his mind. He sharply criticized the way that Dr. Walter Washington ran Alcorn State University, for example. "You just felt the coercion. It was just awful: the kind of seeming reticence that the faculty, the staff people, operated under to do anything, for fear they might cross Dr. Washington. Everything had to be cleared with him." He also criticized a television station for blacking out an address by Dr. King and chided black journalist Percy Greene for going on the payroll of the Sovereignty Commission.

The Taylors had been registered in Jones County and in New York and had voted in all the elections while they were there. In Meridian, they didn't vote in the municipal or county elections, only state and federal elections. "That was not emphasized as important as it is now. We know now that's where the power is. But at that time, the main thing was gubernatorial and national elections. There was not too much resistance to our voting in national elections."

After six years at St. Paul's, Reverend Taylor moved to Hattiesburg in July 1957 when he became district superintendent.

I met Vernon Dahmer at the registrar's office in Hattiesburg. He was there trying to get registered. He just got turned away by Luther Cox, like I did. Dahmer's sister was there registering. They knew Dahmer, but they didn't know her and registered her because they thought she was white. They didn't know she was related to him.

Luther Cox asked me, did I belong to the NAACP? I told him, yes, and he said did I know that was a subversive organization? And I says, no, I didn't know, and I didn't think the Justice Department knows it, either. He says, "Well, I got to wait and get some things straight before you people can register around here." I didn't know what the situation was as to blacks voting in Forrest County before I moved down there.

Reverend Taylor did not return to Luther Cox's office.

I had expected Cox wouldn't let me register. When he turned me down, I mailed an affidavit that I drew up to the Justice Department. Somebody came down from the Justice Department and asked me what happened and about my education. I told him that I was a graduate of Columbia University, was in a class with John Eisenhower, the president's son. Here's a man who has a master's degree, in a class with the president's son, and can't vote. But nothing happened at that point.

*This boy . . . Clyde Kennard asked me to go with him when he went
to register as a student at Mississippi Southern, and I gladly went.
Kennard didn't belong to my church. I think I knew him through Mr.
Dahmer. Dahmer was a people person, always concerned about the
conditions that existed for blacks in Hattiesburg. He was very much
wrapped up in trying to get the vote, but wasn't getting too much support. I guess that's one reason why he was attached to me, because I
was one of the few who had taken the bold step, which he tried to get
so many to do.*

Reverend Taylor met N. R. and Addie Burger when Taylor came to Hattiesburg as the Methodist Church's district superintendent. They were
"church people," and he went to Rowan High School to visit Mr. Burger and
spoke there. Taylor knew many of the teachers and principals in Mississippi
well.

*I was kind of a thorn in the flesh of some of them because of their lack
of awareness and being involved in trying to move forward in areas of
community action. Mr. Burger was one of the few principals that put
his head on the block. Burger's position was that he would support his
teachers if they went in to register to vote, and he did.*

The Taylors moved to Laurel in 1959 because it was the geographic center of the district. He was in and out of Hattiesburg until 1963 when his
six-year term as district superintendent ended. "I was already registered
in Laurel in March 1962 when I testified in the *Lynd* case. I don't remember any discussion about registering as a transfer voter from Lauderdale
County. I took a test in Laurel."

He laughed:

*My wife took the test in Laurel, too, but she didn't answer the ques-
tions. You had to give what a section of the constitution meant. History
having been my major, that wasn't no bother to me. My wife just wrote
down, "It means what it says." And they didn't question it. Of course,
they thought she was probably smart . . . We went to register together.*

Reverend Taylor lived in Hattiesburg for a little over two years. With
Judge Cox restricting our testimony to the period when Theron Lynd was
registrar, we were limited to the final eight months. His first visit to Lynd's
office was on March 19, 1959, the same day Vernon Dahmer and Pearlina

Barnes attempted to register. One of the women in the office told them the office was not yet set up for registration. Taylor returned a month later only to be told he "must see Lynd," who, of course, was not there.[4] That was it. His testimony was brief and straightforward.

The picture left for a neutral observer was of a distinguished, highly literate clergyman found qualified, not just in New York, but in two other Mississippi counties, who paid one more visit to the office than the most illiterate white person would have paid, and still had not become registered to vote in Forrest County.

CHAPTER 17

THE LEADER, VERNON DAHMER

At first glance, Vernon Dahmer did not stand out among our witnesses. His tenth-grade education at the Bayside School in the Kelly Settlement paled beside the master's degrees of the teachers assembled by Principal N. R. Burger at Rowan High School. Dahmer had no connection with the city's major employer, the Hercules Powder Company. He was not a minister like the Reverends Taylor, Chandler, Pittman, or Hall.

But Dahmer, along with B. F. Bourn, was the mainstay of the county's tiny, furtive but durable NAACP chapter, and he was its president until the year before his death. Most of all, he was the community leader: generous, courageous, respected. While he owned property on Mobile Street, in the midst of black Hattiesburg, his major holdings, his home and his heart were in the open farmland north of Hattiesburg, almost to the Jones County border, known as Kelly Settlement. There he had two hundred acres of the best land east of the Delta. His thirty-acre cotton allotment was Forrest County's largest. His mechanical cotton picker was one of only five in the county. And he didn't keep it to himself.

J. B. Smith, a white man about Vernon's age, farmed three hundred acres five or six miles away up in Jones County. When Dahmer bought a new mechanical cotton picker, he moved it to Smith's field because Smith had the earliest cotton in the area. Dahmer kept it there for three days, picking that cotton.[1]

Ellen Dahmer, Vernon's mother, had inherited land from her father Warren Kelly, a descendant of the white slave owner, O. B. Kelly. Like a number of white slave owners, O. B. Kelly had sired children by a black woman. She was Vernon's great-great-grandmother. But unlike most of these white men, Kelly had left significant property to his black children.

Kelly's black descendants were sophisticated and educated. When George Dahmer, recently arrived in Forrest County, asked Warren Kelly for his daughter Ellen's hand, his future father-in-law made it clear to him that to make himself eligible Dahmer had best get himself off to Jackson State to get some education. Vernon was the eighth of their twelve children.

George Dahmer owned his own large farm with cotton, and some corn, the cash crop. Vernon Jr. told me his grandfather emphasized to him:

> *"When you've got the land, you can survive . . . but once you lose the land, you've lost control of your own life. You have your responsibilities: to yourself and to those around you, your family and your community." And I think that really reflects what my dad was with the civil rights movement.*
>
> *When I was growing up in the early forties, my daddy identified himself as a Republican, because that was the party of Abe Lincoln. He let you know what was right and what was wrong. And he was a leader; he didn't send you no place he wouldn't go himself. We went to Sunday School, where he taught, every Sunday. He was always involved in those things that represented the best part of the individual and of the community, sort of a Boy Scout leader for the community kids.*[2]

Vernon Jr. had been in the middle of his twenty years of air force service when I was visiting his father often in the early sixties, but I had known his brother Harold at the time. Jay Goldin, another young Civil Rights Division lawyer who later was New York City's comptroller, was sometimes with me when I stopped by. Nothing delighted Vernon more than getting two city boys up on his tractor to demonstrate the farming life.

Vernon and his first wife, Winnie Laura Mott, had divorced. In 1949, his second wife, Aura Lee Smith, died after a long illness. Ellie Jewell Davis was his third wife. She attended Alcorn for two years and finished up at Tennessee A&I in Nashville. In 1950, she came to Forrest County to teach at the Bayside School where Vernon had gone to school and had come to serve on the school board.

They were married in March 1952 and had two children of their own to add to the six Vernon had with his first two wives. "Miss Jewell," as she became known throughout Kelly Settlement, termed her late husband "educated . . . widely read on the issues, on most anything that was important."[3]

One of those things that was important was equal rights, whether it was joining the NAACP in the late forties along with B. F. Bourn, B. F.'s cousin James, and Reverend Pittman, or being a part of what James Bourn called the Gang of Sixteen: blacks who went in, sometimes four at a time, to attempt to register to vote when Lynd's predecessor, Luther Cox, was still the registrar.

A large man, light-skinned enough in complexion to pass for white, which some of his relatives were thought to have done, Dahmer was born March 10, 1908. Douglas Baker, a white Ole Miss student from Hattiesburg, wrote at the time of Dahmer's murder that Dahmer "chose to be a Negro—and chose to be a man. Forfeiting the privileges that could easily have been his, he stood, lived and died for the cause of human dignity."[4]

Dahmer had once known what it was to be registered to vote. But in 1949, he was struck from the rolls in a reregistration, and Luther Cox denied his attempts to reregister. In 1951, still six years before the passage of the twentieth century's first federal voting rights legislation, Dahmer was one of the fifteen *Peay v. Cox* plaintiffs who brought suit against Cox for the way he was administering the state voting law. When that case was not treated on its merits, Dahmer had to keep trying.[5]

The week before the 1952 presidential election, a woman clerk in the registrar's office told him to come back the following week. In early 1953 he and four other blacks were told by a woman in the office that they would have to wait and see Mr. Cox when he was in.

On March 24, 1955, a written constitutional interpretation test went into effect in Mississippi, supplanting the previous either-or procedure. In Forrest County, no white person was required to fill out an application in order to register until November 18, 1960. Until January 31, 1961, no black was even permitted to fill out such a form and attempt to register. Form or no, Vernon Dahmer was still being told in 1955 that he had to see Registrar Cox personally because the women in the office could not register him.

When Theron Lynd took office as circuit clerk and registrar on February 26, 1959, some county blacks viewed the transition with hope. Dahmer and Pearlina Barnes, the wife of a local minister, went to register within two weeks of Lynd's taking office. Under Judge Cox's ruling, Dahmer could only testify as to his attempt with Lynd, a man he'd been seeing on the streets of Hattiesburg for close to twenty years.

Lynd told them that he hadn't been in office very long and wasn't yet set up to register people. When Mrs. Barnes asked when he would be ready, Lynd replied that he didn't know—though he was already registering white applicants.

When our motion for a preliminary injunction was finally heard in March 1962, Dahmer didn't want to be a witness. He asked me if he was really needed. When I told him that he was, he said that he would be there. His testimony helped demonstrate the pattern of discrimination in the county.

CHAPTER 18

THE WHITE WITNESSES AND THE WOMEN WHO REGISTERED THEM

We heard the plaintive cries of Shands, Roberts, Zachary, and Ed Cates as John Doar began examining our first white witness, twenty-two-year-old John Edward Dabbs. And for once what Shands said was true. "Judge, they are changing their whole case. They are trying to make it equal protection and the Fourteenth Amendment as well as voting and Fifteenth Amendment. They never told us about any white witnesses. There is not a single word about them in their last amended complaint."

Our decision to seek white witnesses who had been registered by Theron Lynd's staff at the same time he was turning away our black witnesses was a late one, made after our final amended complaint had been filed on February 5. Just days thereafter, Bob Owen and I began our intensive three-week preparation for the March 5 trial date, visiting and preparing all of our black witnesses. We also were digging up names, using recent yearbooks of all-white Hattiesburg High School. Nineteen to twenty-two-year-olds were likely to have registered after Theron Lynd took office on February 26, 1959, the period to which Judge Cox had limited us for the hearing.

They would be interviewed by agents from the New Orleans office of the FBI. On the basis of those interviews, we would determine which ones to subpoena. We were going to meet our burden under the 1957 Civil Rights Act of showing the systemic discrimination that existed between the treatment of whites and blacks seeking to vote in Forrest County. We, of course, knew that FBI agents "swarming over" Greater Hattiesburg would scarcely stay secret for long. In fact, a few of those interviewed had set off immediately to alert M. M. Roberts.

So we viewed those "plaintive cries" of counsel as just more of the delaying tactics we had suffered through since the case was first filed. We reviewed the bureau reports, did some follow-up interviews of our own, interviews that would have been dangerous to conduct two years later, and issued our subpoenas.

We were ready to call white witnesses, as well as black ones. Doar told the court how recently these witnesses had come to our attention and dictated, in open court, a separate paragraph for each of the white witnesses, a new amendment to our complaint.

John Edward Dabbs and Thomas Dabbs, twenty-two-year-old twins, were the first to testify. Both had registered in July 1960, brought to the clerk's office by their father. Theron Lynd had asked where they lived and how old they were and then filled out their affidavits and certificates to vote. The Dabbs brothers were registered in five to ten minutes, and Zachary later conceded on the record that Lynd had no form for either Dabbs or for the next witness, Robert Irving Newcomer, Jr., twenty-three.

Newcomer had registered in January 1960. He was hostile to John from the outset of his testimony and declared he had interpreted a section of the state constitution. That contradicted what he had told the FBI on February 22 and turned out to be a lie. He refused to talk to Bob before testifying and had talked with Roberts and Zachary.

Newcomer testified that he had found bureau agents sitting in his living room when he got home from work and that several days later, when they brought a statement to his job, he had declined to sign it. He did say that he had been registered by a woman in the office without seeing Lynd, something no black applicant had achieved. Newcomer had told the agents that she had filled out a form for him.

M. M. Roberts objected that Doar was "browbeating his own witness," but John failed to shake Newcomer's revisionist history.[1] Ultimately, however, the defendants had to produce what application forms they had for our witnesses. They made it clear for the record they were doing so only "under the direct orders of this Court."[2] There was none for Newcomer.

Charles Andrew Still, Jr., twenty-two, testified that in May 1960 "the one who was behind the counter pulled out the large registration book from under it and asked [him] the data which is registered in that book, and I signed the book."[3] That was all it took for Still to receive a certificate entitling him to vote at the Camp School.

Lafayette "Love" Stewart, twenty-six, from nearby Petal, had registered in February 1960. He had not known his way around the courthouse and had come in a back entrance by the jail, asking for directions in the sheriff's office. Once Stewart had reached the circuit clerk's office, Zachary acknowledged that all Stewart had been asked to do was sign the ledger book.

That was also the case for Harmon Gary Stewart, twenty-four, also of Petal, registered in August 1959 by a woman who filled out his affidavit and certificate to vote.

Jackie Rowe Valentine, also twenty-four, a Hercules truck driver, had registered in January 1962, when our hearing had first been scheduled. A woman behind the counter handled his registration, though Lynd was visible. Valentine filled out an application that included an interpretation of section 116 of the state constitution on the executive powers of the governor and the governor's being barred from succeeding himself. Valentine's interpretation was adequate, as was his recitation of the duties and obligations of citizenship. That did not fit the pattern we hoped to establish, but it had occurred on the eve of trial, and the woman gave him assistance, which blacks never received, as to the prior address to list and which oath to sign, both major points of cross-examination of our black witnesses by Shands. Lynd personally took his oath, not caring that, despite the assistance he had received, Valentine had signed both the General Oath and the Minister's Oath.

Mary Trudie Bilberry, a twenty-two-year-old student registered by the deputy clerk Wilma Walley in January 1961, also filled out an application, including adequate interpretations of section 226, restrictions on jail inmates being leased out for employment, and the duties and obligations of citizenship. She testified that the deputy clerk had told her what her precinct was. Check marks were something we always looked for in analyzing application forms. There were two, by the lines where Ms. Bilberry was to sign her name.

We had subpoenaed the chief deputy circuit clerk Dorothy Massengale and former deputy Wilma Walley. Roberts and Zachary complained that we had brought the operation of the circuit clerk's office to a standstill by requiring both Lynd and his deputies to be in Jackson for the hearing. Accordingly, Judge Cox directed us to call Massengale and Walley promptly. Massengale was first.

Dorothy Massengale was a high school graduate who had worked for Luther Cox for four years before Lynd took over. Lynd later described her as "experienced help" that he needed.[4] She testified that Lynd had directed her in late 1959 to start requiring application forms. She said she had given application forms to both whites and blacks and denied selecting sections of the state constitution based on the race of the applicant. But there was a difference. She would review the forms of white applicants herself, then register them with no one else involved. Only Lynd could register a black.

Wilma Ray Marie Walley served Lynd as a deputy clerk from the day he took office until September 15, 1961, when she enrolled at Mississippi Southern. Ben McCarty, covering the trial for the Associated Press, aptly termed her "shapely."[5] Like Massengale, she testified that she had given application forms to both white and black applicants. She termed her registration of whites provisional, but she had told blacks to give their forms to Mr. Lynd.

Walley conceded there had been a period of time when she had told blacks they must see Mr. Lynd in order to register. She said there was one stack of more than ten cards on which sections of the Mississippi Constitution were written, and she assigned the top card if they were not scattered.

Repeatedly, the defense objected that Doar was cross-examining his own witness, to which John made the obvious reply that Wilma Walley was a hostile witness. Judge Cox disagreed: "She's not an adverse witness. You seem to have that in your mind. You might as well get it removed."[6]

Dugas Shands and M. M. Roberts had been putting off their cross-examination of our white applicant witnesses and of Dorothy Massengale until after the thirty-day continuance they were seeking from Judge Cox. But with Wilma Walley, they wanted to have it both ways.

> SHANDS: The cross-examination of Miss Walley and any other person working there in the office should await the cross-examination of the persons who were brought into this lawsuit by amendment yesterday . . . Otherwise—as a general practitioner of many years, the Court knows the position that we are put in—we will be doing piecemeal cross-examination . . .
>
> THE COURT: You are making this lawsuit sound very complicated, Counsel . . .
>
> SHANDS: Well, Your Honor, we think that fairness and justice demands that we have a full testimony of a witness before we cross-examine a witness.
>
> THE COURT: Well, you just do what you want to do, but if you want to cross-examine her, here she is . . .
>
> Q. Miss Walley, during the time that you were a deputy clerk in Mr. Lynd's office, were you ever appointed a deputy registrar?
>
> A. No, sir.
>
> Q. Such actions as you did were done as deputy clerk and not as registrar?
>
> A. Yes, sir.

Shands continued to lead Walley:

Q. Under those terms you knew that you could not finally register any person, didn't you?
A. Yes, sir.
Q. You didn't attempt to do so, did you?
A. No, sir.
Q. Is the office of the circuit clerk and registrar of Forrest County—during the time that you were there—was that a busy office or not?
A. It's a very busy office. . . .
Q. Were your principal duties in that office in connection with filing of cases, issuing of process, handling of minutes and attending to the office duties of the courts?
A. Yes, sir.
Q. There were circuit court minutes, county court minutes and juvenile court minutes?
A. That's correct.
Q. Did you and whatever other ladies were there as deputy clerks all chip in and do as best you could to render the necessary services about your courts and your papers and your process and what other duties there were as circuit deputy circuit clerks?
A. Yes, we did.
Q. Miss Walley, while you were deputy circuit clerk, did you ever discriminate against anybody because of race, color or previous condition of servitude in connection with the registration process?
A. No, sir.

Walley testified that she handed application forms to black applicants, but did not judge whether or not they passed.

Q. Did you have white persons that came into the office there for the purpose of registering, and when they were told they had to take a test, they just said, "Well, they wouldn't even try it"—and would walk out?
A. I sure have. . . .
Q. While you were deputy circuit clerk, did you permit any persons to sign the registration book?
A. Yes.

Q. Were those the people whose tests you had looked over and, using your common sense and knowledge, you thought in good
faith had completed the tests?

A. Yes, sir.

Q. If there were any who did not complete the test, and if they
did register, was that because of the rush of the duties and the
hurry that you were in and they just got registered as a result of
oversight?

John Doar finally called Dugas Shands on his "cross-examination," ob-
jecting that Shands was testifying:

*This witness is an ex-employee of the registrar of Forrest County. She
is a white woman. Obviously, her . . . sympathies would be for the defendant. It seems to me, Your Honor, that with a witness like this, Mr.
Shands should not be permitted to make these long statements as to
what she did or did not do with respect to registration.*

Judge Cox was not impressed:

COX: You put this lady on the witness stand, I'm sure after knowing what quality her testimony would be, so I can't assume that
you would be too much surprised. It seems to me that she is trying to tell the truth. Mr. Shands . . . is entitled to lead, but I call
counsel's attention to the fact that I value the answer and not the
question . . .

Q. Miss Walley, if you permitted any person to register who possibly
did not complete the test according to the requirements of the
law, why was that?

A. It was probably because I was busy, an oversight on my part, and
not intentional.

Walley then related what had made her resist handling the registration
of African Americans:

One afternoon . . . a Negro applicant came in and asked to register and I gave him an application . . . I went about doing my
chores for the rest of the afternoon. Mrs. Massengale left early,
and about a quarter of five he started asking me questions and

asking me to help him interpret the Constitution and I told him I couldn't.

Then he began asking me personal questions as to how long I had been there and didn't he know me, and didn't I remember him, and I became very frightened. And so after—

Q. Became very what?

A. Very frightened.

THE COURT: Had you registered any colored people up to that time?

THE WITNESS: No, sir.

THE COURT: Had you handled their applications through to completion prior to that time?

THE WITNESS: Yes. . . .

Q. Was that the only incident that occurred of that similar nature?

A. No, sir, there have been a number, one in particular.

Q. What other incident can you recall?

A. There was a Negro woman that came in one afternoon. At first she came in by herself and she asked to see Mr. Lynd, and we told her he wasn't in and she stood there for a good length of time, and—

Q. Did she have anything in her hand?

A. She had her handbag, and then after a while she began to fumble around in it, and she stood there, and we couldn't make up our mind what she was going to do, and so we just walked into another office.

And then a large Negro man came in with her. And he stood around in there with her for a while and then they walked out and stood right outside the door, and we became frightened and called the sheriff's office and asked them to have someone come up and stay with us until we closed.

When they started back in, the Negro man saw the deputy sheriff and just whirled around and left.

Shands tried to lead Walley into saying there was a belligerent or frightening look on the man's face. When she replied with the enigmatic, "You can tell the difference in expressions on people's faces," Judge Cox wasn't satisfied:

THE COURT: What was it that frightened you? That's what he is trying to find out.

THE WITNESS: Well, it was just his way of trying to get familiar that frightened me . . . I mean, you know, he just looked like he wanted to be friendly, too friendly to suit me. . . .

Miss Walley quit her job, but later decided to come back to work part-time.

Q. What understanding did you have with Mr. Lynd when.you came back part-time as to whether you would handle white registrations or Negro registrations?

A. We have the understanding that I would not wait on the counter at all . . .

Q. Did race have anything to do with anyone you did or did not register?

A. No, sir.

Q. Has Mr. Lynd ever instructed you to discriminate against anybody?

A. No, sir.

John Doar then did redirect examination:

Q. What was the name of the Negro man who you say frightened you?

A. I would not remember, Mr. Doar.

Q. When did it occur, Miss Walley? . . .

A. I would say in the year of 1960.

Q. What did you do with that half-finished application form?

A. I put it on Mr. Lynd's desk.

Q. Do you know the name of the Negro lady about whom you testified on cross-examination by Mr. Shands?

A. To the best of my recollection, her name was Mrs. Love.

Q. You testified, in response to a question by Mr. Shands, that if white people were registered who hadn't completed the form, it was because of an oversight, and press of business . . . How frequently did it occur?

A. I don't know.

Q. And would the applicant not fill out the form at all—or would he just fill out the form partially, the white applicant?

A. He would fill out the form.

Q. It would just not be filled out completely, is that your answer?

A. If they were registered without completing the application, it was an oversight on my part.

Q. Well, can you give me any idea how many there were?

A. No, sir.

Q. Were any Negroes registered during the time you were in Mr. Lynd's office who didn't complete the application form?

A. I don't know.

Q. Now, prior to this hearing date two agents of the Federal Bureau of Investigation attempted to talk to you?

Walley testified that she had declined to tell the FBI agents anything.

ZACHARY: Now, if the Court please, we object to the form of that question. This lady exercised her right and told them she did not desire to talk to them. She did not decline to give them information. Mr. Doar is wording it as if she was hiding something.

She had nothing to hide, she was a simple citizen who did not desire to talk to the Federal Bureau of Investigation when they picked her out of the classroom, and she told them so. I think the record ought to reflect that.

THE COURT: I didn't get out of her statement any suggestion or slight inference that she had anything to hide. I will let her explain in answer to your question anything that she wants to say with regard to that matter.

A. Well, they asked me if I would talk to them and I told them that I had left the employment there, and I just didn't care to discuss it. I mean, I would have if they had pressed me, but they didn't. They told me I didn't have to tell them anything. . . .

Q. Do you know a white lady in Hattiesburg named Marcia Rae Wright?

A. Yes, I know her.

Q. Did you handle her registration?

A. I don't remember it, Mr. Doar.

❖❖❖

Twenty-three-year-old Marcia Rae Wright was next. She had been registered in November 1960. Bob Owen had followed up on her FBI interview, talking to her in Hattiesburg. She knew Wilma Walley "to speak to her . . . Wilma registered me and then I signed the registration book. I don't really remember anything else."[7] Zachary conceded they could find no application form for her.

In his final argument, M. M. Roberts later told the court that "the little Wright girl" had come to see him because he had known her family for a long time. She had told him that when she was subpoenaed, "Her daddy was so mad about it, he wadded it up and threw it in the waste basket. She had it ironed out so that you could read it, thinking she had to have it here."[8]

John and James Bennett, whom I had visited the week before the trial, had filled out application forms, interpreting straightforward sections of the state constitution. Walley registered John, filling in the precinct on his form, as did the deputy clerk who registered James.

Steve Ellis Barter, Jr., twenty-three, had consulted with M. M. Roberts before being subpoenaed and again afterward. He had been registered by one of the women deputies in October 1959 and had no memory of interpreting a section of the state constitution.

Helen Marie Coughlin, twenty-two, was the daughter of the Hattiesburg florist. Father Izral had suggested her as a potential witness when I visited him at Sacred Heart Parish. She was a telephone operator for Southern Bell and had registered just five weeks before our hearing began.

She interpreted section 143, No person shall be deprived of life, liberty, or property except by due process of law, writing: "Every citizen has equal rights." Though not a correct interpretation, this was certainly a fine sentiment, as well as the goal of our lawsuit. Coughlin was registered by Theron Lynd despite having signed both the General Oath and the Minister's Oath.[9]

Two months after Lynd assumed office, William Van Hart, twenty-three, was registered by a woman deputy after providing her only with his name, age, and residence. There was no application.

We wound up our presentation of our matching white witnesses by offering two depositions. Bob Owen had deposed James Donald Adcock, twenty-two, on February 12 at the U.S. Attorney's office in Lexington, Kentucky, where he was a student at the College of the Bible. Peter Stockett represented both defendants. Jay Goldin had contacted Adcock three or four weeks earlier.

Adcock went to the clerk's office in June 1960 with a friend, Sandra Phillips. Two female deputy clerks asked Adcock and Phillips their names, addresses, and ages. Certificates to vote were then made out, and they signed the registration book. Adcock voted in the 1960 presidential election. They had no application form for him.

Jay had taken the second deposition from John T. Ames, Jr., twenty-two, in Richmond after Bob and I headed south. Again, Peter Stockett represented the defendants. Ames had been contacted by Bob Owen about two weeks before. He was an Ole Miss graduate attending Union Theological Seminary in Richmond and had gone to school in Hattiesburg with Sandra Phillips and the other deponent, Donald Adcock.

In February 1961, Dorothy Massengale had given Ames an application form and section 258 on the pledging of the state's credit to interpret. Ames's answers were well done, but he signed both oaths, quite possibly because Mrs. Massengale or someone else had checked both signature lines.

The testimony of our white applicants was complete. We would present one final white man: Theron Lynd.

CHAPTER 19

"NEGRO OR WHITE DIDN'T HAVE A THING IN THE WORLD TO DO WITH IT"

Theron Lynd Takes the Stand

The defendant himself was our final witness. John Doar examined Lynd, who told the court that he was forty-two years old and had been president and general manager of Southern Machine Sales, Inc., when elected.

> When I first took office, Mrs. Massengale came to me and requested that she not be required to deal with Negroes applying for registration, and so I talked to her about it, of course, because that was the first knowledge that I had that she did not care to do all of the duties.
>
> I was thrown in a position of having a chief deputy clerk leave my employ if I forced her to do something she had requested me not to be made to do. That was what I had in the back of my mind. And frankly I had just walked into the office cold, and I was interested in keeping experienced help for the court procedure more than anything else, so I told her she wouldn't have to be bothered with that, that I would handle it myself.
>
> And I told her that any white people that came in that in her opinion looked like could qualify, it looked like a good application, just for a matter of expediency and for political reasons, because I was faced with another election in less than a year's time, I told her to go ahead and register them provisionally, subject to my approval.

Q. That's white people?

A. Yes, sir . . .

Q. Has she ever accepted any applications from Negroes?

Lynd clarified that Mrs. Massengale gave out applications to African Americans who asked for them, but did not evaluate the applications they turned in. He conceded that she did process the applications of whites that looked properly filled out.

Lynd did not recall if he discussed that procedure with Wilma Walley, but he did remember after two or three incidents had taken place in the office and due to the request of Mrs. Massengale, "I told them that I would handle the Negro applications for registration . . . the girls didn't want to talk to them and I wasn't going to force them to do it, so I done it myself."[1]

Lynd conceded that he had destroyed application forms after the Mississippi legislature, well aware of the records demand provisions of the federal Civil Rights Act of 1960, authorized destruction. But Lynd testified that, after Francis Zachary advised him to retain forms, he had done so. Lynd said he had not used the good moral character requirement to evaluate applicants.

Q. Mr. Lynd, what are the qualifications you require in order for a person to be registered to vote in Forrest County?

Lynd replied with a calculated modesty:

The only thing that I can say is that according to the law they are supposed to give me the information on that form there, and whatever section of the Constitution they happen to have. Well, I look it over and read that section and then read their answer to it and just give it a layman's commonsense interpretation, because I am not versed in the Constitution of the State of Mississippi, or anywhere else.

Q. Let me ask you specifically do you require that the applicant be a resident of Forrest County?

A. Yes, sir. And I might say that's the reason for asking them a question sometimes before I give them an application, because the law to the best of my knowledge, says they must be a resident of the State of Mississippi two years and the district in which they register one year, except for ministers, who must live in the State two years but can live in the district a period of six months.

They established that the applicants had to be twenty-one years old by the date of the next election.

Q. And do you require that the applicant not be convicted of certain crimes?

A. That's what it says there.

Q. If the applicant answers he has not been convicted of the crimes listed in question 14, do you go into the question of conviction of crimes any further with the applicant?

A. I accept the answers they give unless to my personal knowledge I know, because I keep the conviction records of Forrest County in my office. If one happens to come to my mind, I might question him on it.

Q Now, with respect to the completion of the application form did you require that the applicant know his voting precinct?

A. Well, I wouldn't say that I required it, and I wouldn't say that I didn't require it. It was just—in our office, busy like we are, if somebody says, "Where would I vote?" and "I live so-and-so," I would probably answer it. We have a big map there on the wall with all of the precincts outlined.

Q. Suppose somebody filled out the application and didn't put in the voting precinct but you had his street address?

A. I would probably write in whatever it was.

Judge Cox felt that it was time to assist Lynd: "What you are saying is that the criteria you use for both white and colored are alike?"

LYND: Yes, sir. I would tell anybody where they would vote if I knew where they lived. I didn't make any distinction at all.

Q. What criteria would you use with respect to signing the application forms?

A. I did my best to see that they were all signed properly and filled out properly . . . Sometimes I had more time to do that with one than I did with another.

Lynd sought to develop the theme that lack of time, rather than racial bias, led to discrepancies in how he treated various applicants.

Q. What I am asking, would you tell the applicant where to sign the form or would you not tell them? What was your policy?

Under John Doar's questioning, Lynd sought to emphasize that his evaluation of applicants was race-neutral:

> I didn't have any set form or policy to follow in those. Each individual paper . . . that was lying on my desk I couldn't tell whether it was a Negro or a white one. . . . I just looked at it and in my best judgment as a common sense layman if it was satisfactory I just okayed it and if it wasn't I wouldn't.
> Q. Did you review all of the applications?
> A. Yes, sir, I have looked at all of them. I didn't say I read each and every one word for word.

Lynd reminded the court that he was a busy man with other duties.

John then showed him an application of Addie Burger's and asked why she wasn't qualified. After various objections by Zachary were dealt with, Lynd replied:

> I can see that it wasn't signed as to the application, and I don't know whether I could sit in this witness stand and scrutinize this thing and tell you or not, because I don't know, because I took those things in my office and tried to go over them when I had time . . . In my best judgment I turned it down because I didn't think it was qualified. Just my judgment. I don't know.

Lynd was by no means looking at the forms of our witnesses for the first time since rejecting them. In a memorandum to Roberts I saw much later he had come up with feeble reasons for keeping them off the rolls. He had "looked over Burger, Stegall & Lewis closer."[2]

There may have been a certain clumsiness and repetitiveness to Lynd's testimony, but it was becoming clear that he would deliver us no "smoking gun." Judge Cox wanted to be sure the record showed that Lynd considered himself racially neutral: "Did the applicant's race have anything to do with your decision?"

> LYND: It did not. I couldn't have told you whether she was a Negro or a white person. . . . I know she is a Negro now. She had Mrs. Addie N. Burger, and I don't refer to them as Mrs.
> SHANDS: Did the witness testify that the application was signed or unsigned?
> LYND: I said it was not signed.

SHANDS: Was that the reason you turned it down?

LYND: Well, not the only reason . . . If I looked and that was the first thing I saw I probably didn't consider it further. It was according to what I had to do at the time. Each individual case was on its own. It was not because of the fact that it was a Negro or a white. That didn't have a thing in the world to do with it.

DOAR: Well, do you want to look at that and see if you can tell me what the basis of your rejection was?

A. Judge, I am going to tell you, sitting up here and considering this thing is a whole lot different from sitting in my office and looking at them. I don't have the section of the Constitution here. I don't know whether it is completely copied in here or not, for one thing.

Q. Don't you know that she is the wife of the Negro school principal?

A. I do now.

Q. You didn't know at that time?

A. I didn't think about it if I did. As well as I can remember one of the deputies gave her this application and laid it on my desk along with some others that I probably had. . . .

Q. I would like for you to look at Plaintiff's Exhibit 5 and tell me whether you accepted or rejected Robert Lewis.

A. It has "NQ" on it and I would say I rejected it.

Q. Would you tell me what the basis of your rejection was?

Lynd continued his denial of racial bias:

> I would say that it was because the application is not signed, it doesn't have the election district or the name of the county filled in here—just taking a quick look at it. And I did not reject this application just because it was a Negro or white. I didn't reject any application for that reason and that reason alone.

Q. You read over the application before you considered it, didn't you?

A. Yes, sir. If I was in a hurry and looked at it and saw it wasn't complete, I usually do that and, well, sometimes if I have other things to do I wouldn't consider it any further.

Q. Do you know what kind of school the Rowan high school is in Hattiesburg?

A. It is a Negro high school to the best of my knowledge.

Q. Do you know whether or not that high school has any white teachers in it?

A. I don't know . . .

Q. Did you know he was a Negro?

A. I can't frankly say I did, but if I paid very much attention to where his business was carried on, I probably knew it within my mind. But I did not take that into consideration in looking at this application.

Q. Well, will you look at Plaintiff's Exhibit 1, the application of Mr. Stegall, and tell me whether you accepted or rejected that application?

A. It has got "NQ" on it and I rejected it.

By now Lynd had developed a pat answer:

Well, the first thing I see here, it's not signed. Now, I won't say that was the sole basis for rejecting it. The same thing applies to it as applies to these others.

Q. Can you look at the application now and point out any other reason for the rejection?

A. Not without scrutinizing it. On this witness stand under the pressure I'm under right now, I couldn't.

Under questioning, Lynd claimed not to know "Jesse."

Q. I would like for you to look at Exhibits 12 and 13 and tell me whether or not those applications by David Roberson were accepted or rejected by you.

A. One is on March 2, 1961, and the other on October 12, 1961. The one on March 2nd has "NR" on it, which would indicate to me not registered, and the other one has "NQ" on it, which would indicate not qualified. I don't know. Neither one of them is signed as to the application and this one of March 2nd doesn't have any oath filled out on it and it's not signed anywhere.

Q. Now, with respect to those applications, Mr. Lynd, after you graded them you advised those people that they were not qualified, is that correct?

A. Yes, sir, I'm sure I did if they inquired of me about them.

John Doar asked Lynd if he had ever pointed out to black applicants the crucial need to add their signatures to the application:

A. I don't recall any specific instance where I did or did not.

Q. Do you recall any specific instance where a Negro applicant refused to sign the application after you asked him to?

A. No.

Judge Cox again weighed in for Lynd: Did you keep any from signing at the proper place on the application?

LYND: No, sir, I did not.

THE COURT: Did any of them ask you where to sign and you refused to tell them?

LYND: No, sir.

Q. I want you to look at Plaintiff's Exhibit 3, which is the application of Wayne Kelly Pittman. Do you know Mr. Pittman?

A. No, I do not.

Q. Will you look through and tell me why that application was rejected?

A. For one thing, he has all of the oaths filled out in here and signed, every one.

John asked Lynd whether that was a basis for rejection. "It could be one," was Lynd's coy reply.

Q. Was it one?

A. If I opened it up and looked through it and saw that I probably didn't consider it further. I can't say. It would all depend on what the circumstances were at the time I reviewed it.

Q. He checked it as being a minister on the front, he said he was a minister, and signed it Reverend W. K. Pittman. And he also signed the application form, did he not?

A. In all places, and filled out both oaths.

Q. What would the circumstances have been that would have influenced you in deciding whether or not to accept or reject that application?

Lynd was reduced to bluster: "I can't say, it all depends on what was going on at the time I was looking at this particular application."

Q. What could have been going on, can you give me any idea?

Lynd was always busy:

A. My duties are various and numerous. I don't have time to do just
one particular thing . . . there's a lot of people that come into
our office . . . I try to keep enough people in the office to carry a
normal load of work, and I can't say as to what it was under this
particular case.

Judge Cox again tried to help Lynd by raising the issues of gender and
salary at the clerk's office. Lynd replied that he had two deputy clerks, both
female, and that he couldn't pay what a male clerk would require to live on.
So it went: Poor Theron Lynd—unable to hire a white man to stand up to
our aggressive black applicants.

We had felt it necessary to put Lynd on the stand to see if we could obtain any useful admissions. But all that we had obtained was a litany of his
problems: he was overworked and underpaid. We would have to rely on the
witnesses we had already produced. John rested and renewed our motion
for preliminary injunction.

Judge Cox was not buying our request:

I think the colored people brought that on themselves. I am thor-
oughly familiar with some of the conduct of some of our colored
gentry and I am not surprised at Mr. Lynd's reaction to what he
stated into the record. I think that is a clear justification for what
he did. You people up north don't understand what he was talking about. I don't expect you to. But I do.

. . . I think he did just exactly right in taking those things on
himself. He said he couldn't afford any male help and he used
girls in there and those girls didn't want to be subjected to that
kind of influence and that is understandable.[3]

Francis Zachary chimed in, casting whites as underdogs in this drama:

Judge, the federal government has seen fit to spend thousands
and thousands of dollars on this lawsuit—which is all right but a
part of it is my taxes—but Mr. Lynd has to employ private counsel who have to do other things to make a living. We are not on
the government payroll. We have to search out our witnesses
by ourselves and without the F.B.I. and without the Department

of Justice and we can't take two weeks off and stay in motels in Hattiesburg . . .

I asked Mr. Doar this morning if he would be kind enough to set these hearings at some time when Theron Lynd and all of his clerks and myself and Mr. Roberts and the rest of us did not have to be in the State court in Hattiesburg, and he said, "You have an election coming here in June." In other words, he don't give a flip nor a flapdoodle for Forrest County, he's not interested in the people of Forrest County except for a few Negroes.[4]

With every election potential black voters missed, there was an irrevocable loss of a constitutional right. The defendants wanted thirty days to prepare more cross-examination, but we would not agree to the delay.

M. M. Roberts muttered:

There's a lot of feeling about this because the whole county has been stirred up. Not by the Negroes down there but by the . . . great government we have . . . down there in the nighttime scattering around . . . making it impossible for us to know where we are with our own society in the area where we live . . .[5]

Roberts, Shands, and Zachary got their thirty-day continuance from Judge Cox. We did not wait. We would go to the U.S. Court of Appeals for the Fifth Circuit and appeal his failure to have issued the preliminary injunction.

CHAPTER 20

IKE'S FIFTH CIRCUIT

Getting On with the Job at Hand

When most people think of legal appeals in the federal system, they think of the U.S. Supreme Court. However, between 1954 and 1965 the Supreme Court rendered voting rights opinions in only two cases. Policing the hostility to civil rights of many of the Deep South's federal trial judges was left to the United States Court of Appeals for the Fifth Judicial Circuit. For even small steps toward black voting rights or integrated education, that court had to act forcefully on behalf of the Constitution.

In 1962—indeed since 1929—the intermediate appellate level of the federal judiciary was divided into eleven geographic circuits. The Fifth, just increased from seven to nine judges, covered Texas, Louisiana, Mississippi, Alabama, Florida, Georgia, and the Canal Zone. The three great Eisenhower appointees to that court came from Atlanta, Houston, and New Orleans.

They were successful younger lawyers who took on what they called the "Post-Office Republicans"—the supporters of Senator Robert Taft, in Georgia, Texas, and Louisiana, the hangers-on angling for the patronage positions available in every federal administration when their candidate won the presidency. And take them on they did. With the assistance of William Rogers, they persuaded the Credentials Committee of the 1952 Republican National Convention to seat them as delegates, and they in turn helped put Eisenhower over the top in Chicago.

In 1953, John Minor Wisdom, fun loving and socially prominent in New Orleans, was first of the three offered the chance to sit on the Fifth Circuit. He didn't take it. Then Louisiana's Republican National Committeeman, he preferred to remain in private practice and enjoy helping to dispense the state's patronage. Elbert Tuttle got the job, as Wisdom knew he would.

A decorated World War II veteran, Tuttle had twice been wounded in hand-to-hand combat in the South Pacific.[1] He had grown up in Hawaii, where his Iowa-born father had moved from Los Angeles to work for the

Sugar Planters Association. Elbert entered Honolulu's Punahou School, well known to mainland college admissions directors and now better known to the national public as Barack Obama's alma mater. Tuttle went on to Cornell both as an undergraduate and for law school. His mother's father was an Iowa soldier in the Civil War who had been confined for eighteen months in the notorious Confederate prison in Andersonville, where almost one inmate out of three died in captivity from starvation, disease, or abuse.

As a lawyer in Atlanta practicing with his brother-in-law, Tuttle became identified with unpopular cases. In *Johnson v. Zerbst*,[2] the Supreme Court held that Tuttle's client, a criminal defendant, had not waived his Sixth Amendment right to counsel simply by acquiescing to a trial without counsel. Tuttle had taken the appeal to the Supreme Court on his own, without any help from the American Civil Liberties Union after the Court of Appeals stage, and he got a marine sergeant's conviction reversed. Those recommending Tuttle to the president, including Wisdom, certainly knew that.

By the late 1940s, Tuttle had become a leader of the Atlanta and Georgia Bar. He chaired Georgia's Republican state party following the 1952 convention and introduced General Eisenhower at a big rally in Atlanta, held out of doors because Georgia law forbade whites and blacks from meeting together indoors. It was Bob Woodruff, president of Atlanta's dominant enterprise, Coca-Cola, who introduced Tuttle to George Humphrey, Ike's secretary of the treasury. That led to Tuttle's becoming Humphrey's general counsel in Washington. He told the secretary he would stay for two years, and it took both Wisdom's persuasion and two calls from Rogers, who had become deputy attorney general, to get him to break that commitment and go on the court. Tuttle told a friend he was "retiring" to the Fifth Circuit. Little did he know.

Texas was due for the next appointment. John Brown was a successful admiralty lawyer who had come from his native Nebraska to Houston via the University of Michigan Law School. He brooded about whether to become "a federal employee," as his wife put it, and consulted his fellow Houstonite Judge Hutcheson, a longtime member of the court. Brown won Hutch's praise when he told him he had decided not to do it, that he would remain an advocate. But the next day Brown changed his mind.[3]

Tulane law professor Harvey Couch, the Fifth Circuit's official historian, described Judge Brown as "an ebullient, florid man with a seemingly inexhaustible capacity for enjoying life and a seemingly endless supply of multi-colored sport coats. He possesses boundless energy, an unexpected sensibility, a joviality laced with toughness, and an unfailing desire to get on with the job at hand."[4]

Then, in 1957, the first year of Ike's second term, Wisdom had a second chance.[5] President Eisenhower believed that discrimination in employment violated constitutional principles, and on August 13, 1953, he had issued an Executive Order creating the President's Committee on Government Contracts. Vice President Nixon was its chair, but they had trouble getting a southern member. It was Attorney General Brownell who thought of Wisdom. Maxwell Rabb, Ike's chief White House aide on civil rights, also remembered that Wisdom "was liberal and had a lot of courage."[6]

Despite his role in the 1952 campaign, the earlier offer, and his dutiful service on the President's Committee, in 1957 Wisdom was not assured of joining Tuttle and Brown on the court. Louisiana governor Robert Kennon wanted the position himself, and Kennon was one of three Democratic governors in the South who had endorsed Ike in 1952. He also knew Ike's right-hand man, former New Hampshire governor Sherman Adams. But there was strong black opposition to Kennon. Wisdom won out, and Tuttle, Brown, and Wisdom, aided by Truman appointee Richard Rives, would save their part of the country from judges like William Harold Cox, who were staunchly defending the South's segregated society.[7]

Judge Wisdom attended Isidore Newman, a New Orleans school founded to educate Jewish orphans that had expanded and become recognized for academic excellence. He went on to Washington & Lee in Virginia as an undergraduate and practiced in New Orleans after graduating from Tulane Law School. Wisdom became recognized as the Louisiana authority on trusts, and he was a member of the Urban League and president of the New Orleans Council of Social Agencies. Upon entering his chambers in the federal courthouse that would one day bear his name, the first thing I observed was a 1952 campaign photo of a parade through the streets of New Orleans, with Wisdom in the front seat of an open convertible and Ike and his wife, Mamie, behind, a beaming Ike giving the thumbs up sign.

While a case may be heard by all of an appellate court's judges, sitting *en banc*, a three-judge panel is the norm. The judge who selected the panels for Chief Judge Tuttle, as he had for Tuttle's predecessors, Hutcheson and Rives, was John R. Brown. Tuttle did not exaggerate when he declared upon Brown's taking senior judicial status in 1984 that Brown "played a major and highly significant role in the peaceful revolution that took place in the six states of the Fifth Circuit."[8] And it was the *Lynd* case "that transformed the Fifth Circuit Court of Appeals into the center of action."[9]

Brown grew up in the small Nebraska town of Holdrege, halfway between Lincoln, the capital, and the Colorado border:

> *Holdrege had one Negro. He worked in the barber shop. The best illustration of my feeling that there wasn't any distinction between him and me was, I'd come home from college with a bottle of whiskey in my hand, and the first thing we'd do was go in the back room of the barber shop, and we'd drink out of the same bottle. [T]he spectacle of the way that state-imposed segregation was working was just . . . obnoxious to me, and I found it very easy to engage in these legal actions which brought about a change.*[10]

Realistically, it is much easier to be supportive of black rights when there is only one black in town. It is tougher when black rights may cost your family and friends and peers political power and influence. As judges, Brown, Tuttle, and Wisdom dealt with peer pressures Brown had not faced in Holdrege.

After four years at the University of Nebraska in a combined undergraduate-law program, Brown transferred to the University of Michigan, where he "studied like hell and got drunk once a month,"[11] but still finished first in his law class in 1932.

> *And then I came to Texas in the depths of the Depression. There wasn't all that much open for me in that small community where I was raised. I just called on people: Dallas first, then San Antone and Fort Worth. I didn't have any appointments. I couldn't have gotten any appointments.*

Brown was hired by Newton Rayzor, a brilliant young maritime lawyer in Houston. Except for three years in the army, Brown remained with Rayzor until he became a judge. There was little to indicate that upon entering the judiciary he would become a major force for the advancement of civil rights.

> *I didn't get interested in national politics until about 1948, when a very good friend of my wife, . . . Jack Porter, ran for United States Senate on the Republican ticket. Then he got interested in 1952 in the presidential race supporting Eisenhower. I got to working hard for him, and ended up being the county chairman of the Republican Party in Harris County.*

We were thrown out of the county convention in Houston, because the Taft folks were better organized and had some real old-time politicians. But we were finally seated. Then we went to the state convention, and there we were poured out by the Taft people, ousted as delegates to the national convention. So we were in some flea-bag hotel in North Chicago in the depth of summer—no air conditioning. Well, Texas had an appeal. Louisiana had an appeal. Georgia had an appeal. Elbert Tuttle handled the Georgia case. John Wisdom handled the Louisiana case. Brilliant! I was in the Texas Eisenhower delegation that got seated.

These three enormously talented, but quite different, lawyers had successfully asserted themselves against the entrenched forces of Senator Robert Taft. Now they were federal appellate judges in the country's most sensitive region. Although the civil rights movement that led to the Second Reconstruction occurred largely in the sixties, the Eisenhower years saw its beginnings.

The Supreme Court's 1954 clarion call for school integration had been muted with the directive in *Brown v. Board of Education II* that it be accomplished only with "all deliberate speed."[12] Those practicing massive resistance in the South took comfort in that judicial phrase. In fact, the separate but equal doctrine flowing from *Plessy v. Ferguson*[13] had never been honored in the public schools of the Deep South. It was separate, but hardly equal, and only when the practice was outlawed in *Brown I*[14] did the new physically equal schools for blacks that I found in Mississippi in the early sixties begin to be constructed.

Since the 1950s, federal civil rights legislation has tended to come in presidential years. What became the Civil Rights Act of 1957 was passed only by the House of Representatives in 1956, but enacted the following year. The massive disfranchisement of our southern black citizens was about to be attacked.

But in our system neither a landmark Supreme Court decision nor a new statute brings about instant change. The agents of change generally work their way case by case, jurisdiction by jurisdiction. Thus, while the legislation of the fifties demonstrated the rise of civil rights on the national agenda, the empowerment of blacks in the South had to be accomplished in southern federal courts presided over by southern federal judges, life appointees insulated from the political fray, unlikely to be swept away by new administrations or new policies.

Moreover, the reins on the power to appoint judges were held by Chairman James Eastland of the Judiciary Committee, who could hold nominees, including Thurgood Marshall for the Second Circuit, hostage until the selection of his longtime political ally, William Harold Cox, for the Federal District Court in Jackson.[15]

◆◆◆

On March 7, 1962, our three-day hearing ended. Judge Cox ordered Lynd to reconsider applications from our five teacher witnesses, as well as those of Sherman Jackson and Reverends Chandler and Pittman.[16] We did not wait for the trial to resume in thirty days. The solicitor general controls appeals sought by Justice Department trial lawyers, and on March 16, we formally sought his permission to appeal forthwith to the Fifth Circuit. By April 6, permission granted and briefs filed, John Doar was in Houston to argue on behalf of the United States against M. M. Roberts for Lynd and Assistant Attorney General Ed Cates for the State of Mississippi.

Tuttle, Wisdom, and Hutcheson constituted the panel. Roberts and Cates argued that the appellate court lacked jurisdiction, since the trial was still ongoing before Judge Cox. "You can't appeal from nothing," Cates asserted.[17] It didn't work. Tuttle agreed with Doar that Cox should have ruled one way or the other, giving the loser a clear-cut appeal. Hutcheson provided instruction on injunctive relief: "Time is of the essence in a temporary injunction suit, and if the judge doesn't act he refuses the injunction . . . What harm would it have done to grant the injunction? Who would have been hurt?"[18]

Roberts reminded the panel that "the District Judge is a new man." To which Hutcheson replied: "He seems to act like it."[19] Hutcheson didn't mince words: "He either had a lack of experience for an injunction, and didn't understand what it was, or he just was trying to prevent an appeal. Nobody ever tried a temporary injunction like that in the history of the world, at least in my world."[20]

With registration closing a month later for a Democratic primary, the panel entered an oral injunction from the bench. The written ruling, by Chief Judge Tuttle, came just four days later.

Tuttle relied on the All-Writs Act to grant our motion for an injunction pending our appeal from Judge Cox's failure to allow it.[21] He reviewed how we had been "completely frustrated" in our efforts to provide the right to vote to Forrest County's black citizens, going back almost two years to the records demand filed within a month of John Doar's coming aboard, noting that we had waited ten months before bringing this suit. We had sought to enforce the records demand in January, but nothing worked with Judge

Cox, though an order for the records should have been entered "as a matter of course." Cox had then dismissed our attempt to enforce the records demand as "abandoned," because we had sought discovery in the current case.[22] We had, of course, received nothing. Dilatory defense motions continued. Judge Tuttle declared: "Notwithstanding the well-nigh impossible task of showing the true facts, the witnesses produced by the government proved without question that certain serious discriminations had taken place during the term of office of the defendant Lynd."[23]

He found as facts:

1. No Negro had been registered in Forrest County during Lynd's term of office. . . .
2. No Negro was permitted even to apply for registration prior to January 31, 1961. Those who attempted to do so were told . . . they had to see Mr. Lynd personally . . . .
3. Prior to January 31, 1961, most, if not all, of the white applicants were permitted to register without filling out an application form. . . .
4. From January 31, 1961, to present, obviously qualified Negroes were rejected . . .
5. . . . [N]one of the defendants nor their deputies were able to testify to any individual white person who had been rejected.
6. . . . [T]he defendant's deputies received applications from white applicants, but refused to receive them from Negro applicants. . . .
7. The defendant Lynd and his deputies assisted white applicants . . . , but refused assistance to Negro applicants. . . .
8. The defendant Lynd refused to give reasons to Negro applicants . . . for their rejection, and he required that such applicants wait six months before reapplying . . . although there is no provision in the statute authorizing such conduct.
9. All of the 16 Negro witnesses who testified at the trial were required to write and interpret different provisions of the Mississippi constitution from those . . . that were submitted to white witnesses who testified.[24]

The court pointed out that three of our black witnesses had been required to interpret section 178 on the taxation of corporations having charters longer than ninety-nine years. The final sentence of the section contained fifty-eight words. The court couldn't help but conclude "beyond any question that by any objective standard those (sections) supplied to the Negro applicants were longer, more complicated, and more difficult."[25] Ten white witnesses had not been required to interpret any provision.

In 1960, the total voting-age population of Forrest County was composed of 22,431 whites and 7,495 blacks. At the time the injunction was issued, 10,000 whites and 14 blacks were registered to vote.

Normally when a trial judge is reversed, the appellate court directs the judge to enter an order consistent with its findings. But this panel had seen enough in the record of Judge Cox's handling of the *Lynd* case not to trust him to do that. When the Fifth Circuit entered its own comprehensive order that Lynd stop the various abuses they found, it assumed the highly unusual and time-consuming task of enforcing the order and tying up three appellate judges to do so. The first step had been taken. More would be needed.

Within days, Theron Lynd was violating the order the Fifth Circuit itself would have to enforce. He still didn't get it. During the morning of April 14, T. F. Williams and Sherman Jackson went to his office along with fellow Hercules worker Dewey Johnson. Lynd permitted only Williams and Johnson to fill out forms at the same time, rejecting both. Jackson could not stay but returned the next morning with Reverend Chandler. When Lynd was not there, they left.[26]

That afternoon about 4 o'clock, the three Young Turks, Stegall, Roberson, and Lewis, went to the clerk's office with another teacher, Wayne Sutton. They were also told only Lynd could register them, and he would not be in that afternoon. The next morning Roberson and Lewis returned to the office only to be told the same thing. The clerk didn't know when Lynd would be in.

In the afternoon Lewis's sister Erlexia, a fourth-grade teacher who also was an Alcorn graduate and had a master's degree from the University of West Virginia, accompanied Stegall, Sutton, and her brother to the office. The response of the deputy clerk was the same. About 4:35 the next day Roberson and Lewis were in town. It was the day Lynd was served with the Fifth Circuit's injunction. Through a courthouse window, they saw Lynd in his office and quickly entered. Though "it was close to quitting time," as Lynd told them, they got to fill out forms. Both were rejected. They "didn't quite measure up," Lynd declared and said he didn't have to tell them what they had done wrong. "All the law requires is that I tell you you didn't measure up." Four other blacks applied that day, including three school bus drivers who later had employment problems because of their involvement, Reverend John Wesley Brown, John Henry, and Bennie Hines.

When Willie Thigpen stopped by the office on Saturday, April 21, he was told he had to see Lynd, who was out of town due to a death in the family. On April 23 Stegall and Sutton were among eleven blacks seeking to apply, this time getting to fill out forms once they responded to Lynd's question where they worked. While they were filling out their forms, about eight other blacks entered who were told by Lynd they would have to wait because he would only take two at a time. Stegall and Sutton were rejected. Lynd told Stegall he had "too many discrepancies," but he couldn't tell him what they were. At least Lynd stopped imposing his six-month wait before permitting another try. He said they could come back the next day.[27] Thigpen was also rejected on the twenty-third, as were ten more, including Willie Simpson, on the twenty-fourth, and then Jacob Hunter on the twenty-fifth.

Reverend Chandler was our first witness to be successful, but, injunction or not, it had been far from easy. Between April 16 and April 26, 1962, when finally he was registered, he made nine visits to Lynd's office, filling out two application forms and enduring questioning from Lynd as to whether Chandler had filed a complaint against him.[28] But finally Reverend Chandler was a registered voter in Forrest County. He became the first black, other than two mandatory transfers and one woman thought to have been white, to be registered in Forrest County in more than eight years. With the exception of the two transfers, Lynd had registered 2,400 white persons in his three years in office and not a single black.

Chandler's success, however, did not mean the doors would open for our other witnesses. On May 12, 1962, Lynd again rejected Willie Thigpen. He had re-copied section 13 on freedom of speech and of the press being "sacred," instead of interpreting it. That had not troubled Lynd on May 1 when he registered Ira Willie Bounds, a white man, who also had copied his section rather than interpreting it.

On May 17, Vernon Dahmer and his son Harold tried to register, but the immediate result was again failure. The women in the clerk's office told them Lynd was upstairs in the courtroom. When the Dahmers went upstairs, the courtroom was empty. They came downstairs just as Lynd was leaving his office. For the first time, Vernon Dahmer got to fill out an application form, as did his son. But Theron Lynd told them they had failed and declined to tell them why.

On May 29 Willie Thigpen was turned down for just re-copying section 160 on chancery court jurisdiction. Another rejection followed September 25 just after the contempt trial ended. But Thigpen stayed with it.

We were going to just keep going, a bunch of us. All the time, we would sit around on our break from the job, talking about it. I finally got registered after the contempt trial, and it wasn't all that long after I was registered that my wife was registered.[29]

The tide had turned in Forrest County. SNCC workers Hollis Watkins and Curtis Hayes arrived following the March trial and stayed with the Dahmers, encouraging more voting activity.[30] We petitioned the Fifth Circuit to find Lynd in contempt of its April order. The rejected applications filled out by our witnesses and by many new black applicants would demonstrate to the Fifth Circuit judges who traveled to Hattiesburg for a new trial in September that Lynd was in contempt of its injunction.

Judge John Brown had not sat on the initial argument. He praised Judge Tuttle's opinion as one of Tuttle's finest, and Brown went to Hattiesburg with Judges Wisdom and Griffin Bell, later President Carter's first attorney general, but no fan of Tuttle's opinion.[31] Brown described the contempt trial as "kind of an emergency matter."

> We went over there, spent a week. I wanted to start about 7 o'clock in the morning—keep on going. Theron Lynd was about a 350–400 pound man. One day we came back from lunch, and for a half an hour we're going on with testimony coming in. All of a sudden I look out there, and there's no Theron Lynd. We had gotten a special chair for him because he was so big. He sat more or less right out in front of everybody because the regular witness chair wouldn't fit. And I thought, "My God, here we've got a criminal case, and the defendant's not in." So we called a recess, and asked the lawyers "Should we call these witnesses back and have them repeat all this stuff, or will you waive that?" They waived it. The idea, see, of overlooking a 375-pound man was sort of comical.
>
> And the revelations in that trial were just spectacular—smoking guns right and left. This pretty well steeled us in our feeling that this whole apparatus that they set up for blacks who tried to register was just a lot of humbug.

Judge Brown was referring, of course, to the manipulation of Mississippi's literacy test, with black applicants being given long, intricate sections that would challenge even a qualified tax attorney. Indeed, when Hercules custodian Sherman Jackson testified about the section he was assigned, 112—uniform taxation, proportional to value, throughout the state, Judge Cox had exclaimed: "I wanted to see what he would say, because the Supreme Court of Mississippi has had some trouble with this section."[32] Brown was enthralled with the section requiring an explanation of how railroad companies were evaluated for tax purposes. Brown also recalled in my interviews with him: "I'll never forget one answer to the obligation of a citizen. John Doar holds this up: 'Believe in the Lord Jesus Christ. You will be saved.' That white person was approved for registration."

National attention was focused on Mississippi in September 1962 when the contempt trial began, but it wasn't because of the *Lynd* trial. In Oxford, to the northwest, James Meredith, overcoming one obstacle after another, sought to become the first black student at Ole Miss, the pride of Mississippi higher education. But Judge Brown emphasized that there was also ample judicial action concerning Meredith occurring in Hattiesburg.

> *Much of that week was taken up with the Meredith case. Every time we got off at noon, we had Barrett Prettyman or John Doar from the Justice Department. John Doar was before us in the* Lynd *case. We'd issued an order setting Judge Mize's order against Meredith aside. Judge Cameron would then set our order aside. And then we had to set his order aside. This went on all week long. And when I got back Saturday night after being gone all that week, Judge Rives said, "I think maybe we'd better have an end back here." And lo and behold, that's when Justice Black entered the historic injunction for the Supreme Court, which in effect set aside all of Judge Cameron's orders that set aside ours.*

The judges in Hattiesburg were also receiving long-distance telephone calls from the Department of Justice and from other lawyers. Brown explained:

> *I'd say, "We'll see you in chambers." Well,* chambers *was a little dinky cubby-hole, not bigger than 10 foot by 10 foot with one steel desk in it. That was the judge's chambers—but no telephone. To get to a telephone, you had to go through the marshal's jail adjacent to the courtroom. There was a marshal nicknamed "Rabbit." He wouldn't let me go to the barbershop in Hattiesburg without him. I was going to get a shave or a haircut, and he said, that's too close to that damned razor; you're not going to that barbershop, not by yourself.*
>
> *M. M. Roberts kept putting these white people on the stand. And then John Doar would get out their own answers on the voting test. Never seemed to faze him. Doar was such a favorite of John Wisdom and me and Elbert. Not that we gave him anything he wasn't entitled to. But he was so proficient. No bombasts, scarcely ever raised his voice. You just knew he knew what he was talking about. I've heard a lot of cases since then, but those stand out.*

M. M. Roberts had a very different reaction to the contempt trial:

We had five days with these three judges. Minor Wisdom was the most arrogant. We concluded that his first name probably applied to his last because he has little of wisdom in my opinion. Brown is prejudiced against us. He is a native of Kansas and thinks "north of M-D line." On the other hand, he has a brilliant mind.[33]

That "brilliant mind" had these thoughts about southern Mississippi's two federal trial judges:

Judge Mize was a wonderful, lovable character who had been on the bench for many years, and he was almost apologetic when he'd hold against my views. During the time we were setting aside his order, we'd talk to him on the phone and say, "Well, why don't you do this?" "No, I'm sorry, I can't do that." So I would have to issue another order.

Cox—I don't know whether he ever thought they would ultimately prevail, but he didn't give a damn. They were going to try their best, use all the power he had, to see that nothing was done to the status quo. "Lovable" was not a word that would get applied by too many people to Judge Cox. Did you ever see the movie that Charlie Chaplin did, "The Great Dictator," playing both Mussolini and Hitler—that long conference room where people had to walk for almost a block to come to him? All of Judge Cox's motions were heard in a weird long room, with a long, long table. You stood at the end of the table, and he was at the other end, just like Mussolini.

Judge Brown had no preexisting feelings about the concept of a literacy test:

If it was required in Texas, it would have never bothered me. I first became aware of it in the voting rights cases, and I could see the horrendous opportunity for very crass discrimination on such loaded, difficult legal problems. How do you explain the provision of a Constitution? It's an easy way out.

One of the interesting things that John Wisdom and I did was develop the doctrine of the deep freeze [or freezing theory]. And it's still the law, whatever you used to do for whites, you do for blacks. As avid an advocate of civil rights as Judge Rives was, the idea that to remedy the unconstitutional, you had to engage in like unconstitutional

*actions was something he simply couldn't tolerate. But ultimately we
developed that doctrine.*

Biographer Jack Bass credits Wisdom with stating the first constitutional rationale for affirmative action. It came in *United States v. Jefferson City
Board of Education*, an opinion best known for transforming the law on
school desegregation cases:[34]

*The Constitution is both color blind and color-conscious. To avoid con-
flict with the Equal Protection Clause, a classification that denies a
benefit, causes harm or imposes a burden must not be based on race.
In that sense, the Constitution is color blind.*

*But the Constitution is color-conscious to prevent discrimina-
tion being perpetuated and to undo the effects of past discrimination. The criterion is the relevancy of color to a legitimate government
purpose.[35]*

Before he died in 1999 at the age of ninety-three, Wisdom told Bass he
was unsure which was more important: how far blacks had come in overcoming discrimination, or "how far they still have to go."[36]

The contempt trial began September 17, 1962, and continued through
the twenty-second. The Young Turks testified, as well as Reverends Chandler and Pittman and Willie Thigpen and T. F. Williams. It would have been
nice to have a prompt decision, but Lynd was not adjudged guilty of civil
contempt until July 15, 1963. Forty-three blacks who had tried to register
after the injunction was served upon Lynd were ordered placed upon the
rolls. Among them were the three Young Turks, the three school bus drivers, Vernon and Harold Dahmer, Sherman Jackson, Reverends Sam Hall
and Dewey Johnson, Iva Sandifer, Wayne Sutton, Willie Thigpen, and T. F.
Williams. Earline Boyd, who had made ten or eleven attempts and finally
been registered by Lynd in March 1963, was also included.[37]

One by one, our remaining witnesses, their spouses, and others in the
black community became registered. The battle was pitifully slow. It would
not be won in President Kennedy's too-short lifetime. In the second of the
circuit's contempt findings against Lynd two years later, Judge Brown expressed his frustration: "At the snail's pace to date, it will take decades to
eradicate the evil."[38]

But Lyndon Johnson took up the cause and went beyond the fallen president. Kennedy's proposed Civil Rights Act of 1963, announced in a speech
the night Medgar Evers was assassinated, became enacted as the Civil

Rights Act of 1964.[39] The Voting Rights Act of 1965, with its suspension of literacy tests and appointment of federal examiners and poll-watchers, was necessary to complete the job.[40]

When it was challenged by South Carolina and other affected southern states, Chief Justice Earl Warren recalled on behalf of the Supreme Court our Forrest County witnesses who were rejected despite their baccalaureate and M.A. degrees,[41] the Hattiesburg teachers barred from taking part in the democracy they were acquainting their students with, and the way the order of the Fifth Circuit had been defied in Forrest County.[42] "An insidious and pervasive evil . . . through unremitting and ingenious defiance of the Constitution" had been ended.[43]

Chief Justice Warren delivered the Supreme Court's imprimatur to this vital radical legislation, but Judges Tuttle, Brown, Wisdom, and Rives had conducted the necessary earlier skirmishes in the judicial trenches. They are missed, both as human beings and as judges who got on with and accomplished the job at hand.

CHAPTER 21

AFTER THE TRIAL

It was a very warm, sleepy August evening in the early nineties in Montgomery, Alabama. There was no traffic in the streets and the sidewalk in front of the Civil Rights Memorial was empty. But the water flowed constantly down the black granite wall of Maya Lin's graceful memorial onto the circular table inscribed with the names of forty people who had died in the struggle.

My wife and I walked slowly around the edge, looking for the name we had come to see: Vernon Dahmer. Soothing as the flowing waters were, they had also largely washed the paint out of the letters of Dahmer's name, making it easier to trace with our fingers than to read. But this seemed fitting: compared with many of the names on the monument, Dahmer's was then little known.

On January 10, 1966, the top civil rights story of the day was the refusal of Georgia's legislature to seat Representative-elect Julian Bond for his opposition to continued U.S. military involvement in Vietnam. That night Vernon Dahmer was murdered at his home in Kelly Settlement. There had been a radio announcement that Dahmer, long Forrest County's leading proponent of black voting rights, would collect poll taxes from would-be voters to turn in to local officials. That was believed to be the impetus for his murder. There was actually an element of futility in the sequence of events: a federal court would soon declare the state's poll tax unconstitutional.

On March 28, 1966, the top civil rights story of the day was the Supreme Court decision upholding the federal government's right to prosecute, under the Reconstruction conspiracy statute, the alleged killers of civil rights workers Michael Schwerner, Andrew Goodman, and James Chaney in Neshoba County. That day agents of the Federal Bureau of Investigation arrested thirteen members of the White Knights of the Ku Klux Klan—the "secret" Klan splinter group based next door in Jones County—for violating Dahmer's civil rights by murdering him. Still being sought was the ringleader, White Knights' imperial wizard Sam Holloway Bowers, Jr., who surrendered a few days later. FBI sources described Bowers as "armed and dangerous."[1]

"THE VERNON DAHMER PROJECT" AND THE PROSECUTIONS OF SAM BOWERS

Six bored, unemployed Confederate veterans began the Ku Klux Klan near Nashville, Tennessee, in 1865.[2] It was first an almost farcical mystical society, but the sheets they wore as they galloped their horses through town created the stir they had hoped for and, understandably, scared black onlookers. But within two years, other, older men began using the Klan as a vehicle for guerrilla action against the South's hated conquerors.

With the entire South but for Tennessee divided into five military districts under army rule, and close to 200,000 southern white voters disenfranchised for aiding the Confederacy, even some respected leaders such as General Nathan Bedford Forrest, in whose name Mississippi would create Forrest County in 1912, seized on the Klan as their "patriotic" organizational vehicle. Forrest, one of Robert E. Lee's legendary cavalry officers, became the first Grand Wizard of the Tennessee Klan in April 1867. But the Klan would not be merely a political force. Lynchings and other murders, floggings, and mutilations erupted across the South in all their savagery. Within two years, General Forrest was so sickened by the vicious conduct he had helped unleash that he ordered the Klan to disband.[3]

It was too late. His voice was no longer heeded. However, major civil rights legislation enacted by Congress beginning in 1866 and including the Enforcement Act of 1871, known as the Ku Klux Klan Act, as well as strong executive action by President Ulysses S. Grant in South Carolina in the early 1870s, helped check Klan terrorism; and the restoration of political rights to almost all former Confederates in May 1872 deprived the Klan of one of the festering sores that had provided its impetus.[4]

For a time the Klan receded as a force in American life. It made its formal return in 1915, chartered by the state of Georgia and headed by Atlanta promoter William Joseph Simmons. The cross that soon burned over nearby Stone Mountain symbolized the Klan's twentieth-century incarnation.

The Klan was anti-Catholic, anti-Semitic, anti-immigrant, but its greatest impact was upon blacks. Promoters slicker than Simmons increased Klan membership to almost five million by 1925, with units in almost every state. When the Depression occurred and Klan violence again began to draw public criticism, membership dwindled. In 1944 the then Imperial Wizard of the Klan announced its disbandment.[5]

But demise of Georgia's chartered version did not signify the end of Klan activity. Rather it signaled a coming free-for-all for the Klan name and power. *Brown v. the Board of Education* aroused the massive southern resistance to school integration I have discussed, and the Klan was a beneficiary. In 1961 there was a new corporate charter in Georgia, this for the United Klans of America, the creation of thirty-one-year-old Robert Shelton, previous Grand Dragon of Alabama's segment of the "U.S. Klans."[6]

Mississippi had seen little Klan activity for years until the voting rights struggle focused on the state in the sixties. On a November night in 1963, three crosses, attributed to a Louisiana-oriented Klan fragment, blazed at the outskirts of a black community near Natchez. Reporter Don Whitehead terms that the "first warning that the Klan had returned to Mississippi."[7] But the same dissention that had gripped the Klan nationally afflicted it in Mississippi. Among the dissidents was a thirty-nine-year-old Laurel vending and pinball machine operator, Sam Holloway Bowers, Jr.

Grandson of a four-term Mississippi congressman, and claiming roots back to the first president of the Virginia House of Burgesses, the dapper Bowers became the first imperial wizard of the White Knights of the Ku Klux Klan of Mississippi. Born in New Orleans in 1924, Bowers had grown up along the Gulf Coast and in Jackson, enlisting in the navy early in World War II. He was honorably discharged in December 1945. Before returning to Mississippi, he studied engineering in California during 1946 and 1947. In Laurel in Jones County, just north of Forrest, Bowers accumulated some wealth as a partner in Sambo Amusement Company and at one point operating a movie theater.[8]

In December 1963, in anticipation of the Mississippi Freedom Summer being organized by the new student-based civil rights umbrella organization, COFO, the Council of Federated Organizations, some two hundred dissident Mississippi Klansmen voted to set up new klaverns. Bowers prevailed in a short-lived power struggle and became, as Charles Marsh termed him, the "High Priest of the Anti-Civil Rights Movement," operating with religious zeal to eliminate the "heretics" of the civil rights movement.[9]

The 2,500 employees of Laurel's Masonite Corporation were fertile ground for Bowers as he played on their fears of increased power for blacks and of losing control of "white men's jobs." The gas station attendant, the pulpwood worker, the tenant farmer—often uneducated and poorly paid— frequently heeded the Klan's anti-black, anti-Semitic message.

Among Bowers's first demonstrations of the White Knights' power were displays of solidarity with the killer of Medgar Evers, Byron De La Beckwith, during the second of his trials. At about 11 P.M., April 10, 1964, during shift changes for the local police, ten crosses were burned in and around Jackson. The next morning, when testimony was to begin, about seventy-five white men, probably Klansmen, entered the courtroom early, rising as Beckwith came in and remaining standing until he was seated.[10]

On the night of April 24, crosses burned on the courthouse lawns of sixty-four of the state's eighty-two counties to celebrate Beckwith's second mistrial. Though they really functioned in no more than ten counties, the White Knights were broadening their base of free, white, native-born Protestant citizens, their proclaimed purpose "to preserve Christian civilization, protect and promote white supremacy and segregation of the races, to fight Communism and to extend the dignity, heritage and rights of the white race in America."

The journalist Bill Minor described it:

When all the ballyhoo started about these students coming down and going all over the state and conducting Freedom Schools and Voter Education Schools, that's what triggered the organization of the White Knights of the Ku Klux Klan. Because Bowers lived in Laurel, that was the center of it there, and they had more than 6,000 members . . . the White Knights went like wildfire across the piney woods section of South Mississippi. Bowers mesmerized the people. But the White Knights . . . didn't get in the Delta. The Delta had the Citizens Council . . . Main Street downtown Klan.[11]

So except for the relatively minor operation around Natchez, there had been a Klan vacuum in Mississippi. And you didn't have to get a franchise from Stone Mountain. You just called yourself a Klan, printed up your literature, and got your robes. The person selling White Knights robes was Sam Bowers.

The arrest, staged release, and subsequent murder of COFO workers Schwerner, Goodman, and Chaney during the summer of 1964 shocked the country, brought Allen Dulles to Mississippi as President Johnson's personal representative, and roused that slumbering power, the FBI.[12]

On January 11, 1965, a federal grand jury composed of twenty-two whites and a black Gulfport restaurant cook, with a Jackson insurance executive as its foreman, was reconvened by Judge Cox in Jackson. After four days of testimony, it returned civil rights indictments of Neshoba County sheriff Lawrence Rainey and its deputy sheriff Cecil Price, along with sixteen others, and later Sam Bowers.[13] But Bowers had additional problems. He knew, of course, that he was a target of the FBI and federal prosecutors, but his White Knights also became a target of Robert Shelton. Pike County in the southwest corner of the state had been Shelton's 1964 Mississippi beachhead, and in the summer of 1965 he embarked on a major recruitment campaign, beginning with a huge rally, and a twenty-foot-high burning cross, near Meridian, just north of Bowers's home base.

Judge Cox, who himself was threatened and required protection during the trial,[14] had dismissed the felony indictment, but was Bowers doing enough to help the Klansmen who still had to face misdemeanor charges? Some accused Bowers of mismanaging Klan funds. Under organizational siege, Bowers still embraced the climate of violence he had created in and around Jones County. He did try to take the heat off the Laurel area by spreading his violence—and the FBI agents investigating it—elsewhere in the state with bombings in McComb and Natchez. On August 25, 1965, Bowers reportedly gave instruction in Gulfport in the use of plastic bottles to make Molotov cocktails and the use of nitroglycerin as an explosive.

In mid-July Bowers had told an outdoor meeting that Attorney General Katzenbach was holding the prospect of an investigation by the House Committee on Un-American Activities over the heads of Klansmen, a dubious claim considering the low regard mainstream Democrats had for the committee. On October 26, 1965, Bowers was in fact served with a subpoena at a Laurel cafe. His testimony did not occur until after he caused the murder of Vernon Dahmer.

Outside a late December meeting called by Bowers were three masked guards, led by a twenty-two-year-old upholsterer, a ninth-grade dropout by the name of Billy Roy Pitts, who had joined the White Knights two years before. Pitts was one of those selected by Bowers to carry out "the Vernon Dahmer project."[15]

Inside, Bowers pounded on a table, saying they had to do something about the "big NAACP nigger" who was leading this voter registration drive. The Forrest County Klan had done nothing about him, and Bowers was going to take the matter into his own hands. In Klan parlance, Bowers wanted a number three—burning—and, if possible, a number four—murder.

After two dry runs, the eight men selected by Bowers to make the hit on Dahmer met on the night of January 10, 1966. Armed with handguns, shotguns, and jugs filled with gasoline, they set off for Kelly Settlement in two cars. Pitts would testify that Cliff Wilson took two jugs into the carport and ignited the car and truck there, while Smith shot out the picture window. Cecil Sessum tossed the jugs through the shattered window into the living room, then lit the gasoline with a rag burning at the end of a forked stick. Twelve jugs in all were used on the Dahmer property. As "the place roared with flames," Pitts later recalled, they heard a male voice cry out from inside, with Sessum then yelling: "Let him die. That's what we came here for."[16]

Pitts had two assignments: to guard Sessum and to shoot anyone who came out of the house. He later said that Bowers seemed "awfully upset" because Pitts had lost the pistol he had in his holster and because one of the cars had been abandoned when it suffered a flat tire. Bowers was right to be upset; the pistol, when found, gave Pitts a participant's credibility with which to testify—"steady as a rock"[17]—against the others, while the Ford, riddled with bullets with one tire flattened, belonged to one of the White Knights.

The Dahmers had been getting telephone calls all night. Cars came into their yard and driveway, hesitated, then turned around. But the calls seemed to be dropping off. Jewell and Vernon had been sleeping in shifts, but on this night, their sleep overlapped. Jewell awoke first, hearing shooting and seeing flames. Vernon went for the guns he always kept loaded with buckshot.

Their daughter Bettie, ten, appeared to have been badly burned. Vernon handed her out the back bedroom window to Jewell, who had fallen through the window while preparing to get Bettie out herself. Vernon kept shooting at the invaders, trying to hold them off while his family escaped. Their son Dennis had emerged from the back room with his older brother Harold.

Harold backed out the pickup truck and went to call the fire department. But by the time they arrived, the Dahmer buildings were destroyed. Vernon died at the hospital the next day of smoke inhalation and burns inside his respiratory tract. Before he died, Dahmer told a local reporter: "I've been active in trying to get people to register to vote. People who don't vote are deadbeats on the state. I figure a man needs to do his own thinking. What happened to us last night can happen to anyone, white or black. At one time I didn't think so, but I have changed my mind."[18]

More than three hundred angry blacks, led by Charles Evers, who had insisted on succeeding his murdered brother as state field director of the NAACP, marched on the courthouse, demanding action. Evers urged an economic boycott of the city. Grievance lists from the NAACP were presented to the city council, the county board of supervisors, the sheriff and the chamber of commerce.

Dahmer had four sons still on active military duty. Getting home for their father's funeral was not difficult for Master Sergeant Vernon Jr., stationed at March Air Force Base in Riverside, California, or Sergeant George at Homestead Air Force Base in Florida. But, Alvin was a specialist fourth class in Germany, and Martinez, a staff sergeant, was off the Alaska coast. Nonetheless, all were present on Saturday to hear their father eulogized by NAACP leader Roy Wilkins, among others, at Shady Grove Baptist Church in Kelly Settlement.

Within days, a committee inspired by county and city officials and organized by the Hattiesburg Chamber of Commerce met with the five older Dahmer sons to plan construction of a new four-room house on the same land. Materials and labor were being donated and money contributed. The NAACP would have coordinated the rebuilding, but Jewell "chose the Chamber of Commerce so maybe this would bring unity into Hattiesburg."[19]

Testimony against Sam Bowers by an FBI informant in the Klan attributed the following statement to Bowers five days after the firebombing: "Well, what do you think of what my boys did to that Dahmer nigger for me—it's sure going to take the pressure off me in Washington."[20] Bowers was wrong about that. His scheduled appearance before the House Un-American Activities Committee went on as scheduled on February 1.

Bowers took the Fifth Amendment again and again, in the best tradition of the committee's witnesses.[21] He was also wrong if he thought the Civil Rights Division and the FBI would sit back and accept his having assembled and dispatched the assassins of Vernon Dahmer. Ultimately, he was even wrong about the state of Mississippi and its Forrest County prosecutors.

The federal government moved first, but its prosecutions resulted in hung juries. The state cases were tried separately, so that in one prosecution after another Billy Joe Pitts testified as to the planning and the raid and Jewell Dahmer as to the attack and the loss of her husband.

Three Klansmen, Sessum, Smith, and Wilson, were convicted of murder and sentenced to life imprisonment at Parchman penitentiary. Sessum and Smith were paroled in ten years. Wilson's sentence was commuted in seven by his defense attorney, William Waller, who had been elected governor. But the three were probably the first white men ever convicted in a Mississippi state court for a civil rights killing.

A jury took only twelve minutes to find Lawrence Byrd, the Klan "senator" for Jones County, guilty of arson.[22] He was sentenced to ten years but paroled in twenty-two months. In general, where a wife testified that her accused husband was home with her in their double bed, there was a hung jury.

The state tried Sam Bowers first for arson in May 1968. His alibi was having been with his mother in Jackson the night of the raid. The all-white jury was 11–1 for conviction. His first murder prosecution was in January 1969. Two blacks, a retired railroad worker and a beautician, were on the jury which stood 10–2 for conviction when it was discharged.

In late April, before the second state murder prosecution, a federal conspiracy trial took place before U.S. District Judge Dan Russell in Meridian. It occurred in the very courtroom where Bowers had been convicted in October 1967, the original indictments having been restored by the Supreme Court, of conspiring to violate the civil rights—by murder—of Schwerner, Goodman, and Chaney. This all-white jury, equally divided between men and women, acquitted three Klansmen and deadlocked as to the rest, Bowers included. The second hung murder jury was in July. Bowers was out of those woods—or was he?

On February 5, 1994, Byron De La Beckwith was convicted of the murder of Medgar Evers in the long-awaited third trial, thirty-one years after that vicious assassination.[23] At least one person ran to Evers's statue at the Medgar Evers Library on Medgar Evers Boulevard in Jackson on hearing the verdict. Would there be an opportunity for someone to run to the Vernon F. Dahmer Memorial in the Vernon F. Dahmer Memorial Park in Hattiesburg should Sam Bowers be convicted in his third murder trial? The case was reopened by Forrest County district attorney Glenn White.

But White lacked the trial transcript that Myrlie Evers, Medgar's widow, had provided the Hinds County DA and any equivalent for the still available murder rifle that the father-in-law of the Hinds County assistant district attorney, a county judge, had inexplicably brought home after the second Beckwith trial. Both of these had helped to convict Beckwith. Most of all, White lacked Billy Roy Pitts, who, he said, contacted a federal agent when the case was reopened and said he did not want to testify.

Sam Bowers, unlike his ally Beckwith, had maintained a low profile for decades. But if you drove north on Laurel's 16th Avenue, not far from Faithwalk Church or Masonite Road, you would find, right next to Magic Tunnel Jr. Carwash, Sam Bowers eating his lunch at Wendy's.

A biracial committee formed February 8, co-chaired by Douglas Baker, who, as an Ole Miss student twenty-eight years before, wrote that moving letter about Dahmer to the *Hattiesburg American*. The committee explored ways to mount community pressure, and the FBI was helping White. Vernon Dahmer was belatedly receiving some of the recognition his generous, constructive life of leadership always merited.

When Byron De La Beckwith was finally convicted of the 1963 slaying of Medgar Evers, many were asked to comment. What implications might there be for the renewed prosecution of Sam Bowers for the firebombing that had cost Dahmer his life? Yet there was something odd. Few commenting in and around Hattiesburg mentioned Bowers by name. Was this scrupulous concern for the rights of the one-time imperial wizard? Or was it awareness that Bowers was no loose cannon like his friend "Delay," and a fear of retribution from the man from Laurel?

Newly elected district attorney Lindsay Carter took over the murder investigation in 1997. Bowers also was under state investigation on allegations he took part in an illegal gambling operation at his Sambo Amusement business. On January 17, 1998, published reports revealed that Billy Roy Pitts, one of the Klansmen convicted in Dahmer's murder, had never served any of his life sentence. State corrections officials issued a warrant for his arrest.

On February 9, Pitts surrendered to Forrest County authorities. By now fifty-four, he would again be the key witness against Bowers. On February 18, investigators found a transcript from previous murder trials that could be used in a new prosecution. On March 12, notes from FBI files obtained by investigative reporter Jerry Mitchell of the *Jackson Clarion-Ledger*, the leader in bringing to justice the perpetrators of the civil rights crimes of the sixties,[24] revealed that Bowers told an FBI informant that he had tampered with a jury to ensure he never went to state prison in Dahmer's death.

On May 28, Bowers, Devours Nix, and Charles Noble were charged in the Dahmer case. On August 17, Bowers's trial began in Hattiesburg before a jury of six whites, five blacks, and one Asian American. On August 21, as the Dahmer family watched from the balcony, Bowers was convicted of arson and murder and ordered to prison, where he died in 2006.[25] Curtis Wilkie, writing for the *Boston Globe*, called the verdict "the latest chapter in a remarkable ritual of atonement in Mississippi."[26] Vernon Dahmer, Jr., declared: "This is a new Mississippi. I came back home to be with my people, black and white. Mississippi has good people."[27]

A New Life in Chicago

It was a significant step in David Roberson's life when he testified for the United States against his county's registrar of voters both in March 1962 and at the contempt trial in September. He then left Hattiesburg for Ithaca, New York, to become a graduate student at Cornell University on a National Science Foundation Fellowship. From Cornell, David moved on to a successful high school teaching career in Chicago.

On a raw blustery day thirty-three years later David Roberson and I drove along Chicago's Lakeshore Boulevard as Lake Michigan's waves literally crashed ten feet in the air. David had picked me up at a conference at which I was speaking. We drove to his favorite restaurant in the city's Hyde Park section, within sight of the University of Chicago campus.

I gave him a set of the pictures I had taken when Stephanie and I visited his native Nichburg, Alabama, the preceding year. He had obviously made the correct decision when he had followed his younger brother Lloyd to teach in the Chicago public schools. I had seen firsthand his rapport with his students when I visited his classroom at Roberto Clemente Community Academy. But it was far more than that, or his union activity. It was Chicago's two classical music stations, his nearby tennis club, and the Argonne National Lab where he would continue to serve as a guide after retiring after thirty-eight years at the end of the school year. He had outgrown Hattiesburg before he had ever left it. His son, who had spent two years at David's alma mater, Alcorn, was making the military a career and serving a three-year stint in Okinawa. David, divorced, remained a regular at the family's annual Thanksgiving get-together in Moss Point, Mississippi.

"He Spread Himself Thin in a Lot of Ways"

Years after the trial, Roberson's friend, Chuck Lewis moved from teaching at Hattiesburg's black high school to administration in the nominally integrated citywide system. He was in charge of testing for the whole city system and then headed adult education programs. In 1982, Jackie Hosey Dedeaux, then a student at William Carey College in Hattiesburg, had a summer job working for Lewis as he coordinated GED programs for the Hattiesburg school system. She found her boss "gregarious and full of life." He always kept her laughing, and she was well aware of his various girlfriends dropping by the office.[28]

Lewis should today be a senior statesman, one of the success stories of black Mississippi. Instead he died by his own hand in 1985. His friends were shocked. Addie Burger described Lewis to me as "a very scholastic type of person who just loved to study, particularly chemistry, but he lived by himself half a block from me. He had a lot of business activities too. He spread himself thin, you know, in a lot of ways."

One of those ways was buying two 18-wheel trucks, which he leased to Deep South Trucking. His old friends remained critical of his partners in that venture, Stegall suggesting Lewis was taken for a lot of money in a confidence scheme. Chuck Lewis died from self-inflicted gunshot wounds early in the morning of January 18, 1985.

"I KNEW WHERE I STOOD"

Reverend Taylor was suffering from glaucoma when I last talked with him. His reading was limited, and he was within a month of his seventy-sixth birthday. He had built up Central Methodist Church in Jackson, the largest church in the conference, after completing his six-year stint as superintendent for the Laurel district in 1963. After he retired from Central Methodist in 1978, he had served as campus minister for the Wesley Foundation of the United Methodist Church, was Tougaloo College's chaplain for a semester, and often preached there.

In my lifetime, the most significant thing was the Civil Rights Revolution. It was a revolution. Since that time, things have moved a little bit slowly. It might be at this point one step forward, two backwards. But I do think that it liberated not only the black man, but the white man in the south—to a large extent, liberation for two people. The black man came to understand that he was human, had rights, that he was a person who could perform effectively and efficiently, given the opportunity. He knew it all the time, to a certain extent, but didn't know the extent. But he learned during the civil rights movement.

The white man began to understand that so much of what he had conceived to be truth was myth. And he was liberated from that, from the fears which he had of black people being not human. He was liberated from that. In the words that Frederick Douglass spoke over a century ago, you can't keep a man down in the ditch unless you hold him down. I think the south has learned that. I don't think the nation has learned it, altogether, though.

See, I lived in the north for four years. I came back from New York convinced in my own heart and mind that the hope for liberation for black people was much better in the south than in New York City. I had experienced in what was New York City society, the Mayor's Committee on Alternative Care of Children, meetings where I had all the amenities and politeness accorded to me. I'd have them call me Mr. Taylor, very courteous.

But when it came to actualities, the agencies which I represented could not get the kind of consideration that white agencies did not even have to ask for—even though I was called "Mister." In the south I might have been called "Boy," but I knew where I stood.

"Turnaround"

When I returned to Mississippi and made the first of my visits to Eloise Hopson, she was already the only surviving child in her family. Her two younger brothers had been murdered in Cleveland and Philadelphia, respectively, where they lived. With the help of the Fifth Circuit, she became registered to vote and voted regularly in every election.

Looking back after thirty-plus years, Miss Hopson spoke of society's changes:

I'll give you an example of turnaround. In the late fifties, I had a television repaired at a place downtown. When I went to pick it up, the owner said, "Drive around in front, and I'll have a repairman put the television in your car." Well, you had parking on both sides, and there was a line of cars in front of the store. I couldn't get directly in front because there was another car double-parked. I pulled up behind this one that was double-parked so the man could bring my television out. A policeman gave me one good tongue-lashing about double-parking, and talked to me so ugly and mean, I thought any minute he was going to hit me with that night stick. I was wrong, of course, but while he was standing there, giving me a tongue-lashing, this white woman walked out of the store and was getting in the car double-parked right in front of me. He tipped his cap and said, "Good mornin', Ma'am." That different kind of behavior wouldn't happen anymore.

Recently, I rushed to get across an intersection, but the light changed really before I got into the intersection. Usually, if somebody's already accelerated and in the intersection, another driver will wait and let you through. But the minute that green light flashed on, a truck started out. I had to slam my brakes to avoid the collision. Well, I didn't see the policeman, but he saw me. By the time I'd gone a block and a half, he pulled up beside me and asked me what happened. I admitted that I was in the wrong. He said, "Did you see the caution light?" I said, "Yes, I saw it, and I was trying to get away, so I wouldn't have to wait on the red light." So he lectured me about that was dangerous, and the caution light was there to let me know to stop because the light was soon going to change. We talked real nice, and he said, "By the way, Ma'am, do you know you were driving with an expired sticker?" I said, "Oh, my goodness, I surely am. I've got it right in the glove compartment. I just forgot to put it on." I got it out, and he said, "Would you like me to put it on for you?" I said, "I surely would. I'd appreciate that." But I have known the time a policeman would have ticketed me for no other reason than because I was black.

We now have some black police officers here in Hattiesburg. Forrest County has a black county supervisor, James Boykin. I taught the chairman of our city school board, who is black, James DuPree. We have black councilmen and members of the school board. Some black women are holding important positions in the Hattiesburg school system: assistant principals in junior high schools and the principal of an elementary school. The assistant superintendent of the Hattiesburg Public Schools is a black man. So there is more opportunity, and the residential patterns are changing. We have open housing now. There are maybe one or two exclusive areas where they have put up archways, you know, and there are no blacks in there. But I think it's financial because you can't legally have an area where blacks can't buy.

Eloise described to me a talk by Charles Evers at Mississippi Southern:

Charles Evers is a real comical speaker. He said, "One thing you white folks got to learn, and that is, as soon as a black buys out in your area, you get ready to move. And you run right out in the country. And when you get out there, there we are because we've been out there all the time." It brought the house down.

Eloise took early retirement at the age of sixty, but led an active life. During the school year she had about eighteen private piano students, as well as adult students year round. She belonged to several business clubs, and to the Delta Sigma Theta sorority. At her church she taught Sunday School, sang in the sanctuary choir and directed the youth choir. She had been a member of the United Methodist Women, not just in Hattiesburg, but in the Core Planning Group for the Southeastern Jurisdiction.

A life member of the NAACP since the early sixties, she remained in touch with the national scene, and visited her South Carolina students living in Philadelphia. She told me: "I was a happy teacher; students liked me because I liked them, too. I believe you are successful if you're doing what you like to do."

In her final years, Ms. Hopson suffered a stroke and Alzheimer's Disease, needing a companion. As Alzheimer's progressed, the feisty irreverent qualities of the woman who went to Jackson to testify and later laughed at Theron Lynd were replaced by a sweet gentleness. She surely knew me, I wanted to believe, but Penton Street where she lived no longer seemed the same.

On April 5, 1999, friends, church members, and her former students gathered at her beloved St. Paul United Methodist Church. Hymns she had sung: "O, How I Love Jesus," "Jesus Is All the World to Me," and "There's Something About that Name" were sung for her prior to burial back in her hometown of Enterprise.

T. F. WILLIAMS: IN RETIREMENT

Despite the Voting Rights Act, Theron Lynd continued as circuit clerk until his death at the age of fifty-seven in 1978. T. F. Williams described Lynd's successor to me:

> You got Ms. Brown up there now as Registrar. Believe it or not, I hold voter registration at my church, Priest Creek Baptist Church. Black History Month—we hold voter registration, catch all the children coming up 18 years old. And I got over one hundred applications. We go to the church and make them out, and I take people to her office, and she signs them in.

Marian Brown, a self-described "little country girl" from Yazoo County in the Delta, came to work for Lynd two months after our March 1962 trial. She was a thirty-two-year-old apolitical innocent, the mother of three sets of twins, a resident of Forrest County for only seven years, and had never herself registered to vote until being hired as deputy circuit clerk.[29] There wasn't much competition for the job with Lynd under Justice Department siege. She loved the job, learned from and was loyal to Lynd, and succeeded him after his death.

Mrs. Brown was no radical. She employed two of her daughters and had no black employee. But she understood, aided by the Voting Rights Act, that race no longer could be a barrier to voting. She not only gave T. F. the registration forms he took to Priest Creek Baptist Church, she appointed T. F. to a committee to work out the details when there was a reregistration. Mrs. Brown also complied with a request of the local NAACP by opening her office, not just on the two required Saturdays before the next election, but till 7 P.M. two or three nights a week. Theron Lynd's punctual closing of the office on the dot of 5:00 in the face of black applicants was no more.

Hercules records reflected T. F.'s advance through the ranks, the second or third black to crack the white man's jobs at the Hattiesburg plant. Nine months after he testified in Jackson, he was made an electric craneman. His improved performance was officially praised. In 1973, T. F. became a mill room relief operator. In 1979, the year before his retirement, a job evaluation noted that he excelled at quantity of work, job knowledge, and attendance. When T. F. retired, as a mill room operator, it was apparent to all who knew him that this hard-working, intelligent man richly deserved the status, the praise, and the $7.13 an hour he had attained.

But T. F. did not retire from civic life. He became president of the Francis Street Apartments, a subsidized housing development at Martin Luther King Drive. He was also president of the water association, a nonprofit organization made necessary when Hattiesburg mayor Bobby L. Chain, whom Williams called "the great segregator," left Palmer's Crossing out of the Hattiesburg water district. "I got a professor and a preacher, and we organized. The federal government let us have $260,000, and we got a water system in here. Now I'm buying water from the city."

U.S. district judge Dan Russell, who handled the Forrest County school desegregation case, selected T. F. as one of three blacks to monitor issues such as busing and fairness in employment. Palmer's Crossing's sparkplug became appreciated far beyond Satchel Avenue.

"I Wanted My Freedoms, but Not at the Expense of My Children"

Willie Simpson's health was already failing when I talked to his wife and him in 1989. Chemistry may have been an impediment to Simpson's receiving his high school diploma, but there were no educational impediments for their five children. Willie recalled when Olivia, the baby of the family, was born on May 30, 1946:

I remember that, for the rest of my life. I couldn't hit that baseball that season until she was born. Then I busted it. I hit that ball so hard it went through that infield onto the outfield. Olivia went to Jackson State and Alcorn and is teaching high school in Yonkers, New York. She got her master's degree from State University of New York.

After my retirement, I had a stroke in 1985. But I'm glad that I tried to vote back then. Man, I wanted my freedoms, but not at the expense of my children. No. I've been just as happy as a lark. After baseball season, I enjoyed life from when I was small until I was grown. Because I adapted to what's what.

Willie Simpson died in 1990. He had adapted to what was what and that what came to include full citizenship.

A Different Judge in the Southern District of Mississippi

Judge Cox had shown both courage and recognition of the need for decorum in his presiding over the 1967 trial for the conspiracy-murders of Michael Schwerner, Andrew Goodman, and James Chaney,[30] but the 1970s moved on, he came closer and closer to going over the edge in his behavior. By 1977–1978 it had become pronounced.

If you wish to practice in a United States District Court, you must be admitted by that court as well. Membership in one's state bar is not enough. At one admission session a young white woman approached Judge Cox who asked what kind of legal work she would be doing. When she replied that she would be working for a civil rights organization, he said, "I won't admit you." It was the other judge in the Southern District who did later admit her.[31]

Henry Travillion Wingate, an African American, was a graduate of Grinnell College in Iowa and of Yale Law School who served both as a Mississippi assistant attorney general and as an Assistant United States Attorney. During one motion session in Judge Cox's courtroom, Wingate, who was about thirty at the time, inadvertently said something that annoyed the judge. "You nigger," the judge exclaimed. The courtroom grew still and tense, but Wingate, showing a maturity Cox rarely demonstrated on the bench, ignored Cox's comment and simply completed his motion argument.[32] Shortly after Cox took senior status, the same Henry Wingate, strongly supported by Senator Thad Cochran, was nominated to a newly created Southern District judgeship.

Not surprisingly, Judge Wingate understood the importance of the right to vote:

> [T]he disenfranchised is severed from the body politic and condemned to the lowest form of citizenship, where voiceless at the ballot box . . . [he] must sit idly by while others elect his civic leaders and while others choose the fiscal and governmental policies which will govern him and his family.[33]

From the Disfranchised to a Warden for Her Precinct

Addie Burger had not just testified against Theron Lynd, she had testified before the grand jury that failed to indict Luther Cox:

> Across town, we have a U.S.O. building that was built during World War II. The city bought it and restored it to its old ways and looks. It's named for my husband; N. R. Burger Building they call it. It's a kind of community center, with an auditorium and a stage where you can have all kinds of programs. It has a very spacious lobby in front, side rooms and is really nice.
>
> It was just too bad that we had to go through that. Now nobody thinks about it, you know, the right to vote. You just think everybody . . . I feel good about what I did in going back all those times to Theron Lynd and by going to testify in Jackson. It was breaking down a tradition, opening a way for those to come . . . you know, the black citizens of the city to a life that they should have been a part of . . . the civic life, the life of a town, as well as qualified to vote. The changes have led to having black representation on the council and in the courts, and the various boards. Rowan High School is a voting precinct for Ward 5, and I have been one of the wardens in charge of that precinct.

"It's Mr. Thigpen, It Ain't Boy"

Asked about changes in Forrest County, Willie Thigpen told me:

> The situation here in Forrest County now is 100% better in every way. Now you are recognized. I can't say how folks feel, but I know how they treat you. They treat you like you're a man. You walk in a store and get

in line. You don't have to step aside if a white man comes in. You get up to the counter, it's "Mr. Thigpen," it ain't "Boy."

Thigpen, by then a pipe fitter, retired from Hercules on a disability in 1973. He died of congestive heart failure twenty years later, survived by his wife, Iola. Through his efforts and those of his fellow workers and our other witnesses, Willie Thigpen had been a first-class citizen for thirty years.

CHAPTER 22

MISSISSIPPI TODAY

In the fall of 1963, we moved back to Boston just before President Kennedy's assassination, when I was appointed an Assistant U.S. Attorney for Massachusetts. I did not return to Mississippi until I began work on this book.

Shortly after leaving the Jackson airport in late June of 1989, I stopped at one of the multitude of Waffle House restaurants that populate the South. There I saw an African American man seated with his arm around a blonde white woman. Neither seemed to fear imminent attack. That was a quick jump start in my realization of how much Mississippi had changed in the intervening twenty-six years.

When I reached Hattiesburg, Eloise Hopson gave me a different example:

When I first came here, there was a garment manufacturing place called "Big Yank." Black women could not work there, except as maids. They couldn't work at the machines. And you know the reason, the white women said, "If you let the black women work there, we won't have anybody to babysit and do our housework." Therefore black women were not permitted to work there. They do now. And at the Dairy Queen today, there were five teenagers working. Three were black and two were white. That's a massive change since the civil rights days.

And the major factors were the employment provisions of Title VII of the Civil Rights Act of 1964 and the Voting Rights Act of 1965.

But a particular development unique to Mississippi occurred on April 1, 1982: the sale by the Hederman family of the *Clarion-Ledger*, the *Daily News*, the *Hattiesburg American*, and six weeklies to Gannett.[1] Until Rea Hederman became editor of the *Clarion-Ledger* prior to the sale, their papers were, as Gene Roberts and Hank Klibanoff put it, "vindictive, poorly written, and error-ridden. Their management of the news helped explain why Mississippi remained the most reactionary state in the South."[2] Without Gannett's implementing fairness in both staffing and news coverage, Mississippi could not have changed. Jerry Mitchell would not have worked for the older Hedermans.

As a visiting law professor at Ole Miss during 2000, I had the opportunity to teach students in both Legal Ethics and Civil Rights, and observed the slowly growing number of African American students. One of my white civil rights students told me of the minority scholarships being awarded by the private academy he attended that had been founded to avoid school integration.

While Stephanie and I were in Oxford, Nick Lott became the first African American elected to head the university student body. As at other schools in the Southeastern Athletic Conference (SEC), African Americans dominate the football, track, and basketball teams at Ole Miss.[3] There was no lack of enthusiasm among white supporters of Ole Miss football for the team's great African American running back, Deuce McAllister, who went on to star with the New Orleans Saints. "Deuce for Heisman" bumper stickers abounded on cars and pickup trucks throughout the area. Ole Miss has had African American head basketball coaches, and Mississippi State University took the additional step of hiring an African American as its head football coach.

The William Winter Institute for Racial Reconciliation at Ole Miss played a significant role in the healing process, with passage in 2006 of legislation directing the State Department of Education to teach civil and human rights education in the state's public schools, as well as creating the Mississippi Civil Rights Education Commission, a major accomplishment.[4] The Sunflower County Summer Freedom Project, which provides enrichment for African American children, has been conducted at Ole Miss.

In October 2007, more than four hundred gathered in front of the Tallahatchie County Courthouse where fifty-two years earlier the murderers of Emmett Till had been acquitted. A biracial commission deplored the "terrible miscarriage of justice" and expressed its "deep regret."[5]

A setback was the crushing electoral defeat in 2001 of a carefully worked-out proposed new state flag which retained the Confederate flag in a corner. The broad business and university support were not sufficient for the electorate. Forrest County voted 11,207–6,532 against the new flag, a vote approximating the white-black racial composition of the county.[6] I was reminded of what a newspaper editor told me when I set out to visit him in Sunflower County: "Don't forget, Gordon, six miles out of Oxford, you're back in Mississippi."

President George W. Bush's Civil Rights Division, staffed heavily from top to bottom with political appointees, maintained an interest in the state, filing a voting rights action against the black leader of Noxubee County for discriminating against whites.[7]

A special congressional election in the northern tier of the state in the spring of 2008 lessened the Republican grip on Mississippi's delegation in Washington. It was won by Travis Childers, a Democrat who stressed local issues and promised he would not be subservient to Speaker Nancy Pelosi,[8] and he was reelected that fall. A disproportionate number of blacks remain in the Delta-based congressional district of the Homeland Security chair, Democrat Bennie Thompson, the only African American in the delegation.

Mississippi continues to lead Alabama, and all other states, in the number of black officeholders. In the symbolism of change, what could have been more vivid than Ouida Barnett Atkins, daughter of Governor Ross Barnett, teaching at a predominantly black Jackson high school with SNCC leader Bob Moses; or one of the 2008 presidential debates, with the first African American nominee for president, being held at Ole Miss, where he could not have been a student forty-seven years earlier?

In a 2008 tribute to Bill Murphy, one of his own professors who had been driven out of the state in the early 1960s because of speaking up for respecting the law, Ole Miss law professor John Bradley wrote of "the politics of race" having made Murphy and others "whipping boys."

> *The political power of the reactionary group persisted unabated until the early 1970s when Governor William Waller, the first elected after the Voting Rights Act of 1965 took hold, eliminated the Sovereignty Commission and set a tone of moderation on race.*
>
> *Nowadays the rhetoric of the state and the University speak of having embraced enlightenment. Whether the conversion is superficial or real is not tested by good times but only will be answered with a crucible as severe as the test it failed with Bill Murphy.[9]*

My impression is that great opportunity exists for African Americans right up to, but not including the state's power structure. There are exceptions such as former Supreme Court justice Reuben Anderson, a partner in a major Jackson law firm and a significant player in corporate Mississippi.[10] More should come, in the state as a whole as they have in Hattiesburg, and, when that happens, we can look back to the early beginnings, to the brave black witnesses of Forrest County.

EPILOGUE

It was September 30, 2002, at the John F. Kennedy Presidential Library in Boston's Columbia Point, the night before James Meredith was to return triumphantly to Ole Miss to celebrate the fortieth anniversary of his integrating the Rebel campus.

But there was a moving celebration at the library as well. James Meredith, Burke Marshall, and John Doar were all speaking, with the C-SPAN cameras rolling.[1] Stephanie and I were there with Jim Groh, who had flown in from Arizona.

Doar described his initial confrontations with Governor Ross Barnett and Lieutenant Governor Paul Johnson as he attempted to enroll Meredith and his concern that more and more rednecks from all over the state and as far away as Alabama were converging on Ole Miss. Marshall called them "a rag tag mob of rioters."

The question period was half over when a white man in his early sixties, with white mustache and goatee and wearing a black sports shirt and jeans, reached the microphone. Don Byrd had driven up from Rhode Island where he then lived. He told the crowd that he had been one of those rednecks Doar was concerned about: a potential rioter against James Meredith in the fall of 1962.

Byrd was born near Mobile, Alabama, the oldest of seven children. He finished high school in Bay St. Louis, Mississippi, and then enlisted in the army in July 1958, serving in the military police in that racially tense time. Discharged in May 1961, Byrd hitched up Route 49 to Pearl River Junior College, then to Mississippi Southern where he studied journalism with a midwesterner, Frank Buckley, the department head.

James Meredith, unassuming and quiet though he really was, was viewed as a strident gadfly or opportunist. Even in the journalism department, some students wanted to go up to Oxford and "knock the nigger on the head." Byrd was the older guy in the group, and he had a car. He was not against joining in at Oxford. He, of course, did not know two would die there. But he just did not want to drive six hours and have his car shot up.

Then Buckley assigned Byrd to attend the contempt trial of Theron Lynd in Hattiesburg. Byrd likened John Doar in court to a High Noon lawman.

Standing in the crowded auditorium at the Kennedy Library forty years later, Byrd addressed Doar about what he felt at the voting rights trial Doar conducted in Hattiesburg at the federal courthouse.

> *I experienced an epiphany by going there. I had never, ever in my life understood what all the hoo-hah was about, and how you presented that case and bringing in those educated black people who qualified in every possible way to be able to vote and counterposing them with literally ignorant people who had no education and no ability to be able to understand the constitution of Mississippi, which was one of the things they had to be able to talk about. I experienced probably one of the most fundamental changes in my life by watching you do that . . . I came here tonight to thank you, sir.*

I will always remember the intensely focused look on John Doar's face as he listened to this unexpected tribute. NPR's Juan Williams, the lively moderator, asked John if he remembered the trial. Burke interjected, "Oh, yes," and John confirmed dryly that he had not forgotten *United States v. Lynd.*

John then spoke with deep eloquence about what had existed in Forrest County and that he and the young lawyers who worked with him had to teach the country:

> *that no matter how educated a black person was in Mississippi it was very unlikely that he would get a chance to vote, and, if you could breathe and you were white, you voted. That message over a four or five year period in case after case similar to the Hattiesburg case, helped to change the country until the Voting Rights Act of 1965 was passed and that really broke the back of the caste system in the South.*

That was why I had joined the Civil Rights Division—to help break the southern caste system. That was why I left for Mississippi on Friday afternoons.

ACKNOWLEDGMENTS

I had been a trial judge in Roxbury, Massachusetts, for five years when a little girl named Tiffany Moore died in gang crossfire. Motivated violence in my court's jurisdiction was more often becoming random. It seemed to me that if I were to continue as a judge, a break was necessary. The break I selected was participation in a New York University seminar on Fridays, "Race and Nationality in Modern America." I was the only nonacademic. That Humanities seminar, led by Professor David Reimers, led to my returning to Mississippi to visit my witnesses in *United States v. Theron Lynd.*

My friend, the Forrest County Youth Court judge Mike McPhail, helped locate the witnesses. Grants followed from the John F. Kennedy Library Foundation and the National Endowment for the Humanities. John Kramer, dean of Tulane Law School, just two hours from Hattiesburg, invited me to be a visiting professor there in 1991. State senator Patricia McGovern created legislation for unpaid judicial leaves of absence which made that possible, and I also spent both 2000 semesters at Ole Miss Law School. Sara Crafts transcribed the interview tapes, which are available at the Kennedy Library and, as to the women interviewed, at Radcliffe's Schlesinger Library. Gilbert F. Ganucheau and Richard E. Windhorst, Jr., clerks of the U.S. Court of Appeals for the Fifth Circuit, retrieved the Lynd files from storage, gave me duplicates, and provided pictures, some of which appear in this book.

Student assistants who also worked with me in court and assisted in my work on *Civil Rights Litigation: Cases and Perspectives* have been recognized in the prefaces to the first and second editions to that work. I had particular assistance on this book from Richard Link while I was at Tulane and Jon Seawright while at Ole Miss. I have also benefited from the editorial assistance of Andrew Szanton while writing the book and the guidance of Walter Biggins at the University Press of Mississippi. Ed Robin, John R. Bradley, Jr., Burnis Morris, Gay Polk-Payton, Charles Eagles, Betsy Eggert,

Josie Brown, Barbara Flannery, Matt Bush and CBS News helped in various ways.

I am grateful for the help of librarians at Tulane Law School, Ole Miss, the University of Southern Mississippi, and certainly New England Law Boston where I have been an adjunct professor for twenty-four years. Sue Roche, Caroline Young, and Phuong Doan of the New England law staff have been particularly helpful.

My wife of a half century, Stephanie Lang Martin, my personal librarian, has lived with me through both the events described in this book and their being made into this book. I owe her more than words can express.

GORDON A. MARTIN, JR.
March 2010

NOTES

ABBREVIATIONS USED IN SOURCE NOTES

John F. Kennedy Presidential Library, Boston, Mass.: JFK.
Lyndon B. Johnson Presidential Library, Austin, Tex.: LBJ.
McCain Library, University of Southern Mississippi, Hattiesburg, Miss.: USM.

PREFACE

1. See Adam Cohen, Editorial Observer, "The Supreme Court's Hostility to the Voting Rights Act: A peculiar assault on the power of Congress to protect basic rights," *New York Times*, May 13, 2009, A26.

2. *Yick Wo v. Hopkins*, 118 U.S. 356, 370 (1886).

3. 42 U.S.C. 1971. See Robert Mann, "In praise of mild reforms: The Civil Rights Act of 1957 paved the way for much more," *Boston Globe*, August 21, 2007, A11.

4. 42 U.S.C. 1973. Writing for the Supreme Court, June 22, 2009, Chief Justice Roberts stated: "The historic accomplishments of the Voting Rights Act are undeniable. When it was first passed, unconstitutional discrimination was rampant and the 'registration of voting-age whites ran roughly 50 percentage points or more ahead' of black registration in many covered States. [citations omitted] Today, the registration gap between white and black voters is in single digits in the covered States." *Northwest Austin Municipal Utility District No. One v. Holder*, 129 S. Ct. 2504, 2511.

5. *Poverty and Social Justice Challenges Facing the Nation*, John F. Kennedy Library Forum, February 8, 2009.

6. In a major magazine article, "The Kennedys Move In On Dixie: How the two brothers are planning to change the whole political climate of the South, by opening the ballot boxes to hundreds of thousand of Negroes," *Harper's*, May 1962, Louis E. Lomax chronicled the "unprecedented campaign."

7. *South Carolina v. Katzenbach*, 383 U.S. 301, 312 n. 13 (1966).

8. *Id.* at 308.

PROLOGUE

1. Interview with Vernon Dahmer, Jr., at the family home in Kelly Settlement, Forrest County, July 4, 1989.

2. *United States v. Theron Lynd* (S.D. Miss., January 20, 1965) *reversed because of the District Court's failure to find a pattern and practice of discrimination*, 349 F. 2d 785 (5th cir., June 16, 1965).

3. *McLaurin v. Oklahoma State Regents for Higher Education*, 339 U.S. 637 (1950); *Sweatt v. Painter*, 339 U.S. 629 (1950).

4. 347 U.S. 483 (1954) Richard Kluger's thorough account of all aspects of the case is *Simple Justice* (New York: Alfred A. Knopf, 1975).

5. Letter dated April 30, 1952, from Marshall to Assistant Attorney General James M. McInerney contained, along with two of the affidavits, in a notebook maintained by David Norman, when a young attorney in the Civil Rights Division, and provided to the author by Professor Brian Landsberg, McGeorge School of Law, University of the Pacific, also a longtime division lawyer.

CHAPTER 1

1. Strongly supported by Majority Leader Lyndon Johnson, Eastland became chairman of Judiciary in 1956 despite an effort to override his seniority by Senators Herbert Lehman of New York and Wayne Morse of Oregon. Transcript, James O. Eastland Oral History I, 2/19/71, by Joe B. Frantz, Internet Copy, LBJ, 3–4.

2. Neil R. McMillen, *Dark Journey: Black Mississippians in the Age of Jim Crow* (Urbana: University of Illinois Press, 1989), xiii.

3. James Franklin Barnes, "Negro Voting in Mississippi" (Master's thesis, University of Mississippi, 1955), 1, citing Jesse Thomas Wallace, *A History of the Negroes of Mississippi* (Clinton, MS, 1927), 8.

4. *Id.*, 4.

5. Hiram Revels (1870–1871) and Blanche K. Bruce (1875–1880).

6. McMillen, *Dark Journey, supra* n. 2 at 334 n. 45.

7. *Id.*, 41.

8. *Id.*

9. *Id.*, 42.

10. *Id.*, 46, quoting *Laurel Leader*, May 2, 1903.

11. McMillen, *Dark Journey, supra* n. 2 at 229.

12. *Id.*, 230.

13. Kathleen Woodruff Wickham, *The Role of the Clarion-Ledger in the Adoption of the 1982 Education Reform Act: Winning the Pulitzer Prize* (Lewiston, NY: Edwin Mellen Press, 2007), 9.

14. *Voting: 1961 United States Commission on Civil Rights Report 1*, 108. The commission had data for only sixty-nine of the state's eighty-two counties.

15. *Id.* at table 8, 272.

16. 347 U.S. 483 (1954).

17. See *Cooper v. Aaron*, 358 U.S. 1 (1958).

18. *Education: 1961 United States Commission on Civil Rights Report 2*, 58.

19. Barnes, master's thesis, *supra* n. 3 at 38–42. After World War I, the number of blacks registered in Forrest County was reportedly four. McMillen, *Dark Journey, supra* n. 2 at 46.

20. *Peay v. Cox*, 5th cir. no. 13,494, record, 9.

21. *Id.*, 10.

22. *Id.*, 4.

23. *United States v. Lynd*, S.D. Miss., trial on merits, April 1964, transcript, 215.

24. *Id.*, 16.

25. Interview with R. C. Jones at his home in Hattiesburg July 4, 1989.

26. Myrlie Evers-Williams and Manning Marable, eds., *The Autobiography of Medgar Evers: A Hero's Life and Legacy Revealed Through His Writings, Letters, and Speeches* (New York: Basic Civitas Books, 2005), 6–13. Evers became the NAACP's field secretary for the state later the same year.

27. Interview with Bill Minor at the state capitol in Jackson, November 1991. See Curtis Wilkie, "The Conscience of Mississippi: Bill Minor specializes in riling rascals and reactionaries," *Boston Globe*, April 1, 1997, D1, and Lawrence N. Strout, "Wilson F. (Bill) Minor and the *New Orleans Times-Picayune*," in David R. Davies, ed., *The Press and Race: Mississippi Journalists Confront the Movement* (Jackson: University Press of Mississippi, 2001), 209–231.

28. Minor interview. Sebe Dale should not be confused with his son, Sebe Dale, Jr., a respected longtime chancery judge who, beginning in 1979, held the same chancery judgeship that his uncle T. Price Dale once held.

29. *Peay*, record, 5.

30. Miss. Code §3226 (1942).

31. Miss. Code §3227 (1942).

32. Miss. Code §3228, 1162 (1942).

33. *Peay*, plaintiffs' brief, 16.

34. "Samuel H. Sibley: Senior Circuit Judge: Fifth Circuit," 33 *American Bar Association Journal* 313 (1947).

35. *Chapman v. King*, 154 F. 2d 460, 464 (5th cir.), cert. denied 327 U.S. 800 (1960).

36. 140 F. 2d 662, 666 (5th cir. 1944), reversed 325 U.S. 91 (1945).

37. Harvey C. Couch, *A History of the Fifth Circuit 1891–1981* (The Bicentennial Committee of the Judicial Conference of the United States, 1984), 69.

38. John Brown, "Hail to the Chief: Hutcheson, the Judge," 38 *Tex. L. Rev.* 140, 142–143 (1959).

39. Author interview with Judge Tuttle in his chambers in Atlanta, December 1991.

40. *Peay v. Cox*, 190 F. 2d 123, 125 (5th cir.) cert. denied 342 U.S. 896 (1951).

41. *Id.*, 126.

42. The materials provided me dealt not with Forrest County, but rather Greenwood in Leflore County. My most important work there followed the February 28, 1963, shooting of SNCC worker Jimmie Travis, a Tougaloo College student and former Freedom Rider. An important voter registration drive had commenced in the county. Not only had Travis been wounded while driving nearby, the county board of supervisors had cut off surplus food distribution as a form of retaliation. Four of us from the division, Nick Flannery, Jim Groh, John Martin (not a relative), and I, divided up the homes of the county's black residents and started in separate directions, knocking on doors, documenting how little food black families had on hand and how soon they would go hungry if food distribution did not resume. Our report convinced the Department of Agriculture to resume the program by taking over its entire cost. I was asked to prepare a draft answer for President Kennedy should he be asked about Greenwood at his next press conference.

43. "The state that couldn't spy right," *Boston Globe*, September 21, 1997, D3.

44. Yasuhiro Katagiri, *The Mississippi State Sovereignty Commission* (Jackson: University Press of Mississippi, 2001).

45. *Id.*, xxviii–xxix.

46. J. Todd Moye, *Let the People Decide: Black Freedom and White Resistance Movements in Sunflower County, Mississippi, 1945–1986* (Chapel Hill: University of North Carolina Press, 2004), 59–61. Katagiri, *supra* n. 44 at xxix. Governor Barnett later named Brady to the state supreme court. "Barnett Raises Racist to Top Court," *New York Times*, July 19, 1963.

47. Moye, *supra* n. 46 at 56–58. Interview with Minor in Jackson, December 1991. One indication of the national respect for Minor was his selection as the first recipient of the $25,000 John Chancellor Award for Excellence in Journalism by the Annenberg Public Policy Center at the University of Pennsylvania. "Names & Faces: Major award for Minor," *Boston Globe*, May 22, 1997, E2. See also Lawrence N. Strout, in *Press and Race, supra* n. 27 at 201–232.

48. Katagiri, *supra* n. 44 at 4–5.

49. *Id.*, 8.

50. Phil Stroupe, "State To Hire Secret Racial Investigators," *Jackson Daily News*, May 16, 1956, reviewed in the Eastland Collection, Special Collections, J. D. Williams Library, University of Mississippi, February 2007.

51. Katagiri, *supra* n. 44 at 36.

52. *American Civil Liberties Union v. Mabus (ACLU I)*, 719 F.Supp. 1345, 1348 (S.D. Miss. 1989).

53. Katagiri, *supra* n. 2 at 39. This was confirmed by Sovereignty Commission files, reviewed February 5, 2000, Mississippi State Archives, Jackson.

54. Katagiri, *supra* n. 44 at 38–42.

55. *Id.*, 19. See Caryl A. Cooper, "Percy Greene and the *Jackson Advocate*," in *Press and Race, supra* n. 27 at 55–83, and Gene Roberts and Hank Klibanoff, *The Race Beat: The Press, the Civil Rights Struggle, and the Awakening of a Nation* (New York: Knopf, 2007), 368–369.

56. David R. Davies and Judy Smith, "Jimmy Ward and the *Jackson Daily News*," in *Press and Race, supra* n. 27 at 88, quoting a January 28, 1990, retrospective by the *Clarion-Ledger*'s new owner.

57. Katagiri, *supra* n. 44 at 40–41.

58. Jay Driskell, "Amzie Moore: the Biographical Roots of the Civil Rights Movement in Mississippi," in Susan Glisson, ed., *The Human Tradition in the Civil Rights Movement* (Lanham, MD: Rowman and Littlefield, 2006), 138.

59. Various reports in Box 17480, Sovereignty Commission files.

60. *ACLU I, supra* n. 52 at 1349.

61. Oral History, 45, USM.

62. Sovereignty Commission file document 1-27-0-6-1-1-1 at 30, obtained from the University of Mississippi Law Center, May 1999.

63. David G. Sansing, *Making Haste Slowly: The Troubled History of Higher Education in Mississippi* (Jackson: University Press of Mississippi, 1990), 148; Nikki Davis Maute, "Black History Month: Black leader faced tough times," *Hattiesburg American*, February 3, 1991.

64. Sovereignty Commission files, document 1-27-0-6-1-1-1 at 30, obtained from the University of Mississippi Law Center, May 1999.

65. *Id.*

66. *Id.*, 31.

67. Sansing, *supra* n. 63 at 152.

68. Jerry Mitchell, "Records: Would-be student framed: Sovereignty Commission records detail the 1958 plan," *Jackson Clarion-Ledger*, September 9, 1991, 1A, 5A. In April 2006 Mitchell, the country's top civil rights investigative reporter during both of those decades, received a George Polk Award for his persistent reporting which led to a new state prosecution for the 1964 murders of civil rights workers Schwerner, Goodman, and Chaney.

69. *Id.*

70. Sansing, *supra* n. 63 at 152–153.

71. Mitchell, *supra* n. 68 at 5A.

72. Evers-Williams, *supra* n. 26 at 200.

73. Sansing, *supra* n. 63 at 153.

74. Evers-Williams, *supra* n. 26 at 183.

75. *Kennard v. State*, 128 So. 2d 572, 576 (1961).

76. UPI, "Court Rejects Kennard Plea: Leaves State Conviction Valid," *Jackson Daily News*, October 9, 1961, 1.

77. Sansing, *supra* n. 63 at 153; Evers-Williams, *supra* n. 26 at 273.

78. ACLU I, *supra* n. 52 at 1353.

79. Mitchell, *supra* n. 68. Mitchell's reporting has brought him more than twenty national awards and made him a Pulitzer finalist for beat reporting in 2006. Adam Liptak, "Pardon Unlikely for Civil Rights Advocate," *New York Times*, May 4, 2006; University of Southern Mississippi press release, *Clyde Kennard, Denied Admission to Southern Mississippi in 1950s, Exonerated in Forrest County Circuit Court*, May 18, 2006.

CHAPTER 2

1. John T. Elliff, *The United States Department of Justice and Individual Rights 1937–1962* (New York: Garland Publishing 1987), 546. Rogers was Herbert Brownell's deputy attorney general. In *Enforcing Civil Rights: Race Discrimination and the Department of Justice* (Lawrence: University Press of Kansas, 1997), Brian Landsberg relates the history of the division's first forty years.

2. John T. Elliff, "Aspects of Federal Civil Rights Enforcement: The Justice Department and the FBI, 1939–1964," V *Perspectives in American History* (Cambridge, MA, 1971), 605.

3. See Nancy J. Weiss, *Farewell to the Party of Lincoln: Black Politics in the Age of FDR* (Princeton: Princeton University Press, 1983). In 2005, the United States Senate formally apologized for its failure to have enacted anti-lynching legislation.

4. Elliff, "Aspects," *supra* n. 2 at 606–607.

5. Section 241 was a conspiracy statute that could be utilized to prosecute private individuals. The problem was that, as of the unit's creation, the unit found that legal authority for utilizing 241 was limited to slavery, fraud, and intimidation in connection with federal elections or federal witnesses, homestead cases, and free speech violations relating to a federal subject. Section 242 then provided misdemeanor sanctions (maximum confinement for one year and a maximum fine of one thousand dollars) for the willful deprivation "under color of any law, statute, ordinance, or custom . . . of any

rights, privileges or immunities secured or protected by the Constitution or laws of the United States."

6. See, e.g., Burton Hersh, *Bobby and Edgar: The Historic Face-off Between the Kennedys and J. Edgar Hoover that Transformed America* (New York: Carroll & Graf, 2007), 334.

7. Memorandum from Assistant Attorney General McInerney to Thurgood Marshall.

8. Memorandum from the U.S. Attorney to the Criminal Division dated February 4, 1953.

9. Memorandum from AAG Warren Olney III to the U.S. Attorney dated February 13, 1953.

10. I had observed in going about the Deep South the number of new schools for blacks built just after the *Brown* decision in a feeble attempt to make separate a little less unequal.

11. E.g., regarding one 1955 bill: "This purpose is a laudable one with which the Department of Justice is in full accord. Whether this particular measure should be enacted constitutes a question of policy concerning which the Department of Justice prefers to make no recommendation." Herbert Brownell, *Advising Ike* (Lawrence: University Press of Kansas, 1993), 88.

12. Elliff, "Aspects," *supra* n. 2 at 647.

13. *Id.*, 643, citing J. W. Anderson, *Eisenhower, Brownell, and the Congress: The Tangled Origins of the Civil Rights Bill of 1956–1957* (University, AL, 1964), 34.

14. *Id.*, 650.

15. Notes on interview, November 19, 1975, Scott Rafferty Papers, Box 1, 4, JFK. Rafferty's interviews were research for his senior thesis at Princeton.

16. See *Cooper v. Aaron*, 358 U.S. 1 (1958).

17. Robert A. Caro, *The Years of Lyndon Johnson: Master of the Senate* (New York: Knopf, 2002), 875. Caro provides an engrossing account of Lyndon Johnson's handling of this important legislation, 844–998.

18. *Id.*, 904.

19. *Id.*

20. *Id.*, 941.

21. The Reconstruction statutes, which are still of great significance, are dealt with in Roy L. Brooks, Gilbert Paul Carrasco, and Gordon A. Martin, Jr., *Civil Rights Litigation: Cases and Perspectives* (Durham: Carolina Academic Press, 1995), 727–728.

22. *Master of the Senate, supra* n. 17 at 950.

23. *Id.*, 974.

24. *Id.*, 988–989.

25. *Id.*, 985–987.

26. *Id.*, 996–997.

27. David A. Nichols, *A Matter of Justice: Eisenhower and the Beginning of the Civil Rights Revolution* (New York: Simon & Schuster, 2007), picture caption 8.

28. *Master of the Senate, supra* n. 17 at 997.

29. Elliff, *Department, supra* n. 1 at 546.

30. Wan J. Kim, *The Department of Justice's Civil Rights Division: A Historical Perspective as The Division Nears 50*, March 22, 2006, 3.

31. Interview, December 16, 1975, Scott Rafferty Papers, Box 1, 1, JFK.

32. Rafferty interview July 3, 1975, Box 1, 1.

33. *Id.*, 2.

34. Rafferty interview, November 19, 1975, Box 1, 3.

35. *Id.* Eisenhower had appointed what he considered to be six "moderates" to the Civil Rights Commission. However, Senator Eastland delayed their confirmation hearings for almost two months, presumably so they could not get started on their work. Mary Frances Berry, *And Justice for All* (New York: Knopf, 2009), 12–14, 22–23.

36. Rafferty's Caldwell interview, 2.

37. Interview with author, July 23, 1992.

38. Rafferty's Norman interview, 1.

39. Elliff, "Aspects," *supra* n. 2 at 670.

40. Notes of interview, December 16, 1975, Rafferty Papers, Box 1, 1.

41. Elliff, *Department, supra* n. 1 at 548.

42. Rafferty's Caldwell interview, 1.

43. Rafferty's Norman interview, 1.

44. Rafferty's Flannery interview, 1.

45. Rafferty's Putzel interview, 1.

46. *New York Times*, August 14, 1959, quoted in Brian K. Landsberg, *Free at last to vote: The Alabama Origins of the 1965 Voting Rights Act* (Lawrence: University Press of Kansas, 2007), 27.

47. Rafferty's Norman interview, 1.

48. See "Harold R. Tyler, 83, Lawyer and Former Federal Judge," *New York Times*, June 27, 2005, C21.

49. See http://goprincetontigers.ocsn.com/genrel/080100aaj.html (accessed April 7, 2003).

50. Interview with Doar by the author in New York, May 16, 2003.

51. Elliff, *Department, supra* n. 1 at 550.

52. Rafferty's Caldwell interview, 3.

53. Author's Doar interview.

54. Rafferty's Putzel interview, 1.

55. Rafferty's Caldwell interview, 2. Abby Ginzberg chronicled Doar's career well in her film *John Doar: Trailblazer for Justice* (Albany, CA: Ginzberg Video Productions, 2006). Most vivid is Doar's averting bloodshed in Jackson following the assassination of Medgar Evers when he moved out into the street between the police and demonstrators.

56. Rafferty's Norman interview, 1.

57. See Elliff, "Aspects," *supra* n. 2 at 651.

CHAPTER 3

1. Nancy Weiss, *Farewell to the Party of Lincoln: Black Politics in the Age of FDR* (Princeton: Princeton University Press, 1983).

2. Interview by Berl Bernhard, November 29, 1965, 11, JFK.

3. Interview by Anthony Lewis, December 4, 6, and 22, 1964, in *Robert Kennedy in His Own Words* (New York: Bantam Books, 1988), 69.

4. Remarks by Harris Wofford at the John F. Kennedy Library Forum, A Tribute to Sargent Shriver, December 12, 2005.

5. Bernhard interview, 30.

6. Mark Stern, *Calculating Visions: Kennedy, Johnson, and Civil Rights* (New Brunswick, NJ: Rutgers University Press, 1992), 26.

7. *Id.*

8. Folder 21, M. M. Roberts collection, USM.

9. Bernhard interview, 25.

10. Scott Stossel, *Sarge: The Life & Times of Sargent Shriver* (Washington: Smithsonian, 2004), 163–165.

11. Bernhard interview, 19.

12. "Swallowing the Elephant," *New York Times*, September 19, 2004, 11.

13. Lewis, *In His Own Words, supra* n. 3 at 70. Byron White, Kennedy's future deputy attorney general and member of the United States Supreme Court, later asked Wofford, jovially it appeared to Wofford, what he thought about Kennedy's call to the judge. Wofford replied: "'I fly out to Notre Dame once a week for my class, and I just had a whole class on the question: Should Bob Kennedy be disbarred because he called the judge in the King Case?' And White said, 'Well, what did you conclude?' . . . And I said, 'I thought it was unprofessional, but not enough to disbar him, but it was pretty bad.' And White said, 'Well, you'll be very pleased to hear that I'm the one who recommended to Bob that he call the judge.'" Interview of Wofford by Larry J. Hackman, February 3, 1969, 124, JFK. A slightly different account of the conversation appears in Wofford's *Of Kennedys & Kings: Making Sense of the Sixties* (Pittsburgh: University of Pittsburgh Press, 1992), 94.

14. Anthony Shriver, *Kennedy's Call to King*, JFK.

15. Interview of Harris Wofford by Larry J. Hackman, May 22, 1968, 77, JFK. Georgia State University historian Clifford M. Kuhn refers to Wofford's "various accounts" of the incident since 1965 and sets forth his own evaluation with useful footnotes. He stresses Vandiver's role with both Kennedys. "'There's a Footnote to History!' Memory and the History of Martin Luther King's October 1960 Arrest and Its Aftermath," 84 *Journal of American History* 583 (September 1997).

16. Theodore H. White, *The Making of the President 1960* (New York: Atheneum, 1961, Buccaneer edition), 350.

17. *Id.*

18. *Id.*, 387.

19. Transcript, *James O. Eastland Oral History*, Interview I, 2/19/71, by Joe B. Frantz, Internet Copy, 6, LBJ.

20. Douglas Martin, "Burke Marshall, a Key Strategist Of Civil Rights Policy, Dies at 80," *New York Times*, June 3, 2003, A1, C17.

21. Interview with author, November 10, 1989; interview with Anthony Lewis, June 13, 1964, 42, JFK; interview of Harris Wofford by Larry J. Hackman, February 3, 1969, 122, JFK. White was named to the United States Supreme Court by President Kennedy in 1962. Wofford, later president of Swarthmore College and Director of the Corporation for National and Community Service under President Clinton, scored a stunning victory for the United States Senate from Pennsylvania in a special election in 1991, defeating former governor and U.S. attorney general Richard Thornburgh. He was, however, defeated by Rick Santorum in the next general election.

22. Interview with T. H. Baker, U.T. Oral History Project, October 28, 1968, LBJ.

23. Bart Barnes, "Burke Marshall, 80, Dies; JFK's Civil Rights Enforcer," *Washington Post*, June 3, 2003, B6.

24. Wofford interview by Hackman, February 3, 1969, 122.

25. *Id.*, 123. At Robert Kennedy's assassination, distinguished political journalist

James Reston wrote: "In many ways the personal characteristics of Robert Kennedy were very much like the dominant characteristics of the American people. We are an ambitious, strenuous, combative, youthful, inconsistent, abrupt, moralistic, sports-loving, non-intellectual breed, and he was all these things. . . . He was a passionate and pugnacious man." "Washington: the Qualities of Robert Kennedy," *New York Times*, June 7, 1968 (op-ed).

26. Notes of interview, Scott Rafferty Papers, Box 1, 3, JFK.

27. Notes of interview, July 1, 1975, Scott Rafferty Papers, Box 1, 1, JFK. Not everyone was a Marshall fan. Richard H. King, reviewing Taylor Branch's *Parting the Waters*, made this harsh and, I believe, unfair comment: "Doar's work in the South was offset by his boss Burke Marshall's pedantic federalism and lack of constitutional imagination." *Journal of American History* (June 1990): 268.

28. Baker interview of Marshall.

29. Notes from Marshall interview, January 27, 1976, in New Haven, Scott Rafferty papers, 6, JFK.

30. *Id.*, 1.

CHAPTER 4

1. "Luther Cox Rites At 3 Sunday," *Hattiesburg American*, December 13, 1958, 1.

2. Elliott Chaze, *Hattiesburg American*, July 16, 1963, 1.

3. *Id.*

4. E.g., "Stanley Dalton Candidate for Circuit Clerk," *Hattiesburg American*, January 2, 1959, 1. The *American* carried the candidate announcements on its front pages between January 2 and January 6.

5. "Mrs. Autry is Candidate for Circuit Clerk," *Hattiesburg American*, January 3, 1959, 1.

6. *Hattiesburg American*, January 6, 1959.

CHAPTER 5

1. In his memoir, *Some of It Was Fun: Working with RFK and LBJ* (New York: Norton, 2008), 42, Nicholas Katzenbach says, "Bobby added some two hundred young and dedicated lawyers to the Civil Rights Division." The 100 mark was not reached, however, until 1965, the year after RFK left the department to run for the Senate, and there were not 200 till 1996. Brian K. Landsberg, *Enforcing Civil Rights: Race Discrimination and the Department of Justice* (Lawrence: University Press of Kansas, 1997), 78.

2. See two books by Howard Ball: *Murder in Mississippi: United States v. Price and the Struggle for Civil Rights* (Lawrence: University Press of Kansas, 2004) and *Justice in Mississippi: The Murder Trial of Edgar Ray Killen* (Lawrence: University Press of Kansas, 2006); James Dao, "The Town and the Accused: Indictment Makes Start at Lifting a 40-Year-old Cloud Over a Mississippi County," *New York Times*, January 8, 2005, A11.

3. Walter Lord, *The Past That Would Not Die* (New York: Harper & Row, 1965), 119.

4. In *The Race Beat: The Press, The Civil Rights Struggle, and the Awakening of a Nation* (New York: Knopf, 2006), 64, Gene Roberts and Hank Klibanoff describe Sitton as "a tenacious reporter who did his own legwork, who didn't rely on official sources, who reflexively felt the need to cover the same ground as investigators, and who trusted his own judgment to guide his articles."

5. V. O. Key, *Southern Politics in State and Nation* (New York: Knopf, 1949), 577.

6. When *Washington Post* reporter Robert E. Lee Baker visited Dawson in Terrell County, "he found a town where white authorities were brutalizing and terrorizing the Negro residents and systematically pulling trapdoors every time they came close to registering to vote." Roberts and Klibanoff, *supra* n. 4 at 197. In an informative memoir, the division's second assistant, St. John Barrett, discusses the first case brought under the 1957 Civil Rights Act, which was in Terrell County. *The Drive for Equality: A Personal History of Civil Rights Enforcement 1954–1965* (Baltimore: PublishAmerica, 2009), 30–37.

7. I first saw the attorney general at St. Matthew's Cathedral on a Catholic Holy Day as he was returning from receiving communion and I was approaching.

8. *New York Times*, July 15, 1962. Burke Marshall described the Albany situation as "frustrating" to President Kennedy: "They were imposing very rigid restraints on free speech. People were arrested as soon as they appeared on the streets with a picketing sign or anything. . . . The President said . . . it was not only that they didn't give them any rights to any fair treatment, but they wouldn't even let them complain about not having it." Anthony Lewis interview, June 13, 1964, 70, JFK.

9. George Newlin, ed., *Princeton Class of 1952, The Book of Our History, 1952–2002* (Hagerstown, MD: Reunion Press, 2002), 507.

10. *Id.*, 506–507.

11. *Class of 1952* (Princeton: Princeton University Press, 1964), 274.

12. Application in the possession of the author.

13. My greatest disappointment while in the division was our inability to protect the teaching position of Ernestine Talbert. She was a resident of George County and had attempted registration there. Her one-year contract in adjoining Greene County then was not renewed. Judge Rives was the only one of "The Four," the judges who changed the Fifth Circuit, sitting on the appeal after we lost in the district court. Concurring in the adverse holding, he found it undisputed that her being a witness in our voting discrimination case was at least one reason for her not being re-employed. But the panel believed that the trial judge's finding that we had not met our burden of showing that her dismissal was for the purpose of interfering with the right to vote was "not clearly erroneous," the standard on appellate review. *U.S. v. Board of Education of Greene County, Miss.*, 332 F. 2d 40 (5th cir., 1964). I described the voting situation in George County in "Southern Fear and Negro Voting," *Commonweal* 80, no. 5 (April 24, 1964), 135.

14. *United States v. Lynd*, 301 F. 2d 818, 821 (5th cir. April 10, 1962).

15. Interview with Judge Henderson in his chambers in San Francisco, July 27, 2007. His career was set forth in 2005 by Abby Ginzberg, Ginzberg Video Productions, Albany, CA, in a moving film, *Soul Of Justice: Thelton Henderson's American Journey*.

16. M. M. Roberts papers, M27, Box 6, Folder 11, USM.

17. *Id.*

18. Dean W. Colvard, *Mixed Emotions: As Racial Barriers Fell—A University President Remembers* (Danville, IL: Interstate Printers & Publishers, 1985), 16.

19. Walter Lord described our search, including my visit to the church; *supra* n. 3 at 125.

20. Also coming to Mississippi from the same seminary was Bernard F. Law, later archbishop of Boston and a cardinal, who was the courageous editor of the diocesan paper, *Mississippi Register*. See my article, "The Church in Mississippi," 100 *Ave Maria*, No. 24, December 12, 1964, and my op-ed, "A voice of courage in Mississippi," *Boston Globe*, January 27, 1984, 15.

21. Interview dated December 16, 1975, Scott Rafferty Papers, Box 1, JFK.

22. In his excellent account of the Kennedy Justice Department, Victor Navasky refers to this as "Interrogative Overkill." *Kennedy Justice* (New York: Atheneum, 1971), 102. It was still two years before the bureau would establish a major office in Mississippi.

23. Interview with former Special Agent Steinmeyer at his home in Kady, Texas, March 2000.

24. 93 *Cong. Rec.* 27–28 (daily ed., January 3, 1947), quoted in Brian K. Landsberg, *Free at Last to Vote: The Alabama Origins of the 1965 Voting Rights Act* (Lawrence: University Press of Kansas, 2007), 22.

CHAPTER 6

1. Strongly supported by Majority Leader Lyndon Johnson, Eastland became chairman of Judiciary in 1956 despite an effort to override his seniority by Senators Herbert Lehman of New York and Wayne Morse of Oregon. Transcript, *James O. Eastland Oral History I*, 2/19/71, by Joe B. Frantz, Internet Copy, LBJ, 3–4.

2. Interview by Anthony Lewis, December 4, 6, and 22, 1964, in *Robert Kennedy: In His Own Words* (New York: Bantam Books, 1988), 109.

3. Author interview in New Haven, November 10, 1989.

4. *Id.*

5. Victor S. Navasky, *Kennedy Justice* (New York: Atheneum, 1971), 250–251.

6. Kay Bray, "Cox Given Senate Okay for Federal Judgeship," *Jackson Clarion-Ledger*, June 28, 1961, discusses the pro forma confirmation hearing that followed; *Report of Proceedings before the United States Senate Committee on the Judiciary on the Nomination of William H. Cox*, June 27, 1961.

7. See generally, Marie M. Hemphill, *Fevers, Floods and Faith: A History of Sunflower County, Mississippi, 1844–1976* (Indianola, 1980).

8. John Dollard, *Caste and Class in a Southern Town* (New Haven: Yale University Press, 1937; New York: Doubleday, 3d edition), 62.

9. Hortense Powdermaker, *After Freedom: A Cultural Study in the Deep South* (New York: Russell & Russell, reissued 1968), Appendix A.

My involvement in Sunflower County in November 1962 concerned voter education classes conducted in Ruleville during the summer by James Bevel of the Southern Christian Leadership Conference. The county's voting-age population then was 13,524 blacks and 8,785 whites. A substantial majority of the whites were registered, but only 114 Negroes.

SNCC workers, including Robert Moses and Charles McLaurin, arrived after the SCLC classes. Both groups taught voter education classes and accompanied black applicants to the courthouse. On August 30, six registration workers were arrested and charged with violating an ordinance by distributing without a permit leaflets about the classes and the registration process. Robert Moses was arrested the next day for distributing door to door a leaflet protesting the first six arrests.

My job was to assess the success of the registration attempts. Thirty-two blacks applied between August 14 and 21, but no one returned for their results. On November 26, Hattie Sisson, Irene Johnson, Ruby Davis, and Rebecca McDonald found Registrar Campbell in his office. Campbell registered all but Mrs. McDonald, who had only completed the fourth grade. Ida McIntosh also passed. However, Registrar Campbell told

McLaurin that Mrs. McIntosh asked that her name be removed. Sunflower blacks told me that the white woman for whom Mrs. McIntosh did domestic work brought her to the office for that purpose. Being registered did not cause Hattie Sisson to forget that her house had been shot into.

10. *Mississippi Lawyer*, July 1961, 6.

11. Navasky, *supra* n. 5 at 265. Rogers subsequently said that he rigorously screened prospective nominees well before sending them to Segal's (ABA) committee and that "the most useful role they played was a veto role. Senators viewed the appointments as political patronage jobs: We'd call Bernie, his committee would rate them unqualified, and then we'd call the senator and say, 'We can't get it past the ABA.'" Cynthia Mayer, "Heavy-Hitters: The Irrepressible Bernie Segal," *American Lawyer*, March 1984, 12–14.

12. Jack Bass, *Unlikely Heroes: The Dramatic Story of the Southern Judges Who Translated the Supreme Court's Brown Decision into a Revolution for Equality* (New York: Simon & Schuster, 1981), 85.

13. *Id.*

14. That traditional role was restored by President Obama. "The A.B.A. and Judicial Nominees," *New York Times* editorial, April 14, 2009, A20.

15. Jerome Corsi, *Judicial Politics: An Introduction* (Englewood Cliffs, NJ: Prentice-Hall 1984), 122; Herbert Brownell with John P. Burke, *Advising Ike: The Memoirs of Attorney General Herbert Brownell* (Lawrence: University Press of Kansas, 1993), 177.

16. *Id.*, 123.

17. Mayer, "Heavy-Hitters," *supra* n. 11 at 12.

18. "Oral Reply of Lawrence Walsh to the House of Delegates" at the 1959 ABA mid-year meeting in Chicago (mimeo.), 17, set forth in Joel Grossman, *Lawyers and Judges: The ABA and the Politics of Judicial Selection* (New York: Wiley, 1965), 94. Walsh and Senator Eastland exchanged effusive letters when Walsh left the Justice Department after Kennedy's election, Eastland writing February 9, 1961: "I have never been associated with any person anywhere whom I admire more than I do you." Department of Justice Attorney General 1960s File, Eastland Collection, Williams Library, University of Mississippi.

19. "Presidential Judicial Appointments—1961: Nominated and Confirmed," dated September 13, 1961, in William H. Orrick, Jr., Box 8, JFK.

20. Interview of Joseph F. Dolan, who coordinated the Kennedy administration's review of judicial recommendations within the Office of the Deputy Attorney General. Interviewer: Charles T. Morrissey, December 4, 1964, 74, JFK Oral History Program.

21. Interview of John Seigenthaler by Jack Bass, September 7, 1979, Tulane Law Library, Box 6, 19.

22. June 10, 1961, letter from Eastland to White, Cox File, Eastland Collection, Williams Library, University of Mississippi.

23. Thirteen years later, Jaworski would serve as special prosecutor during the Watergate scandal. A later committee chair, Robert Meserve, a distinguished Boston lawyer, told me he found it necessary to visit Cox in Jackson when he learned that Cox was denying black lawyers access to the normal lawyers' entrance to his courtroom.

24. Bass, *Unlikely Heroes, supra* n. 12 at 165.

25. The Fifth Circuit Court of Appeals Reorganization Act was approved by Congress October 14, 1980, and signed by President Carter a day later to be effective October 1, 1981. The Fifth Circuit was reduced to what has been called "an oil and gas circuit,"

Louisiana, Mississippi, and Texas, with Alabama, Florida, and Georgia forming a new Eleventh Circuit.

26. W. C. Shoemaker, "Decision Is Delayed In Negro Voter Suit," *Jackson Daily News*, August 26, 1961.

27. "U.S. Judge Halts 2 Voter Suits," *Commercial-Appeal*, August 26, 1961.

28. "Judge Considering Voter Suit Motion," *Jackson Daily News*, September 6, 1961. Gerald M. Stern, another division attorney, has written about his frustrations with Judge Cox, particularly as to Clarke County. "Mississippi," *Outside the Law: Narratives on Justice in America*, ed. Susan Richards Shreve and Porter Shreve (Boston: Beacon Press, 1998), 153–172.

29. "Justice Dept. Names Names in Forrest," *Jackson Daily News*, October 21, 1961.

30. "2 Negro Vote Suit Actions Dismissed," *Jackson Daily News*, January 18, 1962.

31. *Kennedy v. Lynd*, 306 F.2d 222, 225–226 (5th cir., July 11, 1962).

32. *Id.*, 227.

33. Attorney General's Papers, Box 17480, Folder 15, Mississippi State Archives.

34. Kenneth Toler, "'Riders' Refused U.S. Jurisdiction," *Commercial-Appeal*, August 27, 1961.

35. "Cox Sends Rider Suits Back to State Courts," *Jackson Daily News*, August 27, 1961, 1.

36. Anthony Lewis, "Negro Vote Drive Wins a Court Test," *New York Times*, October 31, 1961.

37. The facts are taken from the complaint and affidavits filed by the government. *United States v. Wood*, 295 F.2d 772 (5th cir., 1961).

38. 295 F.2d at 780.

39. 295 F.2d at 785 n. 1.

40. 295 F.2d at 774.

41. 295 F.2d at 784–785.

42. Lewis, "Negro Vote" *supra* n. 36; "U.S. Gets New Tool To Help Negroes Vote," *Washington Post*, October 31, 1961.

43. 295 F.2d at 789.

44. 295 F.2d at 788.

45. Telephone discussion with author January 8, 2009.

46. Michael R. Belknap, "The Vindication of Burke Marshall: The Southern Legal System and the Anti-Civil Rights Violence of the 1960s," 33 *Emory L. J.* 93, 112 (1984).

47. William Doyle, *An American Insurrection: The Battle of Oxford, Mississippi, 1962* (New York: Doubleday, 2001).

48. Robert Drew and ABC News, *Crisis: Behind a Presidential Commitment* (1963; dvd 2003).

CHAPTER 7

1. Stegall was also the first witness I interviewed when I returned to Mississippi to begin work on this book. I spoke with him at his home in Jackson on July 1, 1989, then the following morning at the Georgia Dawson Elementary School.

2. Discussion prior to John Doar receiving, on behalf of Civil Rights Division lawyers (1960–1967), the Humanitarian Award of the Choral Arts Society of Washington, D.C., at its annual concert in memory of Dr. King, January 11, 2009. Groh was later a law school professor and a United States magistrate judge.

3. Letter to the author dated July 14, 1990.

4. The great soprano Leontyne Price was born in Laurel. Her father worked in a saw-mill and her mother was the local midwife. "They must have been remarkable parents, considering the accomplishments of their two children: Ms. Price, and her younger brother George, who became a brigadier general in the army." Anthony Tommasini (music critic), "Aida Takes Her Story to Harlem: Leontyne Price Reads Her Book and Sings for Schoolchildren," *New York Times*, May 30, 2000, first arts page.

5. 347 U.S. 483.

6. 349 U.S. 294, 301.

7. The comparable recollection of the mural by civil rights lawyer Len Holt in 1964 is set forth in Howard Ball, *Murder in Mississippi: United States v. Price and the Struggle for Civil Rights* (Lawrence: University Press of Kansas, 2004), 119. The mural was still there, but covered by drapes, during a 2007 civil rights prosecution. Harry N. MacLean, *The Past Is Never Dead: The Trial of James Ford Seale and Mississippi's Struggle for Redemption* (New York: Basic Civitas, 2009), 26–27.

8. We in the Civil Rights Division addressed Stegall as "Mr. Stegall," but just as he was one of the "boys" to Theron Lynd, he was "Jesse" in the condescending words of Dugas Shands.

CHAPTER 8

1. Interview with author, October 1991.

2. Bob Pittman, "Capitolizations: Shands Stands Between State and Integration," *Jackson Daily News*, August 13, 1961.

3. Michael De L. Landon, *The University of Mississippi School of Law: A Sesquicentennial History* (Jackson: University Press of Mississippi, 2006), 63.

4. *Id.* at 34.

5. *Id.* at 43.

6. *Id.* at 41.

7. See Jack Greenberg, *Crusaders in the Courts: How a Dedicated Band of Lawyers Fought for the Civil Rights Revolution* (New York: Basic Books, 1994), 318–332.

8. In his chapter "The Warrior," particularly at 34–36, William Doyle summarizes the ebbs and flows of *Meredith v. Fair. An American Insurrection: The Battle of Oxford, Mississippi, 1962* (New York: Doubleday, 2001).

9. *United States v. Ramsey*, United States Court of Appeals, 5th cir., Docket No. 20596, 143.

10. *Id.* at 86.

11. "Vote Witness Is Qualified," *Jackson Clarion-Ledger*, December 21, 1961.

12. John Doar, "Remembering Dr. Martin Luther King," *Taconic Newspapers*, NY, January 11, 1989.

13. *Id.*

14. *Id.*

15. Telephone interview with Robert Kegler, September 8, 2000. See 2009 Year End Report, Civil Rights and Restorative Justice Project, Northeastern University School of Law.

16. Letter dated June 16, 1962, M. M. Roberts papers (USM).

17. Walter Lord, *The Past That Would Not Die* (New York: Harper & Row, 1965), 126.

18. Interviews with Judges Brown and Wisdom in New Orleans, fall 1991.

19. Roberts statement dated January 1, 1981, in his papers, USM.

20. Letter from Roberts to Mrs. Edgar M. Wachtel, June 27, 1980, USM.

21. Letter to Roberts captioned Golden Anniversary of Service G. C. A. H. S., June 15, 1974, USM.

22. Letter from Roberts to Walter Washington, President, Alcorn A&M College, April 27, 1972, Box 3, USM.

23. 1926 Ole Miss Annual, 51.

24. Letter from Roberts to Charles Thurman, October 23, 1965, USM.

25. Dean W. Colvard, *Mixed Emotions: As Racial Barriers Fall—a University President Remembers* (Danville, IL: Interstate Printers & Publishers, 1985), 69; Alexander Wolff, "Ghosts of Mississippi," *Sports Illustrated*, March 10, 2003, 60.

26. Eugene Robinson, "Good Bet on Biloxi," *Washington Post*, January 17, 2006, A17.

27. Wallace Dabbs, "It's hard to believe that at one time Buena Vista Hotel was Coast Magnet," *Jackson Clarion-Ledger*, February 9, 2000, 11A.

28. Conversation in Oxford, Mississippi, January 2000.

29. Law School History, *supra* n. 3 at 60, 96.

30. Letter to the Mississippi Sovereignty Commission, November 29, 1963, USM.

31. Colvard, *Mixed Emotions*, *supra* n. 24 at 82–83, Appendix D; Bill Simpson, "*Board Votes In Favor Of Playing In Tourney: Trustees Stand Behind Colvard By 8–3 Tally*," *Jackson Clarion-Ledger*, March 10, 1963, 1.

32. Colvard, *Mixed Emotions*, 93.

33. *Id.*, 69.

34. Law School History, *supra* n. 3 at 97–98.

35. *Id.*, 111.

36. *Id.*, 111, 119.

37. Letter to Cox, April 28, 1961, Cox file, Eastland Collection, Special Collections, J. D. Williams Library, University of Mississippi.

38. Letter to Lynd and Zachary, July 8, 1961, Folder 21, USM.

39. Letter to Lynd, July 20, 1961, Folder 21, USM.

40. Letter to Shands, August 22, 1961, Folder 21, USM.

41. Letter to Stockett, July 9, 1962, Folder 21, USM.

42. Folder 21, USM.

43. Investigative Report by Virgil Downing, December 13, 1962, 2-64-20, Sovereignty Commission files, Mississippi State Archives, Jackson.

44. Lord, *supra* n. 17 at 129.

CHAPTER 9

1. I interviewed Mrs. Burger at her home, 515 Martin Luther King Avenue, Hattiesburg, July 3, 1989, five years after the death of her husband.

2. Oral History of Nathaniel R. Burger, McCain Library, 3, USM.

3. *Id.*, 19.

4. *Id.*, 20, 22.

5. *Id.*, 39.

6. *Id.*, 36.

7. *Id.*, 53.

8. *Id.*, 25.

9. *Id.*, 45.

10. *Id.*, 38.

11. Ms. Sandifer less kindly called them "Bohemians," saying she saw some "weird happenings" as she walked through Washington Square. Oral History of Iva E. Sandifer, McCain Library, USM, 7.

CHAPTER 10

1. David Roberson was the first witness I visited when I commenced work on this book, seeing him in Chicago in late June 1989.

2. Nadine Cohodas, *The Band Played Dixie: Race and the Liberal Conscience at Ole Miss* (New York: Free Press, 1997), 17–18, traces Alcorn's history, as does the Alcorn State University Web site.

3. *Id.* at 18.

4. *Id.*

5. Mississippi State and Alcorn State University Web sites.

6. Interview with author in Jackson, August 31, 1993.

7. *Id.*

8. Interview with Ms. McLaurin at her newsstand, August 31, 1993.

9. © Columbia Broadcasting System, Inc., all rights reserved; originally broadcast on CBS Reports on September 26, 1962, over the CBS Television Network. Distributed by Films for the Humanities and Sciences.

CHAPTER 11

1. On Sunday, July 2, 1989, I drove from Jackson to Hattiesburg for the first of the number of post-trial visits to Eloise Hopson at her home on Penton Street. At seventy-four she was still vigorous and blunt. Soon she was sharing her Sunday dinner with me, the details of years before still vivid in her mind.

2. Discussion with Ms. Polk-Payton in 2000 at Ole Miss, where she was assistant dean of students at the Law School.

CHAPTER 12

1. Davis Dyer and David B. Sicilia, *Labors of a Modern Hercules: The Evolution of a Chemical Company* (Boston: Harvard Business School Press, 1990), opp. 27. This company history sets out well the background of the litigation as well as Hercules's growth.

2. *Id.*, 41.

3. *Id.*, 29.

4. *Id.*, 42.

5. *Id.*, 139–140.

6. *Id.*, 108. I interviewed Mr. Babcock May 24, 1990.

7. Dunagin provided me with his prepared remarks.

8. Davis and Sicilia, *supra* n. 1 at 331, quoting *Forbes* magazine.

9. We visited Dunagin in March 1990.

10. Charles Dunagin, "Good heart under a tough skin," McComb (Miss.) *Enterprise-Journal*, June 11, 2000, 2.

11. *Id.*

12. *Id.*

13. *Id.*

14. Stanley Nelson, "The night Wharlest Jackson was murdered—Feb. 27, 1967," Concordia (La.) *Sentinel*, June 5, 2008.

CHAPTER 13

1. M. M. Roberts papers, M27, Box 6, Folder 11, USM.

2. I interviewed Sherman Jackson, Jr., at his home in Jackson, October 29, 1991.

3. Author interview at Mosley's home in Hattiesburg.

4. Author interview at Boyd's home in Hattiesburg.

5. *Id.*

6. Transcript, 904–905.

7. *Id.*, 905–906.

8. *Id.*, 912.

9. *Id.*, 913.

10. In May 1990, I reviewed the personnel files of the Hercules workers who were witnesses at this hearing at Hercules corporate headquarters in Wilmington, Delaware.

11. I interviewed Mosley at his home at 1109 Vernon Street, Hattiesburg, in 1989.

12. In February 2007 a state manslaughter indictment was sought against Carolyn Bryant Donham, the woman whom Till supposedly whistled at, but the grand jury did not indict. Her husband and his half-brother had been acquitted of Till's murder by an all-white jury in 1955, though they later bragged about the crime in a *Look* Magazine interview. Jack Elliott, Jr., and Allen G. Breed, Associated Press, "No indictment issued in 1955 slaying of Emmett Till," *Boston Globe*, February 28, 2007, A4.

13. Willie Simpson's health was already failing when I interviewed him and his wife at their home in Hattiesburg in 1989. Chemistry may have been an impediment to Simpson's receiving his high school diploma, but there were no educational impediments for their five children. Simpson died in 1990 with well-deserved pride in those children.

CHAPTER 15

1. Interview with Ms. McLaurin at her newsstand on Mobile Street, August 31, 1993.

2. Memorandum dated December 17, 1958, to Director, Sovereignty Commission from Zack J. VanLandingham re NAACP, Hattiesburg, Mississippi Integration Organization filed as NAACP Hattiesburg 2-70-3, Mississippi State Archives, Jackson.

3. *Id.*

4. Transcript, 827–833.

5. © Columbia Broadcasting System, Inc., all rights reserved; originally broadcast on CBS Reports on September 26, 1962, over the CBS Television Network.

6. The Boyds were interviewed December 17, 1991. Mr. Boyd died December 26, 2008, at his daughter's home in Camden, New Jersey, predeceased by his wife, who had become active in voter registration after the March 1962 trial. Tim Doherty, *Hattiesburg American*, "Voting-rights pioneer dead at 92," *Jackson Clarion-Ledger*, December 30, 2008, 8A.

7. I interviewed Mrs. Burger and Mr. Stegall at their homes in Hattiesburg and Jackson, respectively, in 1989.

8. Testimony in *United States v. Lynd*, U.S. Court of Appeals—Fifth Circuit, No. 19576, September 17–21, 1962, 223–225.

9. © Columbia Broadcasting System, *supra* n. 5.

CHAPTER 16

1. I first visited Reverend and Mrs. Taylor at their then winter home in Lake Placid, Florida, December 14 and 15, 1990. I saw them again at their home in Tougaloo, Mississippi, on the northern edge of Jackson, September 1, 1993.

2. Often ignored is discrimination within a race based upon skin color. See Trina Jones, "Shades of Brown: The Law of Skin Color," 49 *Duke L. J.* 1487 (1999–2000).

3. I obviously admired the courage and ability of Medgar Evers and had been talking with him the week before he was murdered in the driveway outside his Jackson home, the exact spot where he was shot.

4. Transcript, 382–383.

CHAPTER 17

1. *State v. Lawrence Byrd*, transcript, 230, *affirmed sub nom. Byrd v. State*, 228 So. 2d 874 (Miss. 1969).

2. I interviewed Vernon Jr. at the family home in Kelly Settlement, July 4, 1989.

3. Oral history, USM.

4. Letter from Douglas D. Baker to the *Hattiesburg American*, January 13, 1966.

5. One of the twenty-five local lawyers signing Registrar Cox's appellate brief was Stanton Hall, who would sit as judge on the state trials following Dahmer's death. Another was James Finch, who would prosecute the trials.

CHAPTER 18

1. Transcript, 728.

2. Transcript, 1142.

3. Transcript, 735.

4. Transcript, 1109.

5. "Testifies Negroes Frightened Her," *Jackson Daily News*, March 6, 1962.

6. Transcript, 783.

7. Transcript, 807.

8. Transcript, 1201a.

9. In 1992, I called her while in San Diego where she was then living, but she declined to talk with me.

CHAPTER 19

1. Transcript beginning at 1109.

2. Roberts papers, M27, Box 6, Folder 19, USM.

3. Transcript, 1192.

4. Transcript, 1198–1199.

5. Transcript, 1201a–1202.

CHAPTER 20

1. In December 1991, I interviewed Judge Tuttle in his chambers at the Atlanta court-house that was named for him. At ninety-five, he still went to court regularly and vividly recalled the *Lynd* case.

2. 304 U.S. 458 (1938). Harvey C. Couch, *A History of the Fifth Circuit, 1891–1981* (The Bicentennial Committee of the Judicial Conference of the United States, U.S. Government Printing Office), page 61, treats the impact of the case. Professor Couch's student, Will Percy, did an excellent paper, "Judge John Minor Wisdom: Doing Equity in the Deep South," April 15, 1980.

3. I first interviewed Judge Brown in the fall of 1991 at the New Orleans courthouse where he was still sitting with the Fifth Circuit.

4. Couch, *A History of the Fifth Circuit, 1891–1981, supra* n. 2 at 140.

5. I saw Judge Wisdom various times in 1991 while teaching at Tulane Law School.

6. David A. Nichols, *A Matter of Justice: Eisenhower and the beginning of the Civil Rights Revolution* (New York: Simon & Schuster, 2007), 36.

7. *Id.*, 84. Joel William Friedman, *Champion of Civil Rights: Judge John Minor Wisdom* (Baton Rouge: Louisiana State University Press, 2009), 95–98. It was no surprise that both Tuttle and Wisdom later received Presidential Medals of Freedom.

8. 743 F.2d LXVII (*Salute*).

9. Frank T. Read and Lucy S. McGough, *Let Them Be Judged: The Judicial Integration of The Deep South* (Metuchen, NJ: Scarecrow Press, 1978), 220.

10. Interview of Judge Brown in New Orleans December 1991. The judge and I talked again in Boston, October 8, 1992.

11. Jack Bass, *Unlikely Heroes* (Tuscaloosa: The University of Alabama Press, 1990), 101.

12. 349 U.S. 294, 301 (1955). Judge Wisdom told me what that was: an excuse for school districts not to act and judges not to decide cases.

13. 163 U.S. 537 (1896).

14. 347 U.S. 483 (1954).

15. When the dean of New York University School of Law, Richard L. Revesz, was clerking for Justice Marshall, the justice asked him to review the hearings for his nomination to the Second Circuit. The obnoxious treatment to which the justice was subjected during eight months of 1962 is documented fully by Revesz in "Thurgood Marshall's Struggle," 68 *N.Y.U. L. Rev.* 237 (1993). Directly or indirectly, Harold Cox's nomination was the price the Kennedys paid for Marshall's ultimate confirmation.

16. Ben McCarty, Associated Press, "Restudy Of Voting Papers Is Ordered," *Jackson Clarion-Ledger*, March 8, 1962.

17. "Court Orders Halt To Voter Discrimination," Houston *Post*, April 7, 1962, 1.

18. *Id.*

19. Transcript, 96, in the Roberts materials, M27, Box 3, Folder 32, USM.

20. *Id.*, 106.

21. 28 U.S.C. sec. 1651. It was the first of a number of civil rights cases where the circuit employed the statute to order prompt relief. Friedman, *Champion, supra* n. 7 at 259 n. 41.

22. *United States v. Lynd*, 301 F. 2d 818, 819–820 (April 10, 1962).

23. *Id.*, 821.

24. *Id.*, 821–822.

25. *Id.*, 823 n. 1.

26. Where not otherwise specified, black voting experiences are taken from charts the United States filed with the Fifth Circuit for the contempt trial.

27. Affidavits of Stegall and Lewis dated April 28, 1962, filed with the Fifth Circuit two days later.

28. Affidavit of Chandler dated April 28, 1962, also filed with the Fifth Circuit, April 30, 1962.

29. Interview with Mr. Thigpen at his home in Hattiesburg, July 1989.

30. John Dittmer describes this period well in *Local People: The Struggle for Civil Rights in Mississippi* (Urbana: University of Illinois Press, 1994), 179–185.

31. While Bell did not disagree with the result, he described, concurring in a *per curiam* opinion, Tuttle's reliance on the All-Writs statute as a "classic example of the pitfalls to be encountered, with the attendant disruption and delays in the orderly administration of justice when courts depart from the time tested processes of law." *United States v. Lynd*, 321 U.S. 26, 28 (1963).

32. *United States v. Lynd*, transcript vol. 3, 652 (March 5–7, 1962).

33. Letter December 22, 1962, to Charles J. Bloch, a lawyer Roberts had previously called for help with the case. Roberts papers, Box 11, Folder 16, USM.

34. 372 F. 2d 836 (1966).

35. Jack Bass, "How the G.O.P. Created Affirmative Action," *New York Times*, May 31, 2003. In his recent comprehensive biography of Wisdom, *supra* n. 7, ch. 10 and 14, Tulane law professor Joel William Friedman supports Bass's contention.

36. *Id.*

37. 5th Circuit #19,576. The court found Lynd to be in civil contempt and did not decide the issue of criminal contempt.

38. 349 F.2d 790, 793 (June 16, 1966).

39. 42 U.S.C. 2000e et seq. Secretary of the Navy Ray Mabus, Mississippi's governor from 1988 to 1992, named a navy supply ship for Medgar Evers. Associated Press, "New Navy Ship to Be Named for Slain Civil Rights Pioneer," *New York Times*, October 11, 2009, 28.

40. 42 U.S.C. 1973 et seq.

41. *South Carolina v. Katzenbach*, 383 U.S. 301, 313 n. 13 (1966).

42. *Id.*, 314 n. 19.

43. *Id.*, 309.

CHAPTER 21

1. Roy Reed, "13 Mississippi Klansmen Seized in Negro's Death," *New York Times*, March 29, 1966, 1.

2. Don Whitehead, *Attack on Terror: The FBI Against the Ku Klux Klan in Mississippi* (New York: Funk & Wagnalls, 1970), 11. Whitehead states well the evolution of the Klans.

3. *Id.*, 14–15, 18.

4. *Id.*, 18

5. *Id.*, 18–21.

6. *Id.*, 21, 221.

7. *Id.*, 22.

8. *Id.*, 23–24.

9. *God's Long Summer: Stories of Faith and Civil Rights* (Princeton: Princeton University Press, 1997), ch. 2. Surprisingly Bowers permitted Marsh to interview him three times between July 30 and August 3, 1994.

10. Adam Nossiter, *Of Long Memory: Mississippi and the Murder of Medgar Evers* (Reading, MA: Addison-Wesley, 1994), 75.

11. Interview in Jackson, October 1991.

12. Gordon A. Martin, Jr., *The Church in Mississippi; Ave Maria*, vol. 100, no. 24, 14–15 (December 12, 1964).

13. See generally *United States v. Price*, 383 U.S. 787 (1966).

14. Whitehead, *supra* n. 2 at 281–283.

15. *State v. Lawrence Byrd*, transcript, 227.

16. *Hattiesburg American*, January 31, 1969, 2.

17. *Hattiesburg American*, July 27, 1968, 1.

18. "Negro's Views Voiced," *New York Times*, January 11, 1966, 10. See generally Gordon A. Martin, Jr., "Life and Death of a Martyr," *Boston Sunday Herald Magazine*, June 5, 1966, 24.

19. Nikki Davis Maute, "Her Memories of firebombing remain strong," *Hattiesburg American*, February 13, 1994, 7A.

20. *Hattiesburg American*, July 25, 1969, 1.

21. Whitehead, *supra* n. 2 at 242–244.

22. *Byrd v. State*, 228 So. 2d 874 (Miss. 1969).

23. Bobby DeLaughter, *Never Too Late: A Prosecutor's Story of Justice in the Medgar Evers Case* (New York: Scribner, 201); Nossiter, *Of Long Memory*, *supra* n. 10.

24. "Letters to sheriff reveal story behind battle for civil rights," part 4 of a seven-part series, "44 Days That Changed Mississippi," May 28, 2000, 1, was just one of Mitchell's stories that themselves changed the state.

25. The timeline of the 1998 investigation dates appeared in the *Baton Rouge Advocate*, August 26, 1998 (metro ed.) For a vivid account of the crucial Pitts testimony on the third day of the trial, see Curtis Wilkie, "Ex-Klansman details fiery attack on civil rights leader," *Boston Globe*, August 20, 1998 (city ed.)

26. "In Klan verdict, a reckoning with Mississippi's past," August 23, 1998, A2.

27. *Id.*

28. I interviewed Ms. Dedeaux, a supervising probation officer in Gulfport, in New Orleans in 1997.

29. I interviewed Mrs. Brown at her office in July 1989.

30. Whitehead, *supra* n. 2 at 262–263.

31. The lawyer who next sought admission described this to me at Ole Miss, September 21, 2000.

32. I learned this at Ole Miss, September 21, 2000, from a Jackson lawyer who had been in the courtroom.

33. *McLaughlin v. City of Canton*, 947 F. Supp. 954, 971 (S.D. Miss. 1995).

CHAPTER 22

1. Kathleen Woodruff Wickham, *The Role of the Clarion-Ledger in the Adoption of the 1982 Education Reform Act: Winning the Pulitzer Prize* (Lewiston, NY: Edwin Mellen Press, 2007), 7.

2. Gene Roberts and Hank Klibanoff, *The Race Beat: The Press, the Civil Rights Struggle, and the Awakening of a Nation* (New York: Knopf, 2007), 82.

3. Their absence from SEC baseball teams has attracted attention. See "College Baseball: A 'white' game?," *Clarion-Ledger*, May 28, 2000, 1, describing what the paper termed "the bleaching of college baseball."

4. *Wellspring* (The Institute Newsletter), June 2006, 4.

5. *Wellspring*, March 2008, 1.

6. *Clarion-Ledger*, April 19, 2001.

7. Adam Nossiter, "U.S. Says Blacks in Mississippi Suppress White Vote," *New York Times*, October 11, 2006

8. Adam Nossiter, "In a Red State, a Blue Dog Has Republicans Worried," *New York Times*, April 22, 2008, A20.

9. John R. Bradley Jr., "A Salute to William P. Murphy," 77 *Miss. L. J.* 923, 929 (2008).

10. See "Attorney Reuben Anderson named to Mississippi Chemical's board," *Clarion-Ledger*, January 30, 2000, C1.

EPILOGUE

1. Kennedy Library Forum, *Civil Rights and the Integration of Ole Miss*, C-SPAN video 174052. I interviewed Mr. Byrd in Newton, Massachusetts, the month after the forum.

BIBLIOGRAPHY

BOOKS

Ball, Howard. *Justice in Mississippi: The Murder Trial of Edgar Ray Killen.* Lawrence: University of Kansas Press, 2008.

———. *Murder in Mississippi: U.S. v. Price and the Struggle for Civil Rights.* Lawrence: University of Kansas Press, 2004.

Barrett, St. John. *The Drive for Equality: A Personal History of Civil Rights Enforcement 1954–1965.* Baltimore: PublishAmerica, 2009.

Bass, Jack. *Unlikely Heroes: The Dramatic Story of Southern Judges Who Translated the Supreme Court's* Brown *Decision into a Revolution for Equality.* New York: Simon & Schuster, 1981; Tuscaloosa: The University of Alabama Press, 1990.

Berry, Mary Frances. *And Justice for All.* New York: Knopf, 2009.

Brady, Tom P. *Black Monday.* Brookhaven, MS, 1954.

Branch, Taylor. *Pillar of Fire: America in the King Years 1963–65.* New York: Simon & Schuster, 1998.

Brooks, Roy L., Gilbert Paul Carrasco, and Gordon A. Martin, Jr. *Civil Rights Litigation: Cases and Perspectives.* Durham: Carolina Academic Press, 1995.

Brownell, Herbert, with John P. Burke. *Advising Ike.* Lawrence: University of Kansas Press, 1993.

Bryant, Nick. *Bystander: John F. Kennedy and the Struggle for Black Equality.* New York: Basic Books, 2006.

Caro, Robert. *The Years of Lyndon Johnson: Master of the Senate.* New York: Knopf, 2002.

Class of 1952. Princeton: Princeton University Press, 1964.

Cohodas, Nadine. *The Band Played Dixie: Race and the Liberal Conscience at Ole Miss.* New York: Free Press, 1997.

Colvard, Dean W. *Mixed Emotions: Racial Barriers Fall—A University President Remembers.* Danville, IL: Interstate Printing and Publishing, 1985.

Corsi, Jerome. *Judicial Politics: An Introduction.* Englewood Cliffs, NJ: Prentice-Hall, 1984.

Couch, Harvey C. *A History of the Fifth Circuit 1891–1981.* The Bicentennial Committee of the Judicial Conference of the United States, 1984.

Davies, David R., ed. *The Press and Race: Mississippi Journalists Confront the Movement.* Jackson: University Press of Mississippi, 2001.

DeLaughter, Bobby. *Never Too Late: A Prosecutor's Story of Justice in the Medgar Evers Case.* New York: Scribner, 2001.

Dittmer, John. *Local People: The Struggle for Civil Rights in Mississippi.* Urbana: University of Illinois Press, 1994.

Dollard, John. *Caste and Class in a Southern Town.* New Haven: Yale University Press, 1938; 3rd ed. New York: Doubleday, 1957.

Doyle, William. *An American Insurrection: The Battle of Oxford, Mississippi, 1962.* New York: Doubleday, 2001.

Dyer, Davis, and David B. Sicilia. *Labors of a Modern Hercules: Evolution of a Chemical Company.* Boston: Harvard Business School Press, 1990.

Elliff, John. *The United States Department of Justice and Individual Rights, 1937–1962.* New York: Garland Publishing, 1987.

Evers-Williams, Myrlie, and Manning Marable, eds. *The Autobiography of Medgar Evers: A Hero's Life and Legacy Revealed Through His Writings, Letters, and Speeches.* New York: Basic Civitas Books, 2005.

Friedman, Joel William. *Champion of Civil Rights: Judge John Minor Wisdom.* Baton Rouge: Louisiana State University Press, 2009.

Glisson, Susan, ed. *The Human Tradition in the Civil Rights Movement.* Lanham, MD: Rowman & Littlefield, 2006.

Golden, Harry. *Mr. Kennedy and the Negroes.* Cleveland: World Publishing Company, 1964.

Greenberg, Jack. *Crusaders in the Courts: How a Dedicated Band of Lawyers Fought for the Civil Rights Revolution.* New York: Basic Books, 1994.

Grossman, Joel. *Lawyers and Judges: The American Bar Association and the Politics of Judicial Selection.* New York: John Wiley, 1965.

Guthman, Edwin, ed. *Robert Kennedy in his Own Words: The Unpublished Recollections of the Kennedy Years.* New York: Bantam Books, 1988.

Harvey, James C. *Civil Rights During the Kennedy Administration.* Jackson: The University and College Press of Mississippi, 1971.

Hemphill, Marie M. *Fevers, Floods and Faith: A History of Sunflower County, Mississippi, 1844–1976.* Indianola, 1980.

Hersh, Burton. *Bobby and Edgar: The Historic Face-off Between the Kennedys and J. Edgar Hoover that Transformed America.* New York: Carroll and Graf, 2007.

Johnston, Erle. *Mississippi's Defiant Years, 1953–1973.* Forest, MS: Lake Harbor Publishers, 1990.

Katagiri, Yasuhiro. *The Mississippi State Sovereignty Commission.* Jackson: University Press of Mississippi, 2001.

Katzenbach, Nicholas deB. *Some of It was Fun: Working With RFK and LBJ.* New York: Norton, 2008.

Key, V. O. *Southern Politics in State and Nation.* New York: Knopf, 1949.

Kim, Wan J. *The Department of Justice's Civil Rights Division: A Historical Perspective as the Division Nears 50,* 2006.

King, Mary. *Freedom Song: A Personal Story of the 1960s Civil Rights Movement.* New York: William Morrow, 1987.

Kluger, Richard. *Simple Justice.* New York: Knopf, 1975.

Landon, Michael DeL. *The University of Mississippi School of Law: A Sesquicentennial History.* Jackson: University Press of Mississippi, 2006.

Landsberg, Brian K. *Enforcing Civil Rights: Race, Discrimination and the Department of Justice.* Lawrence: University of Kansas Press, 1997.

———. *Free at Last to Vote: The Alabama Origins of the 1965 Voting Rights Act.* Lawrence: University Press of Kansas, 2007.

Lord, Walter. *The Past That Would Not Die.* New York: Harper & Row, 1965.

MacLean, Harry N. *The Past Is Never Dead: The Trial of James Ford Seale and Mississippi's Struggle for Redemption.* New York: Basic Civitas, 2009.

Marsh, Charles. *God's Long Summer: Stories of Faith and Civil Rights.* Princeton: Princeton University Press, 1997.

McMillen, Neil R. *Dark Journey: Black Mississippians in the Age of Jim Crow.* Urbana: University of Illinois Press, 1989.

Mendelsohn, Jack. *The Martyrs: 16 Who Gave Their Lives for Racial Justice.* New York: Harper & Row, 1966.

Moye, J. Todd. *Let the People Decide: Black Freedom and White Resistance Movements in Sunflower County, Mississippi, 1945–1986.* Chapel Hill: University of North Carolina Press, 2004.

Namorato, Michael. *The Catholic Church in Mississippi, 1911–1984, a History.* Westport, CT: Greenwood Press, 1998.

Navasky, Victor. *Kennedy Justice.* New York: Atheneum, 1971.

Newlin, George, ed. *Princeton Class of 1952: The Book of our History, 1952–2002.* Hagerstown, MD: Reunion Press, 2002.

Nichols, David A. *A Matter of Justice: Eisenhower and the Beginning of the Civil Rights Revolution.* New York: Simon & Schuster, 2007.

Nossiter, Adam. *Of Long Memory: Mississippi and the Murder of Medgar Evers.* Reading, MA: Addison-Wesley, 1994.

Ole Miss Law School Annual, 1926.

Parker, Frank. *Black Votes Count: Political Empowerment in Mississippi after 1965.* Chapel Hill: University of North Carolina Press, 1990.

Payne, Charles. *I've got the Light of Freedom: The Organizing Tradition and the Mississippi Freedom Struggle.* Berkeley and Los Angeles: University of California Press, 1995.

Powdermaker, Hortense. *After Freedom: A Cultural Case Study in the Deep South.* New York: Russell and Russell, reissued 1968.

Read, Frank T., and Lucy S. McGough. *Let Them Be Judged: The Judicial Integration of the Deep South.* Metuchen, NJ: Scarecrow Press, 1978.

Roberts, Gene, and Hank Klibanoff. *The Race Beat: The Press, the Civil Rights Struggle, and the Awakening of a Nation.* New York: Knopf, 2007.

Sansing, David C. *Making Haste Slowly.* Jackson: University Press of Mississippi, 1990.

Shreve, Susan Richards, and Porter Shreve, eds. *Outside the Law: Narratives on Justice in America.* Boston: Beacon Press, 1998.

Stern, Mark. *Calculating Visions: Kennedy, Johnson, and Civil Rights.* New Brunswick, NJ: Rutgers University Press, 1992.

Stossel, Scott. *Sarge: The Life and Times of Sargent Shriver.* Washington, DC: Smithsonian Books, 2004.

United States Commission on Civil Rights. *Voting: 1961 Report 1. Education: 1961 Report 2.*

Wallace, Jesse Thomas. *A History of the Negroes of Mississippi.* Clinton, MS, 1927.

Weiss, Nancy. *Farewell to the Party of Lincoln.* Princeton: Princeton University Press, 1983.

White. Theodore. *The Making of the President, 1960.* New York: Atheneum, 1961.

Whitehead, Don. *Attack on Terror: The FBI Against the Ku Klux Klan in Mississippi.* New York: Funk & Wagnalls, 1970.

Wickham, Kathleen Woodruff. *The Role of the Clarion-Ledger in the Adoption of the 1982 Education Reform Act: Winning the Pulitzer Prize.* Lewiston, NY: Edwin Mellen Press, 2007.

Wilkie, Curtis. *Dixie: A Personal Odyssey Through Events that Shaped the Modern South.* New York: Scribner, 2001.

Wofford, Harris. *Of Kennedys and Kings: Making Sense of the Sixties.* Pittsburgh: University of Pittsburgh Press, 1980.

NEWSPAPERS AND PERIODICALS

American Bar Association Journal, 1947

American Lawyer, 1984

Ave Maria, 1964

Baton Rouge Advocate, 1998

Boston Globe, 1984, 1997–1998, 2007

Boston Herald, 1966

Commonweal, 1964

Concordia (LA) *Sentinel,* 2008

Duke Law Journal, 1999–2000

Emory Law Journal, 1984

Harper's, 1962

Hattiesburg American, 1958–1959, 1963, 1966, 1968–1969, 1991, 1994

Houston Post, 1962

Jackson Clarion-Ledger, 1961–1963, 1991, 2000–2001, 2008

Jackson Daily News, 1956, 1961–1962

Journal of American History, 1990, 1997

McComb Enterprise-Journal, 2000

Memphis Commercial-Appeal, 1961

Mississippi Law Journal, 2008

Mississippi Lawyer, 1961

New York Times, 1961–1963, 1966, 1968, 2000, 2003–2006, 2008–2009

New York University Law Review, 1993

Perspectives in American History, 1971

Sports Illustrated, 2003

Texas Law Review, 1959

Washington Post, 1961, 2003, 2006

Wellspring, 2006, 2008

TABLE OF CASES

American Civil Liberties Union v. Mabus (ACLU I), 719 F.Supp. 1345 (S.D. Miss. 1989).

Brown v. Board of Education, 347 U.S. 483 (1954); 349 U.S. 294 (1955)

Byrd v. State, 228 So. 2d 874 (Miss. 1969).

Chapman v. King, 154 F. 2d 460 (5th cir.), cert. denied 327 U.S. 800 (1960).

Cooper v. Aaron, 358 U.S. 1 (1958).

Johnson v. Zerbst, 304 U.S. 458 (1938).

Kennard v. State, 128 So. 2d 572 (1961).

Kennedy v. Lynd, 306 F. 2d 222 (5th cir., 1962).

McLaughlin v. City of Canton, 947 F. Supp. 954 (S.D. Miss. 1995).

McLaurin v. Oklahoma State Regents for Higher Education, 339 U.S. 637 (1950).

Northwest Austin Municipal Utility District No. One v. Holder, 129 S. Ct. 2504 (2009).

Peay v. Cox, 190 F. 2d 123 (5th cir.) cert. denied 342 U.S. 896 (1951).

Plessy v. Ferguson, 163 U.S. 537 (1896).

Screws v. United States, 140 F. 2d 662 (5th cir. 1944), reversed 325 U.S. 91 (1945).

South Carolina v. Katzenbach, 383 U.S. 301 (1966).

Sweatt v. Painter, 339 U.S. 629 (1950).

United States v. Board of Education of Greene County, MS, 332 F.2d 40 (5th cir.), 1964.

United States v. Lynd, 301 F. 2d 818 (5th cir.), cert. denied 371 U.S. 893 (1962); #19576 (5th cir. September 17–21, 1962); (S.D. Miss., January 20, 1965) reversed 349 F. 2d 785 (5th cir., June 16, 1965).

United States v. Price, 383 U.S. 787 (1966).

United States v. Ramsey (5th cir. Docket No. 20596).

United States v. Wood, 295 F. 2d 772 (5th cir. 1961).

Yick Wo v. Hopkins, 118 U.S. 356 (1886).

Unpublished Items

Barnes, James Franklin. *Negro Voting in Mississippi.* Master's thesis, University of Mississippi, 1955.

Miscellaneous

Alcorn State University Web site.

CBS Reports*: Mississippi and the Fifteenth Amendment,* shown September 26, 1962, distributed by Films for the Humanities and Sciences.

Civil Rights and Restorative Justice Project, Northeastern University School of Law, Year End Report, 2009.

Drew, Robert, and ABC News. *Crisis: Behind a Presidential Commitment.* 1963; dvd 2003.

http://goprincetontigers.ocsn.com/genrel/080100aaj.html, visited April 7, 2003.

John Doar: Trailblazer for Justice. Albany, CA: Ginzburg Video Productions, 2006.

John F. Kennedy Library Forums 2002 (C-SPAN video 174052), 2005, 2009.

Mississippi State University Web site.

Soul of Justice: Thelton Henderson's American Journey. Albany, CA: Ginzburg Video Productions, 2005.

USM press release, *Clyde Kennard, Denied Admission to Southern Mississippi in 1950s, Exonerated in Forrest County Circuit Court,* May 18, 2006.

INDEX